Journey to Enlightenment

Ross Bishop

With thanks to Amanda and Selena for help with my writing, to Steve for the cover art, Karen for graphic design, Toan for the coffee and Christina for making it all possible.

Ross

Blue Lotus Press

First Edition
Copyright ©2008, Blue Lotus Press

Other books by Ross Bishop:
Healing the Shadow
Truth

ISBN -13: 978-0-9669822-2-0
ISBN -10: 9669822-2-3

Printed in Canada by Hignell on recycled paper
Cover art by Steve Hartman
Graphic design by Karen Brand, www.kbranddesign.com

CONTENTS

FROM THE AUTHOR

People ask me why I became a shaman. Truthfully, I didn't have much choice in the matter. You see, God and I had not been on good terms for much of my life. My early years were pretty tough. Most of the time I was confused and angry, but I repressed my feelings inside.

My life orbited around compensating for my "inadequacies." Everything I did was built around my need to feel accepted and worthwhile. I cared about other people, but my connection to them was built around my need to be liked. I thought I was opening my heart, but I did not know what real love was because I had never known it. With all my pain, I was afraid to open to another person. So, like everyone else, I lived on the surface. As Carlos Rey wrote, "Our dreams are what we are meant to be. Our life is what we settled for." I rationalized everything. When I had a difficult time, which was often, the first thing I did was get down on myself. Then I got angry at God.

This allowed me to hide behind my feelings of unworthiness, not look at why my life wasn't working and not change anything. I didn't have to look at my shame as long as I was immersed in it. It allowed me to not deal with a self that I was convinced was defective. And as some of you know, you can milk that game for a long time and get lost in struggle and drama, without getting anywhere.

From the outside things looked OK. I was living the great American dream, and I was miserable. I didn't know how bad things were because pain was all I had ever known!

Interestingly, at the same time that my life was in so much turmoil, there was also a profound spiritual connection that I could not ignore as hard as I tried. And I tried! And although I felt like a pinball in an arcade game, life was busy putting me through lesson after lesson to chip away at the beliefs I took refuge in. I didn't understand what was happening at the time, because in life you mostly see through hindsight. All I really knew was that I hurt!

Desperate to find another way, I began to do Zen meditation under the tutelage of Dainin Katagiri, Roshi, a Zen monk who profoundly affected the lives of many of the people he taught. So there I was, being pulled like a moth into a flame, in spite of my anger and resistance. It felt pretty schizophrenic sometimes, and I certainly didn't like it!

But something (maybe it was just that I was hurting and feeling really lost) pulled me to me sit in meditation faithfully morning and evening for six months. I began to change. I slowed down; I began to breathe for the first time in my life. I went deep. And it scared the hell out of me! It was like I had taken the back door into all the pain I had spent the rest of my life carefully avoiding. It is ironic now that I look back on it. Here I was, face-to-face with my pain and I really didn't even know what it was, much less what to do with it!

I don't have many words to explain what drove me to take the next step, but I knew that there was more I needed to explore. I also knew that the life I had been living wasn't going to get me where I needed to go. So, I walked out of my old life and began to search for a real one.

And after a couple of particularly gut-wrenching experiences, I began to look at my life and myself through new eyes. Eventually, I began to see that who I thought I was rested on many untruths. Although the process was still painful, it was a different kind if pain than I had previously experienced. In the past, I had hurt from fear and resistance. Now I was hurting because I was being challenged and changed to become who I really was. I was being reshaped. Giving up old beliefs is not easy. It means giving up a great deal of who you thought you were – and that can be very scary.

I began to realize that I was not the person I had grown up believing I was! I found that it wasn't necessary to jump through hoops and please people in order to be liked. I was "encouraged" to give up my old beliefs in favor of a more enlightened perspective.

I'd love to say that I saw the light and chose this path because I knew it was for my highest good. I didn't. Much of the time, especially in the early stages, I had to be dragged through the mud by the nose. I only changed because there was nowhere else to turn. Besides, I certainly didn't want to go through those experiences again! But, it is a tough way to learn.

Today, life is a different story. I can't paint or draw worth a darn. I love music but I'm right brained and I've never been able to get past figuring out notes on sheet music. I couldn't find God in the organized religions and I felt uncomfortable every time I tried to sell my soul to a corporation. I became a shaman because I found that I had a natural gift for the work. I stayed with it because it was the best way I could find to develop my relationship to spirit.

I paid a price to get here, we all do. No one gets a free ride. It is, as I now understand it, an essential part of the process of life here on earth. I still have challenges in my life, but my self worth isn't on the line as it used to be. My challenges today are to go deeper and to live more authentically from the God Space.

Many of you are going through your version of what I experienced. This book is my gift to you. The task I have set for myself is to help you avoid some of the walls I hit and the crevasses I threw myself into. I hope to help you find a more gentle way. And it is possible. I know that now. I prove it every day with the people I work with. It is never going to be an easy process, but you do not have to make it a living hell for yourself either.

After a while, because of, not in spite of, your problems, you will re-connect with the Creator. And, since my life and my ego are no longer standing toe-to-toe in conflict, my spiritual development has become the single most important part of my life. Maybe it always has been. I just didn't know it.

Namasté,

Ross

Introduction

Silence is the language of God.
All else is poor translation.

Rumi

Consider what it would be like to live in Heaven. Life would be peaceful. Your days would be filled with calm and compassion. The problems you struggle with today would be gone. The anxiety, tension, self-doubt and fear that characterize so much of life on earth would simply cease to exist. Your joy would be incomparable. You would have nothing to prove. You would feel loved and accepted. Sounds nice, doesn't it? This is the God Space.

The qualities of the God Space are eternal. We would find qualities like love, compassion, openness, gentleness, gratitude and kindness there. In the God Space energy flows, there are no barriers or impediments to its movement. The restrictive emotional qualities so prevalent on earth such as fear and anxiety are energy contractions that inhibit the free movement of energy. They are incompatible with the movement and free flow found in the God Space.

An enlightened person lives in the God Space. In them we find acceptance, compassion and understanding. Their thoughts and feelings flow easily. They are not inhibited by emotion or fear. They would not judge because with nothing to fear, there would be no need for it.

You might be curious to know that enlightened people don't think (at least as we know it). When information flows freely, you just do what needs to be done. You don't have to think about it. An enlightened person could feel anger, but it would be compassion-based anger, not the fear-driven rage we commonly call anger. In this person there would be no pretense, no need to manipulate. The truth would determine her behavior, not neediness or insecurity.

But this isn't you, is it? Why is that? Today you can be pulled by fear or emotion, and this keeps you from opening your heart both to yourself and to others. Your emotions keep you out of "heaven," as it were, and compel you to "a life of quiet desperation." And when things are at their worst, you live in "hell."

Although they may seem remote, the qualities of the God Space are available to each of us. And across the board, no matter what aspect you consider, whether it is being more calm, having joy, finding passion, having a more tranquil and enjoyable life, being healthier or actually extending life, the God Space offers substantial improvements over typical earthly existence. A spiritual life is more rewarding and significantly more fulfilling than a life filled with fear, anxiety and tension. This makes it easy to build a case for finding inner peace.

The God Space offers peace, joy and contentment and the ego space leads to pain, stress, discomfort and unhappiness. One might assume then, that people would make the search for a spiritual life the single most important, absolutely essential, focus of their lives. Yet we know that this is not the case. On the surface, our resistance to living in the God Space makes little sense. And where things in life do not make sense, there are always deeper and more significant explanations.

Obviously there is a glitch somewhere. And the glitch is that the God Space requires us to live from compassion. To get to compassion, we have to confront our fears of unworthiness. And most people are not (yet) ready to do that. Conscious of it or not, opening our hearts to be compassionate resurrects an old vulnerability that has been the source of considerable pain for us in the past. We fear that we will be hurt if we open ourselves up (again), and we know that being spiritual will require that of us.

Otherwise why would we waste what little precious time and energy we have on earth being held captive by anxiety, fear, anger, sadness, guilt, unhappiness or a hundred other painful emotions? Why would we choose lives of pain and frustration that give us so little comfort and peace? Why would we accept relationships in which we feel frustrated and unsatisfied, remain in jobs where we are treated like robots, disregarded and dumped by the side of the road when the corporation downsizes? No one is really happy, even the rich guys!

Your emotions and your life are driven by what you believe, especially by what you believe about yourself. What are those beliefs? Setting aside the good stuff for the moment, do you see yourself as worthy? Do you really deserve to be loved? Or do you see yourself as unworthy or defective?

Fundamentalist preachers will tell you that you are a flawed and sinful person in need of salvation. Intellectuals maintain that there is no God, and that your life is the result of what you have made of it. What is the truth? No matter which of these philosophies you accept, it is still your fault. Either you are a sinner in need of redemption, or you know better and are just messing up your life. Either way, you lose.

I accept neither premise. That kind of thinking only makes religious people ashamed and intellectuals feel like failures. For the faithful, it creates fear of a false and judgmental God. And for those who don't believe in God, not being more "successful" condemns them as personal failures. They could be better, they are just not trying hard enough, being smart enough, or are not doing enough with their lives. They become that worst of all things in an economically-driven society, "slackers." Salvation in the scientific/economic system will come only when they achieve worldly "success" by wearing expensive fashions, having the right career, living in an expensive house or undergoing science's latest creation, augmentive body surgery.

As you proceed through this book, you are going to find that there is much more going on than either of these simplistic explanations offer.

You are on a journey that is going to chip away at your beliefs until you accept living from the God Space. That journey is called life. Today part of you does not move in harmony with the rest of The Universe. You hold beliefs (primarily about yourself) that limit yourself and pull you off center. You probably believe that if you are exposed to the light of truth, you will be found wanting, that you might not measure up. Don't pass that last sentence off casually. It addresses the core issue that you and the rest of humanity struggle with, and one which is rarely addressed openly and directly.

To stand in the God Space means being exposed, and part of you is afraid to be seen. It lives in the shadow. When exposed, it becomes afraid, anxious and insecure. The result is that when you are urged to move to compassion, you are only able to go partway – especially in regard to being compassionate toward yourself.

Some part of you believes that the separation you feel from the God Space is because of personal shortcomings. You got dumped into this mess without even so much as an explanation. It is natural to assume you were kicked out of heaven. And although this cannot possibly be true, and there is nothing specific you can point to as a cause or an explanation for your feelings, they are strong, nonetheless. The problem is that if you had known what this was all about, the process would not have worked. Besides, no one in their right mind would have signed up for centuries of struggle, anguish, misery and pain.

Your feelings are intended and they are also necessary. They are part of a process that will eventually bring you to know in a profound way, your true connection to the Creator. In time, you will come to understand that your beliefs cannot possibly be true. And then you will release them.

The truth is you are a child of God. You are a part of the God-consciousness. Although you can feel unworthy or unlovable or a hundred other self-limiting things, you cannot **be** any of them. Based on your feelings of unworthiness, your beliefs cause you to fear rejection and abandonment and require that you compensate for your "inadequacies." It is your ignorance of the truth and your compensations for it that set in motion the engine of change that in turn, brings you closer to enlightenment.

When you decide that you are inadequate, you step away from the God Space. Your free will allows you to do that. Without the guidance of the God Space, you then must find another source of direction. You seek shelter in your ego and your mind and try and think your way through life. It doesn't work terribly well. The result of your efforts to compensate for your "failings" is to create more problems for yourself.

In a curious twist, your problems, driven by your beliefs, generate pain so that you will eventually pay attention to the fears and anxieties (contractions of thought) that created them in the first place. This brings you full circle to confront the source of your problems – your beliefs. The idea of confronting your beliefs is important because you possess a host of avoidance mechanisms designed to avoid doing that very thing.

Pain is a signal that you are out of alignment, not that something is wrong with you . . . but we usually do not see it that way. Eventually, you come to realize that you have been chasing ghosts, that your assumptions have been in error and that there was nothing wrong with you in the first place, but it takes a while.

The understanding you gain from confronting your beliefs is a vital step in the path to enlightenment. Releasing your beliefs allows you to live in a state of grace, unadulterated by fear and emotion.

Letting go of beliefs is like making your first bungee jump. You stand at the edge, about to leap off a cliff, with your heart somewhere up in your throat. I will never forget the feeling of looking over my toes, into the abyss. Everything that I had learned about being safe was about to be violated. All of my conditioning and my experiences had taught me that what I was about to do was going to kill me. Every fear response was screaming, "Danger! Danger!"

I knew the ground, and I was familiar with walking. I did not know flying. I knew what it felt like to fall. I could only imagine what it would feel like to hit the ground going a couple of hundred miles an hour! And after all, we all know that people can't fly!

In truth, I was very safe, but I did not "know" that. I was in a new context, a new paradigm, and the ways I functioned in my "old" life didn't apply in this new realm. I was about to transcend into a different reality, and the rules were different!

It is the same with making a spiritual transformation. The spiritual leap takes you into a different world with which you are largely unfamiliar. The rules are different there too!

To make a successful bungee jump, I would have to transcend my fear and put my faith in things outside my immediate control – in God, in the people who made the bungee cord and in the crew assisting me. Flying was going to require a different understanding. It operated under rules that I was unfamiliar with, and I would need to experience flying in order to really understand it. All the books and theories in the world could not give me the experiential knowledge I would need to make the transition to the new way of being. Making the jump was going to require a leap of faith into something greater than I had ever experienced. And standing there, I could really have no idea as to how wonderful it was going to be to fly.

Once you have made the jump, you see that your fears, although perfectly understandable, were also speculative and based in the old paradigm. This recognition frees you to jump more freely in the future, but it is not an understanding you can come to without stepping over the edge. A certain amount of fear is also a natural and healthy part of the process. It keeps you from being totally foolish.

The interesting thing about life is that flying is actually our natural state. We just do not know that yet. We have walked around on the ground since time immemorial, and even though we grouse about the limitations of walking, we are afraid to leap off the cliff to find out if we really can fly or what flying is like. The fear is that it's going to be a one-way trip if we are wrong.

Remember the Disney movie, "Dumbo The Elephant?" Jumbo Jr., (nicknamed Dumbo because of his huge ears), was capable of flight, but he was landlocked by his belief that "Elephants couldn't fly." That is what the world had taught him and he bought it. Just like you have. It took some "magic" feathers (faith in something greater than his previous experience and conditioning) for him to confront his limiting beliefs and break out of his self-imposed prison. He had good help, but when it got down to it, he had to do it himself! No one could do it for him.

Einstein said, "We all sit in the prisons of our own ideas." What is your prison? Each moment contains an opportunity for you to open your heart. The next moment does too. The question is, "Will you take it?"

Sooner or later, life is going to force you out of your prison, anyway. It is going to show you that you really can fly. If you do not make the leap yourself, life will eventually push you over the edge and make you do it. Today you have the option to make the transition in small jumps through your daily experiences (you call these problems). If you are able to take just some of those opportunities, then life becomes a matter of small transitions. However, if you do not take the smaller jumps, then things accumulate – not so much because the task gets bigger, but because your resistance becomes more entrenched. Many people refuse to make the small jumps, and end up in a crisis, which eventually means that they will have to make the big leap.

Consider what a disease is. Yes, the body fails. But the failure is also a warning. It says "Change or die." People talk about "being hit by the Universal two by four," but that is not entirely accurate. The Universe responds to your resistance. It is your resistance that makes the situation more intense than it needs to be. Making the leap can feel overwhelming until you address your fear. But it is always only a small step, regardless of how it feels.

Life on earth is a process to confront and dissolve the limiting beliefs that keep you pinned to the ground, and like it or not, you are engaged in that process. And although it can feel scary to take the risk and make the leap, there actually is no risk! The outcome is guaranteed! Even with all our diversions, there can be only one outcome. There is only one place that you can go! It may look like an abyss, but there is only Truth. Close your eyes for a moment and imagine yourself standing on the edge of that abyss. As you think about jumping off, what thoughts come? What fears? What holds you back?

Even though The Universe is constantly presenting you with opportunities to open your heart (to fly), much of the time you are not able to do it. There is no judgment here; in fact, there is an abundance of love. You will be given opportunity after opportunity as you need. You're not messed up; you just get scared. And the sooner you recognize the difference, the easier the process becomes.

To people who feel unworthy, life seems unfair. It feels as though God doesn't love them, that He has abandoned them. All they know is that a swirl of emotion periodically rocks their world. They cling to the cliff with all their might. They spend their days trying to bail a hopelessly leaking boat. To them life is, as Elbert Hubbard lamented, "Just one damned thing after another."

But the larger truth is, God is doing the best thing He possibly can to help. It's what God has been doing for all of us all along anyway - by allowing us to feel the limitations of the beliefs we impose upon ourselves. If these people only knew how safe it really was for them to make the "leap" and take flight!

Most people are reluctant to give up the beliefs that brought them this far. It doesn't really matter that these beliefs don't work very well. Their beliefs provide a sense of security. Marines back from Iraq report feeling uncomfortable out on the street without their body armor. Many people are just not ready to take off their old clothes and see what is reflected in the mirror. Yet the truly ironic thing is that what is reflected in the mirror is absolutely breathtaking! That is why life sometimes must give us a push.

Do you remember the last time you picked up a smooth stone from the beach or a riverbed? Thousands of years ago that stone was an unremarkable jagged rock, just like all the others, high up in the mountains. On its trip down to you, it has bounced up against thousands and thousands of other rocks, and each encounter chipped away a rough spot. Eventually, the once-rough rock became round and smooth.

Part of you still has rough edges. On your journey to the Great Sea, you will bump up against other people, and each of those interactions will give you an opportunity to work off your rough spots. It is not a fun process, but you can make the experience much more difficult than is necessary.

In another thousand years, the smooth rock you found will be ground down even further into grains of sand. Then, that sand will become a part of the great, indistinguishable mass of sand that covers the planet. Someday, you too will join the vast expanse of The Universe that has more stars than grains of sand on earth.[1]

Although life can be bumpy, the process has been carefully constructed so you can transition into the God Space in stages. To simply drop you into the God Space all at once would be unkind. The abrupt change would put you into shock.

The question you must ask yourself is, "What kind of journey will I create for myself?" In other words, "How much pain will I put myself through by resisting the inevitable?" Some people will go kicking and screaming, but it is a journey that each of us must make. I'm not asking you to like the process. You're not supposed to.

Given our druthers, most of us would prefer life's pokes and prods to simply disappear. We would be happy if our fairy godmother came along and zapped all of our problems away.

Fantasies are seductive. We get transported to a perfect world without having to confront our limiting beliefs. Without lifting a finger, we eliminate the things that hold us back, get in our way and otherwise keep us from being happy. In our fantasies we can be rich, successful, courageous, famous or desirable without having to face any of the fears that pin us to dreary obscurity. Enlightenment asks us to deal with our limiting fears and beliefs. Fantasy gets us temporarily off the hook.

The truth is, if you could have given up your fears and anxieties long ago, you would have. No one wants a life filled with fear, anxiety and pain, and yet most of us have one. Some of us carry a great deal of pain. We want to heal and to be free of fear and limitation, yet doing that seems beyond our reach. We try and try, and sometimes it seems as though we don't accomplish much. We look for answers in the stars, read books, take supplements, go to church, do therapy, learn yoga and consult all manner of physicians and

healers, and although these things help, the magical key escapes us. We look
to God for help and feel frustrated and abandoned when our pain and
problems continue. Yet the answers to the fundamental questions elude us.

Well, they don't really elude us. The truth is, we avoid them. We allow
ourselves to get caught up in the daily concerns of life because of the dark
and foreboding fears that lurk in our shadow. The experiences of our past lives
and the pain of our recent childhood have convinced us that we are not
worthy, and we are not prepared to confront those beliefs. So, we live on the
surface, often without even knowing why. Thus, we are inclined to leave
spiritual considerations to the mystics of India and priests of the Vatican, not
because these matters are esoteric or unfamiliar, but because we are reluctant
to delve into them.

Interestingly, we persistently avoid doing the one thing that would make
a real difference. We don't confront the beliefs that make our lives difficult.
We accept our beliefs of unworthiness and deficiency and then work
overtime to compensate for our "inadequacies." It's an interesting point to
consider – we desire peace and bliss, and yet we are willing to settle for so
much less.

Consider your life. You might say you were happy, but are you really? Have
the dreams of your youth given way to the painful realities of adulthood?
Have you settled for less than you really wanted and rationalized away your
dissatisfaction? Have you ever really reached for the brass ring? Sure, you are
getting by, but is your passion stifled? Are you frustrated with your work or
your relationships? Is life really giving you the joy you had hoped?

Having considered your own life, then consider the people around you.
How many of them are really happy? Or, are they basically getting by too?
The next time you go to the store or walk down the street, really look at the
other people. They will probably seem okay, but few of them will seem really
happy. I would wager that most of them have made significant compromises
in their dreams too. James M. Barrie, who created *Peter Pan*, commented:

*The life of every man is a diary in which he means to write one story, and
writes another; and his humblest hour is when he compares the volume as it is
with what he vowed to make it.*

Thoreau wrote, "The mass of men lead lives of quiet desperation." Certainly we have more distractions today than in Thoreau's time, but we still feel uneasy, alone, isolated and far too often, in pain. We are not at peace.

Life on earth can be difficult, sometimes downright miserable. With all the pain and difficulty people endure, it can be difficult to reconcile life's anguish with the image of a loving and compassionate Creator. After all, if He really loved us, why would He let children starve, allow people to die from diseases, and let genocide go unpunished?

But we have free will, and much of what happens here on earth is because we are free to beat each other's brains out if that is our desire. However, free will also gives us the opportunity to make other choices and change. The question is, what do we chose and why? And why don't more of us choose peace and compassion?

The things most people worry about, like careers, paying the mortgage, raising kids, their health, relationship issues, the stock market and retirement are important, but they can also be distractions from our real purpose in being here. They pale in comparison to being at peace and knowing life's deeper meaning.

We do try to deal with our pain, and if you consider the monumental expenditure of money and effort we make to alleviate pain, both individually and as a society, you would think a great many people would be dancing on the hilltops like the Von Trapp family instead of suffering in despair in their bedrooms. This becomes especially confusing when you consider all the affirmations that God loves us and cares about us. It would seem that life on earth should be a great deal easier and more joyful, unless of course, you are an atheist.

The problem is that most of our efforts focus on alleviating pain's symptoms rather than addressing its causes. "If you do 'so-and-so', you won't hurt so much." We focus on behavior. Antidepressants and tranquilizers don't address problems either; they just relieve their symptoms.

Your struggles are expressions of the work that remains to be done and of your resistance to moving through life with grace. These are not expressions of failure. They only speak to where you are in your process. You are tumbling down the mountain, getting your rough edges knocked off. If you look around, you will observe that most of humanity is struggling just like you, as we all tumble down this mountain together.

My purpose in writing this book is to help you learn to work with the process you are in, rather than fight with it. I struggled for much of my life because I did not understand what was happening or what was being asked of me. I saw my problems as personal failures and spun myself down into a dark and painful pit. It is my belief that if you come to understand what is taking place in life, you will not be as inclined to struggle with it as I was. You have a choice. You can look down at your rough edges and see yourself as defective. Or, you can see yourself as a work in process. Poets depict the struggle with life as a heroic undertaking, and once you have begum to transition and move out of the victim space this is true. But until then, life can really suck!

People talk about how they will regret leaving this place, and I must admit that a part of me will too. I love the earth. It is a magnificent and wonderful planet, but at this time in our evolution, it is also a place of great pain, conflict and suffering, but that is a discussion for another time.

Before you proceed, I would like to comment on a few of the concepts you will find in this book:

In the shamanic world, we speak of a person's dark or shadow side. This is where our cloaked power resides. It is where people turn when they become afraid. Our most common expressions of power are the negative emotions constellated around fear, i.e., manipulation, dishonesty, envy, greed, hatred, revenge, evil and the rage we mistake for anger. But power is just power. It's like fire; you can heat your lunch with it or burn the house down. The question is, "How will you use it?"

Shaman speak of "soul loss" when people disconnect from important aspects of themselves. This happens when people see themselves as less than they really are. Their interpretation of their life experience has brought them to withhold their love and compassion because they feel a need to protect.

People want to know what I mean when I urge them to "open their hearts." I use the term to indicate an expression of compassion. Most of us spend our days being guarded. We close out hearts, at least partially. Being open feels threatening. Some people have never really opened their hearts, and they do not know what that feels like. Closing the heart is a learned response. We have all been hurt, so opening up requires us to "unlearn" the need for protection that life has fostered in us.

Looking at life is a lot like looking into a cut diamond. As you rotate the stone you see the same light from different perspectives. We will look at life and spirituality from a number of different perspectives, and there will be quite a lot of overlap between each view.

In regard to the writing style of this book, the King's English mandates that "he" be to be used as a gender-neutral pronoun. I find that style to be offensive to modern women. Yet, to have to repeat "he or she" or "him or her" a thousand or more times throughout the book would be tiresome and cumbersome for both of us. So, since the vast majority of the spiritual audience today is female, I will use the pronoun "she." Gentlemen, you are just going to have to adapt until the language police decide to join the modern world.

I am not a writer. I was a good student in school but I was absolutely destroyed by grammar. As I said, I am very right brained and grammar is a linear, left-brain process. I love to read, and so literature saved me from failing English. So, ironically, here I am, writing books. Fortunately I have a gift for making complex subjects understandable. But I fear that I will never understand things like: who and whom, lie and lay, etc.

There are exceptions to some of the concepts addressed in these pages. Where I felt them to be significant, I have tried to address them. To cover every consideration would have made the book encyclopedic.

I do not claim to have a corner on the truth. There are many paths up this mountain. The concepts in this book are expressions of what I believe to be true based upon years of working with these matters. These are my truths. Over the years, my ideas have grown and developed. This is where I am today.

CHAPTER 1

Change

We need not to acquire anything new,
only give up false ideas and useless accretions.
Instead of doing this, we try to grasp something strange and mysterious
because we believe happiness lies elsewhere.
This is a mistake.
Ramana Maharshi[2]

There are two states of being in The Universe. You are either in the God Space, or you are not. In other words, you either live from a place of compassion, or you are dealing with fear. There are levels of intensity to fear, but it is an either/or proposition. The God Space is a place of peace, joy and harmony. And earthly existence is too often a place of pain, anxiety and suffering. Our pain and fear pull us out of the God Space and prohibit us from holding compassion for ourselves and for others.

When in the God Space, you function according to The Universe's principles of harmony and flow. When you separate from the God Space, you must find other ways to manage. You turn to rational thought and ego as substitutes for Universal guidance.

When you live in the God Space you live in the present. You deal with what is really happening. When you operate through fear and ego, you lose that ability, because the ego cannot operate in the present. It lives in the past. In your separated space, there is unworthiness; there are insults, shame, judgment and criticism from which you must protect yourself. When you believe that you are inadequate or unworthy, you must create barriers both to others and within yourself to your own feelings.

You will go through incredible gyrations to avoid, suppress and manipulate in order to keep your defenses functioning and your beliefs intact, regardless of the truth. Faced with an emotional assault, you "stress" the body as you prepare for fight-or-flight and bring up ego compensations as mental defense.

Because of these constrictions, the vital energy of life does not move easily and freely within you. You tighten your muscles, especially your shoulders, neck and pelvis. You will also contract your organs and your breathing will become shallow. The digestive system shuts down and your immune system will go on red alert.

Have you ever eaten lunch when you were tense? Your digestion didn't work very well, did it? The same thing happens to the mind. It can be very difficult to be compassionate and understanding when your mind is clenched with fear. In either situation the energy within you simply does not move well. And when energy does not move freely, you are handicapped from dealing with life. And then you experience pain.

In his insightful book *The Biology of Belief*,[3] Dr. Bruce Lipton points out that the cells of the body can exist in two fundamental states. The first is what he calls a normal or growth state where the cells take in nutrients, process waste, reproduce and carry out common, day-to-day cell functions. For this normal function, the cells require an open exchange with the environment.

Dr. Lipton calls the second state the "protective" state. It is a different configuration that cells move into under stress. In the protective state, most normal cell functions are shut down as the cells reconfigure and move fuel and other resources to a survival posture. In this state, they (in general) shut themselves off from the environment order to protect themselves from harm.

The important concept Dr. Lipton emphasizes is that in a cell, the normal and protective states cannot coexist. Growth and protection cannot take place at the same time. A cell must be in one state or the other. And if you feel insecure, putting your body constantly on "alert" from perceived threats makes it unable to maintain a normal balance. Healthy cell function will be inhibited, cell growth restricted and cell reproduction affected. And the effects are cumulative. Cellular reproduction must continue, but the DNA strands of stressed cells begin to unravel, creating mutations.

Keep in mind that the 80 to 100 trillion cells of your body are constantly replacing and renewing themselves through cell division. And the amount of stress a cell is subjected to can dramatically affect the quality of its reproduction. Although the body can cope with a certain amount of stress and repair some of the damage, ongoing physical, mental or emotional stress takes a heavy toll. Stress suppresses the immune system, compromising your ability to fight off disease and infection. Stress is particularly damaging to the cardiovascular system.

Excessive stress can lead to everything from heart disease, cancer, MS, arthritis, stroke, liver disease, environmental illness and a host of other problems. Stress stunts growth in children. It can even rewire the brain, leaving us more vulnerable to mental problems and emotional dysfunction such as anxiety and depression. Stress makes it difficult to sexually conceive. The one important consequence that is not immediately evident is how stress shortens our lives. We know, as just one example, that mentally ill people have a lifespan that is on average 20 years shorter than normal.

Your thoughts and emotions also change under stress. When you feel tense you can become defensive and overly sensitive. Stress affects your thinking and your decisions. You can become mentally rigid, obstinate, belligerent, or hyper and erratic. Your thoughts can become jumbled, limiting your ability to function. You will not relate freely and compassionately to yourself either.

Just as you and your cells become toxic under stress (when energy does not move), your relationships become toxic when energy does not readily flow in them either. In the contracted state, you cannot participate openly and freely with others. Letting down the drawbridge and making yourself vulnerable creates a level of exposure you are simply cannot tolerate. Even though you have sincere feelings for the others, you must constantly be on guard. You can exaggerate provocations, become overly defensive and attack, or shut down and withdraw. You resist life. And that causes a great deal of pain for partners, friends and families. Everyone involved with you comes away feeling shortchanged. And you feel pretty lousy too.

Withholding love is tough on children. Children need unconditional love in order to feel acceptable. Most of the time they do not get it. This is what probably happened to your parents when they were young, and it is probably what they passed on to you as well.

These dynamics apply on an even larger scale. When energy does not move freely between groups, it causes difficulties for communities, nations, and ultimately for all humankind.

The ego is a mechanism of separation that creates emotional distance (insulation) between you and a perceived threat as seen through the context of your past. The problem for the ego is that the God Space connects you with everything. It opens the doors to all comers. The God Space creates safety and security through the unobstructed flow of information. But when you operate from the ego space, that kind of exposure can make you feel very vulnerable. While the ego offers the seductive (but temporary) comfort of separation, the God Space provides the security of openness and truth. One of the benefits of living in the truth is that you realize that you cannot be harmed.

Not moving energy affects far more than just cells and relationships. The entire universe operates on these principles. In the universe, energy must move. Water runs downhill, light flows into darkness and air rushes into a vacuum. This is how the universe maintains its vitality. Even the great mountains are being constantly eroded, one rock at a time.

The Universe must apply pressure to anything that resists change. When it applies pressure, it creates a temporary disturbance that creates change and ultimately rebalances the system. This is true for stars, your cat and the cells of your body. Think about a sneeze, a cough, or shivering when you are cold.

Remember when as a kid you stuck your hand out the car window to feel the wind push it? Well, that's like The Universe pushing on your ego-based and fear-driven beliefs. Fear and anxiety are incompatible with the God

Space. Your fear-based beliefs stick out to The Universe just like your hand used to stick out to the wind from the car. Your beliefs disrupt the harmony of The Universe. And, The Universe is obliged to apply pressure to them. Every dissonant thought or action ripples out into The Universe and is met with a corresponding pressure "encouraging" you to change them. It is as natural for The Universe to apply pressure to your disharmonious thoughts and beliefs as it is for light to fill a room or for gravity to pull an apple to the ground.

When it pushes on you, the Universe isn't being cruel or unkind. The purpose of The Universe's pressure is not to rebuke or scold, although it can certainly feel that way! The pressure is an invitation, an opportunity, to face the truth about your beliefs and change them. But changing life patterns (and the beliefs that lie beneath them) presents a significant hurdle. It threatens the structure upon which your life has been built. It does not matter that these are untruths. When you live in fear, it feels like all you have. So, when it comes to making changes, even though your beliefs sabotage your life, you can be very resistant to letting them go. You can handle the smaller difficulties, even though they are unpleasant. But taking it all on at once, feels overwhelming.

Normally, The Universe will simply nudge you, but if you habitually resist its requests for change, it will up the ante to match your resistance. Since the truth cannot change, it is your perception of the truth that is going to have to shift in order for you to take the step that is being asked (ultimately required) of you. We know these pressures as "problems." The push comes in the places where you feel vulnerable and insecure (unworthy or inadequate) and, coincidentally, this is where your fears and beliefs originate.

In reaction, we focus on the situation and blame others or ourselves for our failings. We react. We become defensive. We collapse inwardly and withdraw, or push back with aggression and rage. In focusing on the problem, we miss the greater opportunity being offered to move to compassion. We are not often able to make that choice, however.

People despair that they aren't "where they should be" in life. Things haven't gone as they had hoped. They have tried to be happy, and yet they have been given nothing but difficulties. They are frustrated and often angry with God and the world for the way their lives have developed. Their inner fear, protected by their beliefs, gets in their way.

Most people want to heal. Their intention is sincere, but the emotional pain and fear of the unknown trap them. They can't seem to find ways around the obstacles. Trying to change beliefs through altering behavior and attitudes is a lot like trying to stop a train by standing in front of it. You don't stand much of a chance. But, hopping into the cab and shutting down the engine will stop a train. That is what you can learn to do.

The train that is running your life is made up of beliefs, created through your experiences, some difficult and some pleasant, mostly in childhood. We will focus on the difficult experiences and the beliefs you created out of these, because they cause most of your pain. These experiences affected you in your most vulnerable places, and by the way, this is not merely coincidental.

Your beliefs are part of the protective structure you had to create to get through the difficult times of childhood. The really good options were not available to you; your parent's had those and chose not to take them. The only thing you could do was to adapt your behavior and your beliefs (especially about yourself) to accommodate the situation they created. And if that meant that you had to tear your image of yourself down in order to survive, that is what you did.

It did not matter what was right, or what the truth was; your health and well being depended upon you accommodating their needs. Although your parents did the best they could, it was likely they had not dealt with their own pain. This meant they would be unable to openly respond to your needs and were uncomfortable with your natural self. If things didn't go well, something was wrong with you.

You took their inability to respond as a shortcoming in yourself. "If only I had been ___(fill in the blank)___, they would have been more loving."

Although you had done nothing to create the situation, you felt like you did or, perhaps that you were responsible to fix it. And these are dangerous and totally erroneous assumptions. And almost every child makes them.

Most of the pain you feel today is your unresolved childhood pain being dredged up for the umpteenth time. The pain that you have carried all these years is because you blame yourself, at least in part, for what happened. And although you have condemned yourself all these years for being ___(fill in the blank)___, this could not possibly be true. It wasn't your fault. It could not have been. You did not deserve what happened. But you do not know that – yet, and this is The Misunderstanding.

Not only were these childhood experiences difficult, but you will also find that your interpretation of these events, the crucial element in the formation of your beliefs, was seriously in error. The most powerful influences in your life, the things that drive significant and essential aspects of your behavior, are based on a fundamental misunderstanding. For many years you have held yourself responsible for things you had no control over and that you actually had nothing to do with (although they did profoundly affect you).

Kids are just kids. A child does not have the power to control her parents' behavior. You did not have the power to change their fear or their behavior. You couldn't go to Kid's Court and file a petition about your parents' neuroses or their dysfunctionality. Certainly children can make life difficult sometimes, but that is a different matter.

The Misunderstanding is the source of your emotions and your beliefs. You will eventually come to see it for what it is. Then you can confront your beliefs and heal the wounds that drive your emotions and your behavior. We will investigate The Misunderstanding and how it was created at length in Chapters Four and Five. We will also find in Chapter Nine that your present life circumstances are an extension of a pattern that reaches back through many lifetimes, but I want to say a few words about that now.

The Misunderstanding that occurred with your parents is the same dynamic you carried in from your past lives, and it strongly influences how you feel toward life today. In the painful events of your past, you were most likely an adult, and your ego was, as it is today, the dominant factor in your life. Then as now, it got you into trouble. Unwilling to surrender your ego, you looked to God for help when things went badly. But with your ego dominating the stage, the only thing God could do was encourage you to look at what you had created.

As a result, you died (probably badly), feeling alone and abandoned. That is why that lifetime stands out so prominently in your memory. You brought those feelings of abandonment and worthlessness with you into this lifetime. When you are asked today to surrender to the God Space, your ego's understandable response is, "No way!" And as long as you hold those old beliefs, you will struggle. Struggle is the inevitable consequence of having beliefs. We will explore the role of your past lives in greater detail in Chapter Nine.

There is also a larger perspective for you to consider. As much as you dislike them, your problems are essential to your development. Problems come from the disharmonious beliefs you hold. Sooner or later, your ego-driven conflicts will create enough stress (internal and external) to bring you to question the beliefs that drive your fear-based existence. When you become sufficiently frustrated, you will look for other ways of being, and eventually surrender your beliefs because they do not, cannot, sustain a peaceful existence.

As unpleasant as they are, your struggles provide the experiences that bring you to realize you cannot be the person who secretly hides in your private dark swamp. That is why, until you resolve them, no matter what you do to avoid them, your problems will always mutate into some other form and reappear. They must. The Universe will not tolerate disharmony and this conflict is a vital part of your learning. And the process of The Universe will not be denied. Although you can resist making changes for a time, as long as you hold your beliefs, the pressure for change will eventually overwhelm you. This is guaranteed. It is not an option.

Until you give up your beliefs, your life will remain encumbered. Your problems will not, cannot, vanish, so it is important to understand what problems really are and why they exist. Until then, you will simply feel victimized by life and will be unable to work with the gift of change The Universe offers you.

Something else that life teaches us is that nothing is gained through struggle. When you stop struggling, you will confront your beliefs and tear down your belief structures as you realize that they, not other people, not life and not God, have been the source of your problems. And as you peel away the layers of contracted thought, greater awareness will naturally follow, moving you closer to the God Space.

Is the process difficult? Yes. It is uncomfortable? Yes it is. Does it feel unfair? Yes, it does. Is it worth it? Absolutely.

Transformation for anything occurs through the reorganization of its form. Whether it is the established order resisting social change or you resisting giving up your old ways, The Universe presses relentlessly on each of us, on our families and on our institutions to move toward greater alignment with Universal Principles (compassion). If that which has taken form, whether a rock or an idea, has an investment in keeping that form, it will resist The Universe's incessant pressure for change. Eventually, each thing, whether object or idea, must respond to the pressures for change. The Universe will not be denied. Outmoded political systems, old trees and your beliefs are going to have to eventually give way. Fluid systems adapt, rigid ones break. Each must change so that the universe remains viable and vital.

The life expectancy of any thing, whether a tree, a rock or social institution, will be determined by its rigidity, (its flexibility to respond to the pressures of change), and its strength. Green trees bend in the wind, old trees split and break. Each responds to The Universe in its own way and in its own time. Yet each must respond.

The entire universe operates this way. Where systems are fluid, we can see the process more easily. Take the weather, for example. Weather is a constant flux of local changes that keep the larger planetary weather system in balance. Where there is resistance to change, we find weather disharmony. The disharmony created by the resistance will lead to the creation of a storm. The storm clears away the resistance and returns the environment to a more normal pattern. The greater the resistance, the greater the storm. It is the same with people, bacteria, relationships, families, communities and nations.

At one time, both England and France were traditional monarchies. The desire for individual freedom amongst the people grew in each society to the point that the pressure for change would not be denied. Democracy was going to replace monarchy. King Charles I of England and Louis XVI of France did not want to lose their power or their heads, but they had little choice. Ideally they would have listened to the people and responded to the issues they were raising. But this does not happen often.

As is usually the case, the kings were invested in the system they were committed to and that commitment limited their ability to be receptive to new ideas. They could have relinquished their power and retired in comfort, but their commitment to the idea of "King" demanded that they resist the change. These kings could not conceive that the people would actually turn away from them. It was just too far outside the royal paradigm.

The values the kings embraced and symbolized were out of synch with the changes that had already occurred in their societies. They tried to resist the process, and their resistance to the inevitable pressure for greater personal freedom brought about their downfall and eventually cost both of them their heads! Today France has no king and England's monarchy is ceremonial.

The same thing happens when you resist The Universe's pressure to move toward greater compassion. The Universe asks you to move in harmony, and most of the time you resist, creating a "problem." And just as with Louis XVI, the change has already been mandated, you just don't know it. And like the old kings, you fear what is to come because it challenges your beliefs – what you "believe " to be true. The new paradigm will require a different way of doing things. It challenges your old ways. But losing what is familiar feels like a loss of control. It is the bungee jump situation all over again.

The choice is whether you will make a peaceful transition to the new order or whether, like Louis XVI, The Universe is going to have to push you over the edge through the creation of a crisis - perhaps a disease, business failure, divorce or some other potential loss that will force you to change your beliefs. This is the message of Charles Dickens's, *A Christmas Carol* as Scrooge is forced to look at the consequences of the life he has created.

The opportunity to make changes is around us all the time. Look into any problem and you will find at its core an opportunity for everyone involved to make changes (always toward greater compassion, usually for themselves). People do not usually take these opportunities, but they are always there, nonetheless. Every moment offers the opportunity for you to do something heartfelt. . .

Visit the waiting room of any doctor's office or the surgical ward of a hospital, and you will find people there who have resisted life's urgings to the point that their bodies have failed from the stress. Disease is simply an advanced stage in The Universe's unrelenting process of encouraging us to change. The Universe will intensify any situation until the individual surrenders and opens her heart.

I have an old photo from the 1920s of rows of teamsters with their horse-drawn wagons parked on the streets of Chicago waiting for work. Out in the street in the photo, young men drive by in their new Model T trucks, loaded with goods. The younger men were not intimidated by new technology, but the old teamsters could not adapt, and they and their horse-drawn wagons became irrelevant.

In our lifetimes, we have witnessed the passing (although there are still vestiges around) of the cowboy, hierarchical management, segregation, train travel, video cassettes, handwritten letters, colonialism, the family farm, isolationism, wringer washers, perfume, gender inequality, steamship travel, big cars, cheap gasoline, wind-up watches, cassette tape and blue-collar jobs.

On the cusp are libraries, newspapers, mom & pop businesses, bookstores, houses made of wood and the old style military.

Those who could not adapt and change have struggled. The firms that were big in steamship travel didn't move into the airline business. The auto firms that made minivans and SUV's aren't making hybrids. The Swiss, watchmakers to the world, don't make many digital watches today, although interestingly enough, they invented them! Kodak didn't make the transition into digital photography and the retailing giants of tomorrow won't have stores, they will sell around the globe over the Internet.

Does the pressure for change mean we must experience pain? To a certain extent, it does. But there are different kinds of pain. Doing something new requires the death of the old. Change creates anxiety, but if we approach change with consciousness, the process is manageable. But conscious pain is nothing compared to the unconscious pain we create for ourselves when we resist. And we are very good at resisting! You see this happening for individuals, families, communities and nations all the time.

Don't be masochistic about it, but recognize that it will ultimately lead to your enlightenment. Become a student of life instead of a victim of it. Learn to love the process! Besides, living in the God Space makes daily life incredibly more joyous and peaceful.

When we resist the process, it makes life much more difficult! The pain we experience is a measure of our resistance to giving up the beliefs we are being asked to change. Until we make the transition, the pressure from The Universe will not, cannot, go away. In fact, if we try to avoid it, the pressure will increase, creating greater stress and even more conflict. Whether we like the process or not, it is the essential aspect of life on earth. There is an old cliché, "Good judgment comes from experience, which comes from bad judgment." That is life and growth in a nutshell.

People get confused about what they are supposed to do in life. We are on earth for one purpose, and it isn't about amassing millions of dollars, achieving peace in the Middle East or even finding a cure for cancer. And, no, you didn't come here to serve your fellow man or to make the world a better place either. As I have said before, each of us came here to learn the truth about who we are, and in the process of doing that, we will naturally learn to love ourselves. If you are eventually moved to save the world, by all means do so. But do it because your work on yourself has opened your heart to the point that you wish to serve humankind. Do it for heartfelt reasons.

I am asked many questions about the meaning of life, why we are here, why things are the way they are – that sort of thing. Life can be very frustrating without an understanding of what it is all about. As a friend of mine used to say, "I don't mind being on my knees, I just want to know why I am there!"

We all struggle with the vagaries of everyday life, and learning to be at peace is important, not just because it makes life easier, but because it begins to verge into the larger issues about why we are here.

Think about what it was like before you ever came to earth. You were in the etheric realms doing whatever we do when we are out of body, without much self-awareness. You felt good. After all, The Universe is a pretty wonderful place to be, but we would not have called you spiritually developed, especially in terms of consciousness. "Innocent" and "naïve" are words that come to mind. So, a decision is made – probably by your higher consciousness and God, for you (us) to develop into a more enlightened being.

The way this is accomplished is for you to experience untruth, so that you will develop a very strong dislike for it. It is through living in the shadow that you will choose, eventually, to live in the light. Remember, you have free will, so you must choose.

Now here's the problem: If you know what's going on, the process doesn't work. So long as you know that you are loved and perfect, you cannot really experience what living in the shadow is about. You would look at the experience and say, "That's really awful, and walk away." End of story. You would have no reason to deepen and develop your conscious awareness.

But if, even for a short period of time (although long by human standards), you were to live in a space where you really felt the despair and the pain of being outside the God Space, your learning would be profound. Understand, no one is asking, or assuming, for that matter, that you will like the experience.

So as not to disturb your awareness, you get forced out of the God Space, and your energy is then contracted down to the point that you take on physical form. In that state you can experience pain.

God wants this to be a powerful and meaningful experience, so you get tossed into a place where there are few rules and the shadow energies can predominate. You run into walls and learn by trial and error. It is like you only spoke English and God wanted you to take an intensive course in Chinese, so he drops you into the middle of a city in China to make your way. How would you feel? Angry? Abandoned? Unloved? What would you conclude? That you were not worthwhile? Sound familiar?

So you struggle, and you learn. You are lost and alone, you make a ton of mistakes and as lifetime after lifetime progresses, you get better. Certainly you have slip-ups. Some of them are really bad. You carry the pain of those experiences with you. Sometimes you don't know what the truth is or where you are going, but something keeps you motivated and you keep going. Maybe at times, it's just to get away from the pain, but as you get banged about, you begin to get the hang of things. Even though you are developing inner spiritual strength and awareness, it might not look like that from the outside.

You live your life so as to avoid dealing with a God that you are convinced is not happy with you. You intuitively know that going into your feelings and your pain means dealing with the separation you feel from Him and you don't want to look at that. You felt abandoned by Him before and are afraid to let go of the substitute life structures you have created even though they do a poor job of giving you what you really need.

Regular spiritual practice is difficult. There is a lot of resistance. You have tried to meditate and couldn't, or do it only sporadically. You have read spiritual books and listened to CD's, but the fear of not being lovable and the pain of your initial separation keeps getting in your way, although you may not be conscious of it. In time you will come to learn that all spiritual teachings are only meant to help us retrace our steps to the Original Source.

It means just what it says. Good, bad, indifferent–love it. Beautiful, ugly, joyful, sad, and even painful–love it.[4] That may sound crazy, but that is what living from the God Space means. The path you are on will eventually demand that you learn to love everything anyway, so you might as well get on with it. You are being twisted and pulled into a new form, and no one likes the process, so you are not going to like a great deal of what happens.

In addition to Christ's example, the Creator's teachings and guidance regarding how we should live have been with us for thousands of years. Read the Ten Commandments. What do they say? Love your neighbor, don't lie, don't murder, don't steal, don't covet another's wife, don't worship false gods, etc. Isn't that opening your heart to life? Isn't that "loving everything?"

All along there has only been one truth, one place for you to go, and even though you have fought going there with all your might, you are like a goldfish in a bathtub. The Creator lets you and all the other fish swim around in the tub and experience and learn from each other, and then when you have learned what you can and gone about as far as you can on your own, He pulls the plug and creates a grand crisis for the entire species. Ultimately there is only one place for any of you to go, and kicking and screaming, you enter the final crises before enlightenment. You swoosh down the cosmic drain to the light on the other side.

It is a tough process, but it has been done with a great deal of love. We make things here a good deal more difficult than is necessary, but that is an important part of our learning too.

We get hung up on the idea of earthly accomplishment, but if there ever were such a thing as Judgment Day, God isn't going to ask you if you were a banker or a shoemaker or if you cleaned toilets. He's not going to ask how big your house was or the size of your retirement plan. God really doesn't care about earthly concerns. Money has no relevance in heaven. What is important to Him is how you lived your life. Did you live it with compassion? Were you kind and loving? What did you do for others? Did you help the poor and the sick and the suffering? Or were you too busy? . . . .

Of course there really isn't such a thing as Judgment Day. There is just the hell we create for ourselves by choosing to live outside the God Space. At the Last Supper, Christ offered a new commandment. He said, "Love one another as I have loved you." And that brings us to our first principle, Principle Number One:

LOVE EVERYTHING

It means just what it says. Good, bad, indifferent – love it. Beautiful, ugly, joyful, sad, and even painful – love it. That may sound crazy, but that is what living from the God Space means. The path you are on will eventually demand that you learn to love everything anyway, so you might as well get on with it. You are being twisted and pulled into a new form, and no one likes the process, so you are not going to like a great deal of what happens. In addition to Christ's example, the Creator's teachings and guidance regarding how we should live have been with us for thousands of years. Read the Ten Commandments. What do they say? Love your neighbor, don't lie, don't murder, don't steal, don't covet another's wife, don't worship false gods, etc. Isn't that opening your heart to life? Isn't that "loving everything?"

We ignore God and His teachings; it is not the other way around. After years of struggle and fighting against the process, I see its perfection today, regardless of how it felt to me at the time.

Abraham Lincoln was one of the most compassionate and kind-hearted men ever to occupy the White House. There is a story that when Lincoln was an attorney in Illinois, he was riding in a stagecoach, discussing his philosophy of self-interest with a fellow passenger. Lincoln professed that there was no act that was not prompted by at least some degree of self-interest. At that very moment, they passed a squealing pig that had become mired in the mud. Lincoln had the coach stopped and waded out into the mud to free the pig. Upon Lincoln's muddy return, his seatmate exclaimed, "Now look here, you cannot say that was a selfish act!"

"Extremely selfish," Lincoln replied. "If I had left that little fellow in the mud, the memory of his squealing would have made me uncomfortable all day."

We can view Lincoln's compassion, Mother Theresa's caring or Gandhi's nonviolence and be justifiably awed at their dedicated service to others, but what we often miss in our assessment is that these people had learned to live from Universal Truth and had come to realize the blessings that following those precepts gave them. Although Lincoln was acting from compassion for the pig when he rescued it; he was primarily acting in resonance with his own inner truth. Experience had shown him that being compassionate would make life better for him, and that it became more painful when he did not. He had learned the price he paid personally for not addressing the disharmony that life brought his way. This is particularly fascinating considering that this is the man who was destined to be President during our greatest internal conflict.

When people become self-centered because of their ego-based fear, their natural compassion shuts down. They "do not hear" the squeal of the pig because they are uncomfortable venturing outside their self-created security zone. But if we ignore the pig today, we will be presented with an angry, full grown hog, stuck in the same mud tomorrow. There are many people who go through life railing against the injustices of the world (of which there are many, to be sure); but if we would all do just one simple thing, i.e., hear the squeal of the pig; our world would be transformed overnight.

I say "simple thing," but of course it is not, otherwise we would already be doing it. I will repeat this several times in the book: The concepts behind all spiritual teachings are incredibly simple, but doing them can be quite another matter. Opening to the squeal of the pig illustrates the essence of that dichotomy.

Moving to the God Space means relinquishing the ego. And, that means giving up a good deal of what we believe to be true. It threatens what we think we know. The ego has given us comfort. It has kept us "safe," whereas the God Space feels flimsy, ephemeral and insubstantial.

You do not yet appreciate the wonderful and special being that you are. Until you do, the part of you that holds limiting views will be a source of difficulty. It must. The Universe is compelled to apply pressure (bring to your awareness) the places where you do not move with grace and harmony. This is the way The Universe works. None of us likes being pushed where our hearts are closed. It is threatening and it hurts! We closed ourselves off long ago because we were afraid, and we do not want to get pushed back into that vulnerable circumstance again! You would call this having a problem. The Universe would see it as an opportunity for growth. This is not done to punish or condemn you, but to awaken you to the dysfunction of your beliefs. At this stage in your evolution, you learn a great deal more from your pain than you do from your joy.[5]

My boat struck something deep.
Nothing happened.
Sounds,
Silence,
Waves.
Nothing happened.
Or perhaps everything has happened,
and I am sitting in the middle of my new life.
Juan Ramón Jiménez[6]

CHAPTER 2

Beliefs

"Your task is not to seek for love,
but merely to seek and find all the barriers
within yourself that you have built against it."

Jalal ad-Din Rumi

Sometimes I challenge a group by asking them, "Who are you?" The
room usually goes dead for a few moments and then I get some muffled
responses, mostly things people have read in books. No one really knows.

It's a trick question. If you knew who you were, you would not be here.
It was what you were sent her to learn. And besides, even if you knew, you
couldn't put it into words, anyway.

Although we may not know who we are, each of us carries a set of beliefs
regarding who we think we are. Those beliefs have been formed out of our
experiences. The powerful experiences were the painful ones, and
unfortunately they often lead us to think badly about ourselves. They cause
us to drive around with lives that have flat tires.

When we separate from the God Space, we must create a structure
through which to cope with life. We fill the space of separation with belief.
Beliefs about people, beliefs about society, beliefs about God and most
importantly, beliefs about ourselves. Beliefs allow us to live in an artificial
reality devoid of real compassion for ourselves or for others. If I decide that
I am not lovable, then I will need to create beliefs to support my decision in
order to act on it. I might create the belief that I am unworthy, for example.

You really are a good person, but let's assume that you do not fully
embrace that truth. You harbor doubts because you sometimes get snagged

by fear and have done unkind and hurtful things. So although the truth does exist at a deeper level, but your beliefs prevent you from accessing it. What manifests on the surface are your doubts and beliefs. And as long as you believe you are unworthy or inadequate, your beliefs, inaccurate and flawed as they may be, are going to determine how you act and how you respond to life. They will control the life choices you make, and they will also impede your spiritual development.

Consider how much of your daily existence – your thoughts, choices and reactions - are driven by what you believe about yourself and the world. You have been at it so long the process is virtually automatic, but it is there, nonetheless.

As you sit there, take a breath, close your eyes and simply imagine all your beliefs falling away. Feel what life would be like if you were to drop all of them. For many people this is a very freeing moment. Notice that without your beliefs you are still functional, (and a great deal freer than you were just a few moments ago!). And, yet, nothing has changed except your perspective.

Of course, the moment you move back into "reality" you will tighten things back up and lose that relaxed freedom. But it is important for you to know that it is there and that when you tighten back up, you are making a choice. This becomes especially important when you consider that all of your beliefs are untrue – all of them, AND that you no longer need them.

What does the person you see in the mirror believe about herself? What is her story? What is the baggage that she carries into every relationship? We know that her beliefs are based on her experiences, but do her conclusions about herself reflect the truth? Or, do they reflect The Misunderstanding?

Because they are based in untruth, when she acts on her beliefs, she gets into trouble. Sometimes her beliefs get you into a good deal of trouble. In fact, her beliefs are the source of all your troubles.

Every belief you hold will eventually create a problem for you. Actually, most of them create problems for you all the time! Beliefs are constrictions to the flow of energy. They are a ripple in the otherwise calm universal pond and cannot remain as such. Sooner or later, The Universe is going to apply its infinite energy to your beliefs and "encourage" you to change them. This brings us to Walker's Rule. Walker's Rule will be our Second Principle. It states:

ANYTHING YOU DO NOT LOVE
WILL BECOME A LESSON

I could have said, "Anything you do not love will become a problem," but in truth, situations and problems are always lessons. That is why they exist. Think about where your lessons in life come from. Every lesson has to do with you not holding the God Space. Your problem came to teach you to love more openly and deeply. Whenever you step off the path, there will be a nudge urging you back. When this learning process confronts us, we call it having a problem. I call it a learning opportunity, God calls it life.

Walker's Rule is really a corollary to the LOVE EVERYTHING Principle, and it tells us why it is so important to learn to LOVE EVERYTHING.

Sooner or later it will dawn on you that there is a great deal more going on here than just you walking down the road of life. We have been led to believe that we are random particles determining our own paths through the world. This is not true and the implications of that are very important. We will be exploring that idea through the next few chapters.

Universal Truths just are. We know them as feelings. They exist beyond words. They are states of being. If I were to say to you, "You are love," the phrase would resonate positively within you. It is just there, you know it to be true. You really don't have to think about it. Notice the difference between the thought, "I believe I am a good person," and the feeling, "I am a good person."

Universal Truths can be discerned by their genuine compassion, they are not beliefs. For example, there is equality, openness, gratitude and compassion. These are states of being. Our inner peace is determined by our relationship to these states. At this stage in our evolution, few people are at peace with themselves, their lives or with God. They live in a separated space only distantly connected to spirit.

In the God Space, you feel prohibitions against killing, lying, cheating and causing harm. There is also support for being kind, helping others and caring for the planet and God's creatures. When you operate in harmony with Universal Truth you feel better, as do those around you. That is the magic of living a life of compassion and gratitude.

Beliefs are crutches to get us through situations we do not feel ready to address. If I can hold the belief that Hispanics, bikers or gays are lower forms of life, then I do not have to deal with the part of me that envies, perhaps covets, what these people have - their values, life choices and the freedom to express them. I do not have to deal with the part of me that their beliefs threaten and that I am uncomfortable with. My disdain for these people gives me permission to not open my heart. If I can look down on them, I give myself permission to dismiss them and discriminate against them.

Prejudice is quite different from disagreement. Implicit in disagreement is respect for the other person's views and choices. I can disagree with her and let her be. Prejudice, on the other hand, cannot stand to have her on the planet. She must be eradicated so that she does not trigger what is happening within me. Recognize the roots of "ethnic cleansing" here."

Consider another situation: It is against God's law to kill, so in order to get soldiers to kill, government and the military must create beliefs of the enemy as an "evil" that must be eradicated. Otherwise it would be very difficult to get people to go against their natural prohibition to do no harm. The general public must also be propagandized, so that parents will allow their children to go to war and be killed and maimed, usually under specious circumstances. The conflict between political manipulation and Universal Truth is why soldiers suffer post-combat stress disorders and have high rates of violent suicide. Five thousand former soldiers commit suicide every year in the U.S.

Beliefs come from many sources, but the one quality that all beliefs share is that they are human-made. God has truth. Humans have belief. Many of our beliefs are learned from social institutions like school or church, others come from our direct experiences, but most of our beliefs come from our parents and families. We are taught them. We are encouraged to emulate our family's values.

There is an inherent conflict between any social entity, whether it is an individual, group, corporation, religion or family, and the conformity needs of society. After all, it is much easier for the shepherd if all the sheep go in the same direction.

When you were a child, your natural exuberance was "inappropriate" in certain social settings. Your natural self had to be toned down. You had to learn "manners" and conform to social norms.

And, in all likelihood, this was not done with respect for who you were. This is a pattern we will see frequently in life – social conformity inherently limits individual or organizational freedom; but things really get out of whack when the need for conformity is driven by ulterior motives and then handled badly.

It is a parent's job to "teach" you about hot stoves and to not run into the street. And while they taught you about survival, there were also messages about life, other ethnic groups, Aunt Emma and the neighbors. Your parent's biases and their views about life, right and wrong and what was proper and improper, were important parts of your learning process.

But the most powerful things you learned came from how you were treated. If your emotional needs were ignored or repressed, or if your real self was unacceptable, you were going to come away from childhood with a number of false beliefs about yourself. You will have been imprinted with your parent's fears, anxieties and the residue of their unresolved life experiences that had been projected onto you.

The God Space does not/cannot create problems. The fear-based beliefs that you hold, even though they have never really belonged to you, are the cause of all your difficulties. That is why the process of life on earth is to get you to let go of the things you believe. Think of your beliefs as "on loan" from

God in order to assist you in the process of learning one day that you really do not need them. Your beliefs are like lead weights you carry around until you get sick and tired of being burdened by them. This brings us to Principle Number Three:

WHAT GETS YOU INTO TROUBLE ISN'T YOURS

In most cases children are not encouraged to develop their own beliefs, especially when they conflict with those of the parents (which is why some kids do just that). Rather, children are encouraged to believe and behave as the family demands. Unless you were encouraged to form your own beliefs, much of what you hold really isn't yours at all. And when you get into trouble, this is what will be getting in your way.

So now we have three Principles to guide us:

LOVE EVERYTHING

ANYTHING YOU DO NOT LOVE
WILL BECOME A LESSON

WHAT GETS YOU INTO TROUBLE ISN'T YOURS

The core values of most religions don't fit well in society much better than most individuals do. Their teachings typically include care for the sick, help for the poor and ethnic and racial equality. Governments on the other hand, have historically existed largely for the benefit of the wealthy (business) classes. Regardless of the political rhetoric, governments have historically shown little real regard for the suffering or hardships of either the poor or minorities. (I find myself wondering how different the government response would have been if hurricane Katrina had hit Orange County or Miami instead of New Orleans.) In any case, being part of society creates an inherent moral conflict for the organized faiths because their core beliefs run counter to political social practice.

Corporations have to learn "manners" also, but this is a somewhat different situation because corporations are beholden to other masters. Left on their own, history shows us that many corporations will pollute the environment, abuse workers and shove shoddy products onto the public, because those things are advantageous to the owners.

This whole topic is a massive discussion in itself. Without getting too deeply into its moral or ethical considerations, the important principle for our purposes is at this stage in human evolution, being a part of society, for a person, a company or a church, means that natural inclinations and beliefs will conflict with, and must be subjugated to, the larger political and social process.

The essence of being a teenager is to struggle between the need for group approval and acceptance of one's individual sense of self. In that same sense, many adults "sell their souls" in order to have the appearance of a relationship or family rather than suffer the humiliation of social failure, even though living by themselves is really what they desire.

When you make anything outside the God Space, for example, a short-term ego-based need, ahead of your longer term spiritual needs, you guarantee the creation of a problem. You place it and yourself into conflict with The Universe. Get married to someone that you really don't love, even when you think you do (which means you are kidding yourself), and you are going to have problems. That second piece of pie will numb the feelings of your hurting inner child for the moment, but down the road, you will look in the mirror and feel poorly about yourself. When you create any institution-a marriage, a new religion, a group, a new form of government, or even a friendship, and pervert the founding vision in order for ego needs, you guarantee the creation of a problem.

Let's illustrate by using religion. If the survival of the religion is at stake, even if the founder was Moses, Christ or Buddha, their teachings and ideals will be savaged to make the church socially acceptable. It happens in every religion, every social institution and in its own way, to every individual and family.

The early Christian Church needed money, desired power, and wanted to expand its dominion throughout the non-Christian (heathen) world. And its existence had been tenuous up to this time. There was considerable motivation for The Church to support the expansionist efforts of various European sovereigns as they sought to increase their own territory and power by conquering native lands. The rulers wanted the Church's blessing for their conquests, and there was a lot of power to be gained in the process.

Yet Christ had explicitly forbidden violence, without exception. He said, "But I say to you, do not resist him who is evil; but whoever slaps you on your right cheek, turn to him the other also."[7] He also said, "But I say to you, love your enemies, and pray for those who persecute you."[8] In the Garden of Gethsemane, Christ told Peter to put away his sword saying, "Those who live by the sword shall die by the sword."[9] He did not add a caveat and say, "Except for the Romans because they are conquerors and oppressors." His commandment was a flat, unqualified, "Don't do it!"

Although Christ had forbidden violence, the Church found a way to slide around the issue. It is called rationalization. And church leaders, politicians and you do it all the time. The Church has found ways to support the wars and colonial conquests of the various European rulers, and later the mercantile democracies that replaced them, up to, and including the present day. A few faiths like the Quakers, Amish, Baha'i and Mennonites have remained faithful to Christ's admonitions, but they are generally dismissed as fringe elements by the "established" religions.

In 1063, Pope Alexander II gave a papal blessing to the Iberian Christians in their wars against the evil Muslims, granting forgiveness of sins to those who were killed in battle. In 1095, Pope Urban II offered the knights of the Crusades immortality and also forgave their sins. Those who died killing the enemy would gain "everlasting glory" as a "living sacrifice." He also offered rewards for the massacre of Jews. On the opposing side, the mullahs offered martyrdom for Muslim warriors. Both sides sought support from God for their respective causes. God, we can safely assume, was not amused.

There is probably no better example of rationalization than the teachings of Muhammad. Inspired by God, and deeply desiring compassion, Muhammad's personal angst was so great that he distorted the messages he received. It caused him to create dogma that in some very important ways, directly conflicts with God's other teachings.

Today our world is being ravaged by those misinterpretations, and the manipulation of them by Islamic radicals for political ends. Muslim radicals have adopted fundamentalist rigidity because they know that a careful examination of their beliefs will not stand up to the light of truth. So, they live, of necessity, in the shadows. This is a good illustration of how a group not choosing to live in truth can affect the rest of us. It is a pattern we have seen repeated many times throughout history.

I do not mean to give a history lesson – but rather to illustrate the process that we are all capable of when we step outside the God Space. Perhaps our lapses are not as dramatic as Pope Urban's or Osama bin Laden's, but individually and collectively, our rationalizations create racial, ethnic and gender prejudice, support corrupt political and religious systems, destroy marriages, friendships and most importantly, impede our movement toward enlightenment.

The odds are good that at some point in your life, you sacrificed your deeper peace of mind in order to have a partner, to no longer feel alone, defective and unlovable. You undoubtedly had feelings for your partner – but were also operating out of neediness. That relationship went sour and probably ended badly. Or, perhaps you held it in limbo for years. Why? Because your "need" to not feel alone was stronger and in conflict with, the parts of you that were not ready to open your heart. You tried to short circuit the natural process and paid the price for it. There really is no free lunch. The same thing is true for Churches, governments, organizations of all kinds and families as well. There really is only one path.

Democracy in America today is a far cry from the institution created by The Founding Fathers. In that same vein, Adam Smith would be shocked by the practices of today's mega-corporations, and Christ would have a very difficult time recognizing the religion created in His name.

In The Sermon on The Mount, Christ spoke of loving enemies, forgiving people their transgressions, not judging, being generous and not piling up earthly treasures.[10] He said, "Lay not up for yourselves treasures upon the earth."[11] You probably didn't know that non-violence and eschewing possessions were fundamental Christian principles, because most Christian faiths no longer even teach them!

In a famous mistranslation, He also actually said, "Blessed are the humble, for they shall inherit the earth." The "humble" are the egoless. I mentioned that at the Last Supper, Christ also offered the new commandment to "Love each other as I have loved you." Racial, ethnic, sexual, economic and gender inequality are irreconcilable with Christ's message to love one another, and yet religions and political and other social groups routinely engage in biases against some or all of God's children. "One Nation, Under God," unless you are female, gay, a minority or an "illegal alien."

Some religions create an interesting paradox. They build their faith on the existence of an omnipotent God who has the power to create and destroy the universe. To them, God designed this incredibly complex and interconnected process of which we are a part - and is capable of all sorts of wonderful miracles. But at the same time, these religions posit the existence of a Satan or a devil that stands almost (but not quite) as God's evil twin.

Intended or not, this poses a real predicament for the faithful. Either the Creator is feeble, without power to banish Satan and the darkness; or He is an omniscient and omnipresent being who created Satan - and is at best disinterested or possibly even malevolent, allowing his children to be unfairly maimed and harmed without benefit of His love and protection. Obviously, neither prospect is enticing.

About 400 AD, Augustine of Hippo added another explanation, one that places responsibility for the problem squarely on man's inherently sinful shoulders. Church doctrine at the time declared, "*Omne bonum a Deo, omne malum ab homine,*" i.e., "All good from God, all evil from man." Augustine believed that God was both omnipotent and benevolent, but that people were evil and flawed and, as a result, deserved to be punished. Acknowledging that his Greek wasn't very good, Augustine then (either purposefully or in error) mistranslated the parable of Adam and Eve from the Greek[12] and created the concept of Original Sin.[13] Augustine's doctrine has kept Western civilization over a barrel ever since.

Adopted by the Church and later exploited by Protestant reformers, Original Sin added copious quantities of shame onto Christians already accustomed to being shamed for their sins by their priests and ministers. It was of little matter to these churchmen that Original Sin was both a mistranslation and an academic invention that had never appeared in the Bible and was completely contrary to anything Christ had taught. These fundamentalist religious leaders had a mission. They had souls to save. And if convincing people they were sinners would fill the pews and the collection plates, so much the better.

I would like to submit another, more reasonable, explanation for our relationship to God. I believe that God is an incredibly compassionate being who has created a perfect and powerful way for us to achieve enlightenment. We know that process as life.

The events of your life are neither accidental or coincidental, nor are they the acts of a cruel or disinterested Creator. In fact, quite the opposite is true. Your life is shaped by what you believe and by The Universe's responses to those beliefs. And although you act on your beliefs as though they were true, this cannot possibly be so. I will say this many times throughout the book, but the process we call life is a series of opportunities to challenge what you believe (especially about yourself) and encourage you to let go of your beliefs. Those opportunities ask you to find another way of being. They ask you to move closer to living in the Truth.

There are no beliefs in the God Space; there is only Universal Truth. And Universal Truth must be felt; it cannot be written or spoken. It can only be known experientially. Making the transition to the God Space requires that you surrender to the Truth, but your beliefs interfere with that process.

Your problems in life, both internal and external, are created because of your beliefs. They are like anchors that keep you temporarily safe, but also keep you from moving forward. You travel in circles, repeating the same experiences over and over, learning little, held captive by your fear-based perspective. Saint Thomas Aquinas wrote that, "If the highest aim of a captain were to preserve his ship, he would keep it in port forever." I am reminded of something that Clarissa Pinkola Estes, author of *Women Who Run With The Wolves*, wrote:

> Ours is not the task of fixing the entire world all at once, but of stretching out to mend the part of the world that is within our reach. Any small, calm thing that one soul can do to help another soul, to assist some portion of this poor suffering world, will help immensely. It is not given to us to know which acts or by whom, will cause the critical mass to tip toward an enduring good. What is needed for dramatic change is an accumulation of acts, adding, adding to, adding more, continuing...

> ...There will always be times when you feel discouraged. I too have felt despair many times in my life, but I do not keep a chair for it; I will not entertain it. It is not allowed to eat from my plate. The reason is this: In my uttermost bones I know something, as do you. It is that there can be no despair when you remember why you came to Earth, who you serve, and who sent you here... In that spirit, I hope you will write this on your wall: When a great ship is in harbor and moored, it is safe, there can be no doubt. But that is not what great ships are built for.

Ships sometimes flounder on the rocks and sink, but you cannot. You are unsinkable! But you do not know that yet. When you cling to your beliefs, you have something to lose. You will only be free when you come to see The Misunderstanding from which your beliefs have been created for what it is, enabling you to then release it. You will then be both free and unsinkable.

In the moment it is easier to be scared or angry. It is always easier to choose the shadow side because it feels safer, or at least less risky, (in the moment) than being open. People slide into the shadow because they cannot find the self-confidence to risk holding the truth. Hiding in the shadow offers the feeling of insulation from pain and fear. You keep your ship in the harbor. The God Space, on the other hand, requires that we stand naked in the light of truth. It demands that we leave the harbor and sail out into the great ocean.

The ironic thing is that the God Space is actually the safest place in the universe to be. But from the ego's perspective, the complete opposite is true. When we step away from the God Space, we feel vulnerable and fear being harmed. Consider the essence of the 23rd Psalm from the perspective of holding the God Space:

The Lord is my shepherd; I shall not want.
He maketh me to lie down in green pastures:
He leadeth me beside the still waters.
He restoreth my soul:
He leadeth me in the path of righteousness for his name's sake.
Yea, though I walk through the valley of the shadow of death,
I will fear no evil: for thou art with me; thy rod and thy staff they comfort me.
Thou preparest a table before me in the presence of mine enemies:
thou anointest my head with oil; my cup runneth over.
Surely goodness and mercy shall follow me all the days of my life:
and I will dwell in the house of the Lord for ever.

When you are out of alignment, the Universe mirrors your behavior back to you in two primarily ways. Internally, pain is generated through your sense of conscience (guilt and shame). These are the God Space based, deep-seated feelings of wrong (not a voice, but feelings) that you experience when you know what you have done is unloving or unkind. This is the inner mirror. It is different from the shrill voice that simply condemns. That is an ego device.

The second mirror is an external one, but instead of being made of glass and reflecting light, this mirror is made up of other people. It uses their reactions to reflect back to us (make us aware of) the places where we do not hold compassion.[14] Think about the way you react when someone is acting inappropriately. That is The Universal Mirror in operation.

The reflected image will come in the form of a hurtful action or an insensitive word from a lover, parent, a co-worker, a friend, or some fool who cuts you off in traffic. We see these actions as starting with the other person, but they do not. Whether the other person is aware of it or not, she is reacting to the disharmony within you. This is the Universe's way of calling attention to the "sticky" places within us that need attention. These are of course, the very places we would rather avoid.

Whether you like the process or not, it is being done to help you grow and evolve. The Universe will present you with opportunity after opportunity to change, until you get it. Anywhere you hold fear, anxiety, self-doubt or shame, in other words, anywhere you close your heart to yourself or to others, is a place that The Universe must push.

Some years ago, American Guru Ram Dass suffered a massive stroke. Rather than allow himself to be debilitated by his infirmity, Ram Dass took his dilemma as a message from The Universe to deepen his spiritual awareness and to address his self-limiting beliefs. In his book and film, Fierce Grace, Ram Dass says that because of what he has been through, his spiritual gift is deeper and greater than ever before. This is the gift that The Universe offers all of us.

People who have a difficult time finding peace in life know how to struggle, avoid and resist. They have had a great deal of practice at it. It is easier to get upset and blame things on something or someone else, or on life or our own unworthiness. And here's an interesting twist: blaming yourself is just another way to avoid the issue. If you view yourself as defective or unworthy, then you have license to excuse yourself for not stepping up to the plate and addressing your beliefs.

Some people wear their failures and victim hood like badges. They use their woundedness to keep themselves from being free. When our egos start running our lives, we can imagine that God is acting against us and that we are unloved. Although this is completely untrue, we can get wrapped up in our difficulties and our pain, and become unable (or unwilling) to see the larger process that is taking place. From this point of view, life feels unfair.

Our street gangs, prisons, shelters and crack houses are full of hurting people who feel that life has been extremely unfair to them. They hide behind dysfunctional behavior or retreat into drugs and alcohol. They express their rage by acting out. Some of these people are so hardened that they seem unreachable. For others, the guilt and shame are overwhelming.

Although some people's lives can be harsh, and it may seem unkind to say this, every person is exactly where they need to be in order to get what they came here to learn. When these tough cases crack, the depth of their transformation is profound. It can be incredible to witness.

I dislike seeing people in pain, but I also know that pain motivates us to change like nothing else can. Each failure brings us closer to the point where we will turn and say, "What I have been doing isn't working. I need to find another way." And that is a powerful and magical moment.

Fundamentalist faiths posture an evil "Satan" that lures people from the straight-and-narrow into hell. It is important to note that (with four exceptions) when the word "satan" is used in the Old Testament, it refers to an obstacle, an adversary, to man's development. What is "development?" To grow and develop is to address and release our beliefs.

The word satan itself is a verb that means "persecution by hindering forward movement." As a noun, it is used to mean "an adversary."[15] Satan, then, is the force that pushes people to express their ego-based, darker desires. It is an obstacle to our enlightenment in the same way that the problems created by our egos present obstacles to opening our hearts, too.

Fundamentalist faiths are generally fear-based and seek to "stamp out" evil by discouraging people from dancing, drinking or otherwise engaging in "lustful and sinful" behavior. Christ drank wine! He performed his first miracle at a party! The Gnostic Gospels, if they are to be believed, maintain that Christ danced with the disciples at the Last Supper. Repression only empowers people's unresolved shadow issues by frustrating their powerful natural drives.

Fundamentalist sects tend to attract people who fear their passions, and want to be told how to live, but repression actually intensifies the individual's inner struggle and increases their chances of "failure." This is why so many fundamentalist ministers "fall off the wagon." In my healing practice, I have worked with many sexually abused people, and the proportionately large number of clients who had been emotionally or sexually abused by their fundamentalist fathers was always a concern to me.

Instead of repressing and thereby aggravating people's natural desires and inflaming their anxieties, these groups could be a positive influence in the culture by helping people find healthy expressions for their natural selves.

It is difficult to see perfection when you are close to it. But if you pull back from the strictly human perspective, you see that everything that happens here, whether we understand or agree with it or not (especially the difficult and painful stuff), serves a purpose in the Creator's greater plan. That which occurs is intended, without exception. Everything here is exactly as it needs to be, regardless of how we choose to see it. It is always perfect.

Your life is exactly as it needs to be in order for you to learn to open your heart. It's not about fairness or who is a better person, and it's not about having a silver spoon or being born under the right stars. It is simply about whatever is needed to get you to live from the God Space. And that brings us to Principle Number Four:

YOUR LIFE IS PERFECT

Your life probably does not feel that way, but that is because when we think of "perfection," we expect "bliss." But the perfection is in the process. You are being changed. Perhaps it would be more accurate to say you are being strongly encouraged to change. The perfection is in the way things occur in life in order for that to happen. How you feel about the process is up to you.

Your view of life becomes significantly different when you accept that nothing can be wrong with you and that everything happens for a reason. This means that there are no such things as foolish or random acts. If it happened, it was intended and purposeful. Stupidity, chance and screwing up are no longer viable explanations. This removes a great burden of guilt and shame from people as incidents become far less personal.

If nothing can be wrong, it changes the self-condemning burden we all carry regarding our "bad" decisions and our "mistakes." Our lessons become necessary (painful but necessary) steps on our path to becoming more whole. You are still not going to like it when someone does something that makes you uncomfortable, but the shift to becoming a student of life rather than a victim of it allows your life to take on significantly broader dimensions.

We can come to see our challenges not as expressions of failure or inadequacy but as opportunities to learn and grow. Instead of being victimized by the vagaries of life and other people's peccadilloes, we are able to step back and see the larger process of human evolution at work. That makes the Creator a Great Teacher and Guide rather than judge and prosecutor.

We may not like the lessons, but our new perspective moves us out of the realm of being punished for our inadequacies. We might not always understand why things are happening, but that does not invalidate the premise.

Does that mean that we would end up with a world full of people not taking responsibility for their actions? No it wouldn't. We are not built that way. Actually, you could be irresponsible today if you really wanted to, but that is not your nature. You do not need what those behaviors offer. The people who are irresponsible are hurt and angry and are acting out their pain.

If our view of life could change, we would no longer have a substantial part of the population living in guilt, shame and unworthiness and expressing the spawn of those negative emotions: alienation, despair, depression, envy, rebellion and other forms of self-destructive behavior. People would be free to heal themselves and their relationships without the onerous burden of shame and guilt that so many people carry around today.

AIDS is not just a disease; it is also an opportunity for us to learn to love one another. So are racial, sexual and ethnic differences. Someday we may get upset about genocide in Africa, but we are not there today. It is through the resolution of our "differences," individually and as a society that we learn and grow. Hatred and war are fed by unresolved differences. It is important to understand how this all works. It is founded upon a very important principle. This is Principle Number Five:

THE EGO CANNOT LOVE

We do not see a great deal of unconditional love in our world. What we mostly see is "ego love," which masquerades as the real thing. It is love with strings, with conditions. It has limitations. When unconditional love is given, it asks nothing in return. That's a big thought, and people often don't want to hear it! The first thing they do is to put up objections – after all, they do love their partners, parents, friends and children. What they are saying is that they love them as much as they can. And it may be the most love they have ever felt, and it may also be as far as they can open today. So, they are being sincere, but most people have little experience with unconditional love. And although we are capable of giving a great deal of love, we rarely give it unconditionally. The ego operates through erecting walls. It is non-loving by definition. We now have five Principles to guide us:

LOVE EVERYTHING

ANYTHING YOU DO NOT LOVE
WILL BECOME A LESSON

WHAT GETS YOU INTO TROUBLE ISN'T YOURS

YOUR LIFE IS PERFECT

THE EGO CANNOT LOVE

There can be a great separation between feeling something and openly expressing it. The difference is whether or not we sincerely own our feelings. Your parents probably loved you as best they could, but that's the rub. It is the conditional love you received from them that formed The Misunderstanding that you carry. Every time you went to the well, with your light shining and your innocent heart open and came back unsatisfied, you felt badly. Then you blamed yourself for being defective or not good enough.

Consider your life. (This is worth taking some time with pen and paper to explore.) Look at the major situations you have experienced, and move beyond the hurt and pain of each circumstance to see the potential for growth and learning contained in each instance. You will find that at the heart of every situation there was an opportunity for you to be more compassionate (especially toward yourself). You will find this to be true IN EVERY CASE. And the more powerful the situation, the more potent the learning it contained.

You can argue with the Creator about this being a stupid process. I did for years, and I will tell you that not only did I waste my time, I was also totally wrong. I don't like the difficulties I have had in my life, but I now recognize that they were created to help me grow and change. The more I learned to open my heart to what was being offered, the easier and more joyful my life became. And that is the secret to having a happy life!

Accepting the offering that life brings does not mean we should not take care of ourselves or seek to right wrongs, for our nature is to be compassionate. We must learn to follow the instincts of our God Selves. If you are truly led to do something about poverty, AIDS or global warming, by all means do so. It is however, important to be sure that God is motivating you, and not your projected inner woundedness. How can you tell? It's actually quite simple. If God is moving you, the momentum will be so clear and unmistakable that it will be beyond obvious. You will not be able to do anything else.

Sugiyama Iwajiro, known to posterity as the Zen Master Hakuin Ekaku, lived in a small village in Japan around 1700. He is the creator of the famous koan, "What is the sound of one hand clapping?"

People came from far and near to receive Hakuin's spiritual teachings. His writings could be rough, humorous, or sometimes even shocking. They were intended to rouse people from complacency into a deeper contemplation of religion and spiritual life. If there was such a thing as fame in Japan in those days, Hakuin had it.

In the village, the daughter of Hakuin's next-door neighbor became pregnant. Berated by her embarrassed parents, the girl named Hakuin as the father. In a rage, the parents went to Hakuin and berated him for their daughter's condition. To their remonstrations, all Hakuin replied was, "Is that so?"

Word of the scandal spread, and the Master was publicly shamed. His reputation was damaged. He remained unmoved.

Daruma, Hakuin Ekaku (1685-1768). The inscription reads:
"Pointing directly to man's heart: See your own nature and become Buddha."[16]

When the child was born, the parents brought the baby to Hakuin. "You are the father, so it is your duty to look after him." Hakuin took the child and once more said, "Is that so?"

The master took loving care of the child. A year later, the distressed girl confessed that the real father of the child was a young man in the village.

Ashamed, the parents went to see Hakuin to apologize and ask his forgiveness. "We are very sorry. We have come to take the baby back. Our daughter has confessed that you were not the father." "Is that so?" is all that Hakuin said as he handed the baby back to them.

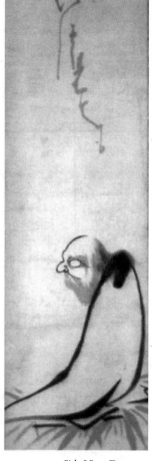

Side View Daruma,
Hakuin Ekaku.

No matter how you slice it, it's about compassion. Certainly it is about compassion for others, but mostly it is about compassion for yourself. Thus far we have dealt with the idea of opening our hearts to others. But if you think that opening your heart to another person is hard, it is child's play compared to doing that for yourself. Today you do not love yourself, and every problem/opportunity you encounter offers you the opportunity to move in that direction.

We put people in jail when they do harm to others. Well, if we had George Orwell's Thought Police around, we could put everyone in jail for the awful things they do to themselves! Not only do we not love ourselves, we beat ourselves up unmercifully! And as Bartholomew said, "If you had a friend who said the things you say to yourself, you'd get another friend!" This is mostly the ego's way of getting you to avoid threats, because if you can be made to feel badly about yourself, you will be less willing to take risks.

If you observe your own process, "the shrill voice" will criticize you for anything and everything. It incessantly nags at you every time you make a mistake. Given the opportunity, it will rip you to shreds. This is not your inner guidance. It is a defensive ego device whose only purpose is to make you feel badly so that you will not expose yourself to rejection. And it will use every means at its disposal to accomplish that.

When you were a child, it was necessary for you to shut your deepest feelings down in order to get through conflicts with your parents, but you no longer need to do that. We are going to investigate this mechanism and how it operates over the next three chapters. We will give you some powerful tools to deal with it.

These are five of the basic components to a happy life. We will add more in the next chapter. Consider this woman's experience:

"YOU CAN'T DO LIFE WRONG"

I heard these words from Ross the first time I attended one of his classes. These have to be the most Empowering words I have ever heard. They were meant just for me. At that time, I KNEW there was no one else in this whole world that was as screwed up, weirded out and confused as I was. There couldn't possibly be anyone else like me out there. After all, hadn't I been the biggest mistake ever created?

From my earliest childhood memories my beliefs were that I was not good enough, not smart enough and not pretty enough. BUT if I tried really hard, others would accept me and then I would be happy and normal. So I tried. I read every book I could get my hands on, but I still wasn't smart enough. My father was an alcoholic, which meant no one could come over to our house, but no one wanted to anyway. After all I was the geeky nerd, and wasn't good enough to be a friend. I craved love and acceptance, but no matter what I did or where I looked, I could never find it. I always believed I was an oddball, a freak. No matter how hard I tried to find acceptance and love it was never there, not the way I needed it, anyway. No one EVER understood me. My mantra was, "You don't understand me. Why can't you understand me?" I carried that mantra from childhood all the way through my divorce. I just never fit in.

I was raised a strict Catholic, and as a child I wanted to be a nun. Even then I felt the pull of God wanting me to come home; I just didn't know how to do it. I raised my kids Catholic, and did all I had been taught in Church and school. I taught religion classes, and tried my best to fit in. Once again, something was missing. I just wasn't a good enough Catholic, person, woman, (fill in the blank with anything you like). I just wasn't good enough. I begged God to change my abusive husband, change my terrible teenager, change my loneliness, and help me find peace and serenity. I tried churches, books, and self-help gurus – all to no avail. I battled depression, and almost lost several times. I had been emotionally and physically controlled and abused all of my life; I never knew I had choices. I just kept hanging on, hoping for the answer to appear.

The day I came to Ross's seminar changed me forever. Ross said that we are all here for the same reason, to find our way back home to God, and WE CAN'T DO IT WRONG. He said that we can do it easy or hard, but no matter what, we are all going home. Wow! That did it for me. It restored my hope. I wanted to know how, and was willing to try anything to feel good inside. I heard him say that the love and acceptance I craved was not going to come from others, but from inside of myself, and he would help me heal my pain, help me get rid of the yucky garbage inside of me. I said, "Deal me in!"

I learned that day about Shamanic Journeying, and met my inner child. She was sweet and good, and full of love for me, and I loved her instantly. We built a relationship, and laughed and played. I loved the time we spent together. Then on one journey, I met another child, a teenager. She was angry and horrid. I wanted to run away. She frightened me, but I had learned enough by then to know that she had a lot to teach me, and that by healing her I would be healing myself. So I stayed and we talked and we worked very hard together. It took several journeys, but with her I was able to face down one of my abusers, and tell him what I felt. I was big and tall and strong, and he could not hurt me anymore. The journey process gave me the strength to look at the old wounds, and heal them. I have used this process many times in various situations to give my inner child the power she needs to heal her wounds, and it works!

My most important journey happened when I asked my inner child to take me to the place where I lost my power. I was taken back to another lifetime to a small farm in Ireland. I was the only female, with a father and three brothers. My mother had died, and I was the one who took care of the men of the house – in all ways. I lived in a hovel of a place, life was very hard, and there was no money and no one else around. I was used and abused by the men of the house, and expected to make their lives easier. I was shut down inside, functioning but not there mentally. There was no hope and no way out. This journey showed me the link between all of my lifetimes, as I saw repeated the same type of pain over and over again. I would put everyone else first, making sure that everyone around me was happy regardless of what was going on for me. I was so horrified and frightened by this poor girl, (I call her Irish), that I left in tears, and came back without doing anything. It haunted me, and knowing that even if I had gotten big it wouldn't have helped her out of there. I didn't want to go back, felt helpless because I couldn't help her.

I journeyed back to be with her several times, I just wanted her to know someone cared. I went back with her further, to when her mother had died, and found that there was an Aunt who wanted to take her in after the funeral, who told the father that she could give her a good life. He refused. In the original story he left and took her home, and then her nightmare began. I changed the story to where the aunt had to pay the father, but she finally convinced him to let her go with her. Irish didn't have a life of luxury, but she grew up healthy, strong and loved. She became a seamstress and fell in love and married. She was happy. I stayed with her until she died, and then I asked her to come back with me, to be with me and guide me, and she agreed. She is now with me in this lifetime, integrated with me, and she helps me to see things more clearly. She is strong and compassionate and I am grateful to her for coming back with me.

Since that journey, I have met several of my other inner children, visited other past-lives and- faced down more demons. And with each journey, I become more complete. I learn my lessons and move on to the next step. Each journey brings me closer to home, closer to God and absolute peace.

Although you live in your private unhappiness, it is important for you to know that you are not alone. I think John Ruskan spoke for most of us when he wrote:

I see that I am often angry. I see that I experience much pain in my intimate relationships. I see that I am still isolated, lonely, and living in anxiety if not downright fear. All this even though I'm trying my best to keep up a dedicated meditation and yoga practice, trying to be conscious of the karma I am generating, trying to be a "loving and spiritual" person. One of the few consoling realizations is that I am certainly not alone. As I look at others, I see the same if not exaggerated condition.[17]

The universal human condition is to feel inwardly fearful, guilty and unworthy. I cannot say that absolutely everyone on the planet struggles with these issues, but everyone I have ever met does, and those who seem to be unaffected by them are only compensating. Any time you see something universal in the human condition, you know something much greater is going on, and that is certainly true in this case.

It is important to ask why you feel unworthy, because that is an essential part of your growth process. And although these feelings are personal, you are also an integral part of a process being shared by all humankind.

Surrendering the ego represents a considerable transformation in the human psyche, and any human system, whether the mind, the lungs, a family or a community, needs time to adjust to new levels of consciousness. Stress of any kind, good or not, disturbs the system. Many more accidents occur to people whose lives have undergone important changes, both positive and negative: marriage, divorce, childbirth, job changes, etc.

If you were to transit into the God Space without preparation, the contrast between the structure and order here and the seeming chaos there, would be extremely unsettling. You would go into shock. Life has been created to help make the transition more manageable. Each problem gives you the opportunity to make a small jump. Think about training wheels.

You can argue that it is taking us too long to leave our egos, and some people will agree with you. But if you look at key indicators in human social/spiritual development like the eradication of slavery, gender equality, elimination of many diseases, individual freedom, ethnic tolerance, health, longevity and conscious awareness, it is clear that even though we still have a ways to go, we are doing much better than we did even just a generation ago. The spiritual practices of our Calvinist and Puritan forefathers were violently abusive and incredibly repressive, and we have come a very long way since then. And, yes, we have a way to go, and, yes, there is a great deal more to be done. But the course of human history shows a clear path of (painfully achieved), growth and transformation.

If you think we ought to be moving more rapidly, I urge you to adopt the principles you will find in this book into your life so they will then ripple out into the larger community. As Gandhi said, "We must be the change we seek in the world."

Do we backslide? Yes. Are there many problems yet to be resolved? Of course there are. Remember, though, that in the Middle Ages people lived in castles because they needed them.

"The Pathless Land"

*The first peace, which is the most important,
is that which comes within the souls of people
when they realize their relationship, their oneness,
with the universe and all its powers,
and when they realize that at the center of the universe dwells the Great Spirit,
and that this center is really everywhere, it is within each one of us.*

Black Elk

It is difficult to describe the God Space. Our language was created to address a tangible reality where objects have three dimensions and boundaries and are separated from one another (at least in theory). In that reality, you and I are separate, the dog at my feet is a distinct entity and across the room is an inanimate object called a table. Each has separate, unique and distinguishing characteristics, and they are further separated by distance and time.

Three-dimensional reality exists because of aggregations of energy. You perceive your body as separate because it is denser than the air that surrounds it. The table and the dog take their particular shapes because of the denseness of their energies and the ways in which those energies coalesce. A rock is denser than water, and its energy comes together in unique patterns; water is denser than air, and so forth.

In the God Space, energy does not coalesce, therefore things appear very differently. In this realm there are no boundaries, there is no separation between "things." In that sense, there aren't even things. Energy moves easily through a vast, constantly fluctuating complex that is more like a cloud than a collection of objects. Time and space are no longer relevant as everything is everywhere and is happening all at the same time. Instead of something being "here" and something else being "there," the center is everywhere and nowhere all at the same moment. There is no beginning and no end. No history, no future, just now. The ego requires a past and future in order to function, and it cannot function in the God Space. As Pema Chandron said, "You cannot be in the present and run your story line at the same time."

These principles apply to thoughts as well as objects in the God Space. In our world you have thoughts and I have thoughts but they are separate. What if we were to become aware of each other's thoughts? Our first reaction is usually fear because of the loss of privacy, but this is really a lack of trust. If we were aware of each other's pain and fear, we could respond more appropriately to what was really going on, instead of having to guess and dance around individual pain and unspoken fear. We could get to the heart of a matter and then get on to other things. And, as just a further consideration, what if there were only one thought?

Since energies flow freely in the God Space, there is an awareness of everything instead of the limited perspective we hold in tangible reality. There are no beliefs, no values, nothing to restrict the flow of information or energy. Therefore, there can be no fear, for there is nothing to be afraid of. Fear lives in the shadow of the unknown. In the God Space, there is only knowledge of everything and compassion, which is our natural state. In the God Space, everything just is. That is why this space is often referred to as "isness."

The concept of the God Space is admittedly alien to a person accustomed to living in three-dimensional reality. Consider this: If you lived in a two-dimensional (flat) world, it would be virtually impossible for you to grasp the concept of height. Height would not exist in your world and it would be extremely difficult for you to conceive of something that "did not exist." Similarly, living in three dimensions, it is difficult for us to comprehend the God Space. Although a higher realm can be felt, the one below it cannot comprehend it. From the ego's view, surrendering to the God Space is like surrendering to a cloud. From the perspective of three-dimensional, rational reality, there is nothing there! To science, God does not exist.

The ego and your beliefs stand in opposition to the God Space. They seek different ends. Beliefs and the ego function on separation and difference; the God Space operates through unity and harmony. In waking reality, the mind controls things. In the God Space, it controls nothing.

In the God Space, there is no thinking, for there is nothing to think about! There is an old cliché that goes, "God does not have to think." When you have total awareness, you just do what needs to be done. You don't have to think about it. This concept can be difficult for Westerners to accept because we are heavily conditioned to depend on our thinking and logic. We have been taught that this is one of man's greatest attributes. After all, it is what separates us from dumb animals and ignorant savages.

When confronted, we generally separate from the God Space, because we are not ready to hold compassion. We move into emotion and think our way through situations. We create beliefs. Thinking and emotion then become substitutes for the guidance of the God Space. They help us to temporarily avoid opening our hearts in places we do not feel ready to address.

In order for the transformation to the God Space to occur, the self must surrender to the vastness that is the universe. This presents the ego with its greatest fear: the loss of self. In the God Space there is no "me." The ego ceases to function because it is irrelevant. The dilemma this presents is that it means giving up that which we think has given us shelter from the hurts and bruises of life. It is a lot like asking an ostrich to give up the sand it hides its head in.

The knowledge of how to come home has been with us for thousands of years, and if it were just about knowledge, you would have made changes to yourself long ago. When it comes to love or living your life, you "know" how to do it, because that comes naturally from the God Space. But of course, doing it is another matter. That is why you have been urged to practice Loving Everything.

There is also an incredible irony here. In giving up the small self, one gains a vast, intimate knowledge and connection with the rest of the universe. Letting go of the small self is a minuscule sacrifice measured against an incredible gain. It is like putting quarters into a slot machine and hitting the jackpot–every time! Yes, you spend your quarters, but look what you gain! The wonderful thing about the God Space is that there is no risk. The outcome is guaranteed before you even make the commitment! And, you get your quarters back!

"But what if I won't be able to do it?" the ego says. "I'm afraid I won't measure up." We fear that our petition to be loved will be rejected and that we will be left standing naked in the awful truth that we are lacking. After all, what would you do if the Creator told you that you weren't worth His time or trouble? That is how it has felt in the past.

This is a fascinating part of the transformational process. Even though almost every human fears failing "the test," it is impossible for us to fail! We are a part of the God Consciousness, and the outcome is pre-ordained. Our lack of awareness of that and our lack of confidence in The Creator is a measure of where we are on the path.

Spiritual dilemmas are unique in that they have only one outcome. There is only one destination, one Truth. No matter what circuitous route you take, you must eventually come to know the truth about who and what you are. That is the perfection of the process, and it applies to individuals, families, nations and to all humankind. You can resist and make life more difficult and more painful than is necessary. I did for years! But it was also a vital part of my learning process. You may feel unworthy, but there is no way you can be unworthy. That truth must eventually win out. There is simply nowhere else for you to go!

Life is not about becoming something different than you are. Life is about finding that it is safe to let go of the protective things you cling to that are not you, so that you can safely stand in the God Space. You are already the magnificent being that you are "becoming." The evolution is not in you; it is in your consciousness, in your awareness. Your "learning," the understanding you will gain, is the crux of the transformational process called enlightenment.

As you begin to comprehend who you really are, fear and anxiety naturally subside. You can make the process more difficult than is necessary, but you cannot fail at it. Your resistance is largely a matter of which end of the telescope you choose to see life through.

People get confused about the idea of free will. Having free will does not mean that you control your life. The person that you see reflected in the mirror does not determine what is going to happen to you. You may want to be the captain of your ship, but the fundamental trajectory of your life is set by a process far greater than your worldly desires.

This larger force, which we could call "love of self" or "soul," shapes and guides events to bring you into contact with the parts of yourself that do not move freely and easily with the rest of the universe. Your soul carefully crafts everything that happens to you; every moment, every occurrence, to bring you the exact experiences you need in order to give you every opportunity to relinquish your beliefs. Left to your own devices, you probably would not choose to confront these issues. Free will means that you get to decide how you will respond to what happens in your life. This is not a small concept.

God cannot simply give you grace because you have free will. This means that if you are to develop, it must be of your choosing. You must decide to let go of the ways you see yourself that keep you in the "safe harbor" of your ego.

Put yourself in God's place. There are billions of souls who do not yet live in the magnificence of who they really are. What would be the most powerful way to get them to know and deeply hold the truth about themselves?

As God, you would create an environment where these people could live from their egos (shamans call this the shadow), outside the God Space (out of harmony) if they chose. When they did that, it would create problems for them, internally and with other people, leading to the experience of discomfort and pain. When the pain became significant, it would generate the self-motivation to release what they believed and move them closer to the God Space. People would then have grown and developed of their own free will.

As God, in order to facilitate their development, you would give them little knowledge of the process they were engaged in, and you would also create a process that would sensitize people to the places where they did not move in harmony with The Universe. This is called childhood wounding, and it happens to every child on the planet. That should tell you something.

If we look at life from only the limited human perspective, it can be difficult to see the greater process at work. People die, accidents happen, hearts collapse and genocide occurs. You pray for contentment, and you get situations that try your patience. You ask for financial ease and you get thrown up against your fear of being successful. Taken out of context, which most people do, life is simply a long series of trials and tribulations to be endured. But those are human values, and a decidedly human perspective.

Consider that God has infinite time and can create life at will. Then the loss of a life in an important teaching or the experience of pain in order to awaken a closed heart are small prices to pay when weighed against the potential gain of moving a soul closer to enlightenment that will last into eternity.

There is an additional factor in all of this. If people use their free will to decide they are worthy, they will hold that truth in the deepest manner possible. When their convictions are challenged, these billions of souls, having once lived in untruth, will hold the magnificence of their beingness not possible in any other way.

"The Pathless Land"

It hurts to feel unworthy and afraid, but these feelings provide the energy that drives the engine of change. Be honest: if it didn't hurt, it is unlikely you would be motivated to change. So long as your well-oiled defenses are operating smoothly and you are getting by, there is little reason for you to change your behavior. This is the downside of having free will. Otherwise, God could just program you like some mindless robot.

Our pain is generated because of our emotions and the choices we make. God does not intend us to suffer. Pain and suffering do not come from God's intention, but they are part of the learning process on earth. We can suffer if we choose. H. G. Wells created a dialogue between a group of men and God. The men complained that life was full of wickedness and suffering, wars and excesses of all sorts, so that life was often unbearable. And God replied, "If you don't like these things, don't do them." Wells would write later, "War is not the will of Heaven, it is the blindness of men."

There is a story about a man who went into a bookstore to buy a book about truth. The clerk offered him my book, Truth, and the man said that he was familiar with my book, but he wanted The Book of Ultimate Truth. The clerk paused, looked at the man and, straightening up to his full height, told the man that they did have such a book, but that it would be extremely expensive.

"How much could it cost?" said the man, "After all, it's just a book."

"Oh, no!" the clerk replied, "It is much more than that! The knowledge of Ultimate Truth will bring you to complete simplicity, costing you not less than everything!"

The man left the store, having recognized the line from T.S. Eliot's, *Four Quartets*:

> *We shall not cease from exploration*
> *And the end of all our exploring*
> *Will be to arrive where we started*
> *And know the place for the first time.*
> *Through the unknown, remembered gate*

When the last of earth left to discover
Is that which was the beginning;
At the source of the longest river
The voice of the hidden waterfall
And the children in the apple-tree
Not known, because not looked for
But heard, half-heard, in the stillness
Between two waves of the sea.
Quick now, here, now, always -
A condition of complete simplicity
(Costing not less than everything)
And all shall be well and
All manner of thing shall be well
When the tongues of flame are infolded
Into the crowned knot of fire
And the fire and the rose are one.

Core beliefs, created in the initial separation from the God Space are typically the last thing people will throw into the fire. People will often sacrifice everything and everyone else in their lives before they will confront the beliefs that comprise who they think they are. How many marriages, prospective or consummated, have been destroyed because one or both partners refused to look at their own fears and anxieties? Instead, they typically turn to avoidance mechanisms such as rationalization or fantasy. They marry people who fit their neurotic patterns because they are reluctant to address what would be asked of them in a healthy relationship.

Consider for a moment the art of air guitar. Playing air guitar is a fantasy. It gives the pseudo-player the accolades that come with success without having to put themselves on the line and actually face failure. It conveniently avoids having to run the risk of critical condemnation, perfect skills through thousands and thousands of hours of endless practice, face rejection by other musicians and critical reviews, play to unappreciative audiences in dead-end bars, spend life on the road living out of a bus, dealing with shady club owners, fickle fans, temperamental fellow musicians and the million other insults that go along with being a successful musical performer, all the while remaining motivated to create and perform at the highest level possible. That's what fantasies give us – all the good stuff without having to address the fears and self-imposed limitations that keep people without driving ambition in the shadows of obscurity.

Whether it's about being rich, attractive or famous, all magical thinking originates from the same source: the desire to avoid dealing with what's inside. Magical thinking is what drives people to buy lottery tickets, gamble at casinos, and for most couples, get married. The myth is that the magic will take away their pain. Regarding marriage, many people hold the mistaken assumption that having a partner will somehow make them more whole, more complete. They fantasize that a partner will take away the "ache" they feel in themselves and their pain from being alone. Unfortunately, the ache is actually their disassociation from their inner selves.

Truthfully, all marriage does is to push each partner to go deeper into the personal issues they were trying to avoid by getting married in the first place! So when things don't work out as they fantasized, people then move into resentment. This is the main reason so many marriages fail. Many women use this same kind of logic around having children. They feel that having a child will ameliorate their pain and feelings of aloneness and incompleteness. It doesn't work that way. It can't.

Consider fantasies about being wealthy. When you have little money, receiving some does make things easier. So in some respects, life does become less burdened. But if you think that people with money are automatically happier, you'd best rethink your assumptions. People who have won the lottery are rarely as happy as we expect them to be, and people who have suffered spinal chord injuries are generally happier than we assume. Certainly life with money is different, but in many ways it is also much more difficult. Keep in mind that if you have unresolved inner issues, having money doesn't make those issues go away. Here are a few stories about people who have won the lottery:

William "Bud" Post won $16.2 million in the Pennsylvania lottery in 1988 but now lives on his Social Security. "I wish it never happened. It was totally a nightmare," says Post. A former girlfriend successfully sued him for a share of his winnings. It wasn't his only lawsuit. Then, his brother was arrested for hiring a hit man to kill him, hoping to inherit a share of the winnings. Other siblings pestered him until he agreed to invest in a car business and a restaurant in Sarasota, Fla., -- two ventures that brought no money back and further strained his relationship with his siblings. Mr. Post even spent time in jail for firing a gun over the head of a bill collector. Within a year, he was $1 million in debt. Post . . . eventually declared bankruptcy. Now he lives quietly on $450 a month and food stamps.

Evelyn Adams won the New Jersey lottery not just once, but twice (1985 and 1986), to the tune of $5.4 million. Today the money is all gone and Adams lives in a trailer. "I won the American dream but I lost it, too. It was a very hard fall. It's called rock bottom," says Adams.

Willie Hurt of Lansing, Mich., won $3.1 million in 1989. Two years later he was broke and charged with murder. His lawyer says Hurt spent his fortune on a divorce and crack cocaine.

Charles Riddle of Belleville, Mich., won $1 million in 1975. Afterward, he got divorced, faced several lawsuits and was also indicted for selling cocaine . . .

One Southeastern family won $4.2 million in the early '90s. They bought a huge house and succumbed to repeated family requests for help in paying off debts. . . Eleven years later, the couple is divorcing, the house is sold and they have to split what is left of the lottery proceeds. The wife got a very small house. The husband has moved in with the kids. Even the life insurance they bought ended up getting cashed in. "It was not the pot of gold at the end of the rainbow," says their financial advisor.[18]

"For many people, sudden money can cause disaster," says Susan Bradley, a certified financial planner in Palm Beach. "In our culture, there is a widely-held belief that money solves problems. People think if they had more money, their troubles would be over. When a family receives sudden money, they frequently learn that money can cause as many problems as it solves."

Having worked with people from every social and economic stratum, I can honestly tell you that people with money have as many, if not more, problems than you do. This is particularly true for those with inherited wealth. Having money brings up a host of issues and problems that regular people just don't have to concern themselves with. And if you're sitting there saying, "That wouldn't happen to me!" your magical thinking has just kicked in.

First, it is important that you understand the reasons your life is not more abundant. Those reasons are because of the ways you do not love yourself, which leads to emotional as well as earthly poverty. These reasons have nothing to do with the world, other people or your parents. They begin and end with you and the feelings you have about yourself. You came to earth to work on and resolve those issues. If God were to simply give you what you wanted, you would learn nothing. It would defeat the entire purpose of your being here. So it is not about money, it is about self-love. Having money isn't going to change that. Being successful can give you recognition from the world, but you still have to look at yourself in the mirror every morning.

Let's look at how it works: Say you want to be free of economic difficulties. You want things to be better. You wish, you hope. You stick affirmations on your refrigerator, make a collage of pictures cut out of magazines or call a psychic or therapist that one of your friends has used. You're not asking for wealth, just for things to be easier. So, you pray. You ask for God's help. You ask to be relieved of your burdens.

On the surface this seems like a reasonable request. But it is actually not. In seeking the result (more money) you are actually attempting to slide around the confrontation with your beliefs that would be otherwise necessary for the change to occur naturally. You want to play air guitar with life. The Universe has created your life situation so you might learn from it, and you want to be let off the hook! It is like asking for a hall pass from life. What you have brought to the table is conditional. You are willing to participate so long as you don't have to give up your beliefs. Unfortunately, you cannot come to the table with dirty hands.

As I have pointed out, because you have free will, there are limitations on what The Creator can do to help you. You look to God and plead, "Please help me heal!" And God looks back and says, "How? With all that ego running your life, it is almost impossible for me to do anything!" Then you feel abandoned. But, giving up the ego is what it is all about. That is why it is called "surrender." Someone sent me this: "Letting go is the first step toward having the trust, the faith, that all things are divine and that all that is divine is in your best interest."

When The Universe responds to your prayer (as it must), it will be to create a life experience giving you the opportunity to see how you push away the love or abundance or whatever else it is that you have asked for. In other words, you will receive a lesson, or a "learning opportunity" asking you to address your limiting beliefs. You will most likely experience failure, and it can feel like torture. After all, you have asked for help, and instead of being given salve, you got sandpaper. To be fair, we must remember that you have not begun in the best frame of mind, anyway.

Yet this is the route you must take in order to receive what you have asked for, because that is where the problem is! The barrier to abundance or love or peace or whatever you desire isn't on God's end, it's on yours! I will say that again, the difficulty isn't on God's end. It's on yours, so that's where you have to go to fix it!

Of course, we don't want to have to give up the sanctuary of our limiting fears and beliefs. We would rather have someone give us peace and joy so we don't have to give up our defenses.

Materialism hit the big time in post World War America. So did stress-related diseases such as heart disease, cancer, stroke and Alzheimer's (unknown before WWII). Do you really believe that these are unrelated? Some people will argue that there are other causes, but in 1904 there was very little cancer in the U.S. Now there is an abundance of it. In 1940, a woman had a 1 in 22 chance of getting breast cancer. Today that rate is down to 1 in 7. Only one in 10,000 women in China will die from cancer. One in 10 in the West will. For men, the death rate from prostate cancer is 70 times higher in the West. Seventy times!

When Japanese people move to America, their stress-related health problems escalate rapidly, especially heart disease. As industrialization sweeps through India, Southeast Asia and China, the stress-related health problems in those countries are skyrocketing. This is the price for not doing inner work and for turning away from the eternal. Having harmonious thoughts is a good first step, but Eckhart Tolle tells us there is more:

> Some spiritual teachings urge us to let go of fear and desire. They are unsuccessful. Trying to be a good or better human being sounds like a commendable and high-minded thing to do, yet it is an endeavor you cannot ultimately succeed in unless there is a shift in consciousness. This is because it is still part of the same dysfunction, a more subtle and rarefied form of self-enhancement, of desire for more and a strengthening of one's conceptual identity, one's self-image. You do not become good by trying to be good but by finding the goodness that is already within you, and allowing that goodness to emerge. But it can only emerge if something fundamental changes in your consciousness.[19]

So, it's not about if – it is about when. You could argue then, that there is no reason to hurry things along. Actually, quite the opposite is true. There is always a consequence for turning away from the God Space. Avoiding the situation is always easier in the moment. Going with the ego is always more seductive. But when we ignore the God Space, we guarantee the creation of a more difficult situation down the road.

When you take a temporary fix, you guarantee that there will be more pain in the future. Always. Every time you postpone a lesson, or turn away from an opportunity, the intensity of the process goes up a notch. Refuse enough times, and you will eventually get hit between the eyes. We call it a crisis.

Today you have the option of making these changes at your pace. Ignore your lessons, and you will eventually get pushed into a corner where circumstances will demand that you make these very same changes. Only then, it will not be of a time and place of your choosing. That's the problem with avoidance. We act as though there were a free lunch, as though there were no consequences for our refusal. We think that when we avoid a situation, we get away with something. Later, when another situation clobbers us, we do not often connect the two – but they are completely related! And that brings us to Principle Number Six:

DO IT NOW

That second helping of desert is going to be tough to get off your waist, but she wants it, and she wants it now! The thing is, you are not really hungry! She needs to be loved! But, if you do not address her longing, and choose to medicate the discomfort instead, the really difficult part will come later, as you do hours and hours on the treadmill to work it off, or worse, leave it on and have a heart attack from occluded arteries. It has to be this way because every time you refuse to love yourself, you are also refusing The Universe!

Heroin may provide a great escape, but at some point you will have to come back to reality, and then deal with being addicted. Having an affair may temporarily ameliorate your relationship frustrations, but you eventually have to go home, live with yourself and look in the mirror. The long-term price is pain and suffering.

So have that second scoop of ice cream and don't deal with others from a place of compassion. What's going to happen down the road? The one guarantee you have is that things are going to get worse. It isn't just about external turmoil. The private hell you create for yourself is going to be far worse than any external situation will ever be. So now we have Six Principles to guide us:

LOVE EVERYTHING

ANYTHING YOU DO NOT LOVE
WILL BECOME A LESSON

WHAT GETS YOU INTO TROUBLE ISN'T YOURS

YOUR LIFE IS PERFECT

THE EGO CANNOT LOVE

DO IT NOW

Logical thinking has dominated Western society for almost 2,500 years. Aristotle and the other Greeks held logic to be man's supreme achievement. The Church embraced logic and used it to defend its positions on scripture even in the face of scientific observation and rational proof, embraced by the emerging scientific community. Early scientists needed a defense against logic, corrupt spirituality and persecution by a domineering Church. Rational thought gave them that sanctuary. David Hume, a skeptical Scotsman and one of the founders of the self-proclaimed Age of Enlightenment, spurned spirituality and exalted rational thought above all things. He once asked of knowledge:

If we take in our hand any volume; of divinity or school metaphysics, for instance; let us ask, "Does it contain any abstract reasoning concerning quantity or number?" No. "Does it contain any experimental reasoning concerning matter of fact and existence?" No. Commit it then to the flames: for it can contain nothing but sophistry and illusion.[20]

Similarly, when Descartes reasoned, "I think, therefore I am." He sought to eliminate all other forms of awareness except for those that could be deduced rationally. Theodoric of York, a medieval doctor, wrote:

Medicine is not an exact science, but we are learning all the time. Just fifty years ago, they thought a disease like your daughter's was caused by demonic possession or witchcraft. But now we know that Isabelle is suffering from an imbalance of bodily humors, perhaps caused by a toad or a small dwarf living in her stomach.

In choosing rationality, science isolated itself from the God Space. Science functions by putting boundaries around concepts and ideas, and then seeks to observe and understand the differences between them, whereas the God Space functions through inclusiveness. To science, light is this, heat is that, gravity is this, electricity is that, and here's what each can be expected to do under various circumstances.

To make scientific distinctions, we have to make arbitrary, human-created determinations, because science does not work with the thing itself. It uses mathematics and factual descriptions. Descriptions are useful, but they are also removed from reality and are limited in the understanding they can provide. Science works with what Gregory Bateson called "maps of reality."[21]

Nothing in the universe exists in categories, especially living things. Rational thought creates artificial barriers to the way the universe really is. And when a truth is reduced to mathematical description so it can fit into the constraints of rationality, it is stripped of its essential nature. The God Space simply works with reality.

Outside the world of science, everything is deeply interconnected. With every breath, you take in atoms created in the stars. Every time you exhale, you disperse atoms that will someday reach the stars.

Considering boundaries, at what point does the air you breathe or the food you eat cease to be separate and become you? Science would say that you and this book are separate, yet as you connect with my thoughts, the boundary between "you," "book" and "me" becomes an academic distinction. Where is the place where your thoughts and my thoughts are separate? Where do "I" end and "you" begin? Do I reside in the ink on this page? Or do you and I fashion something completely new and different as your thoughts merge with my thoughts in creating a structure of ideas that did not exist before? Where are your thoughts? Just in your brain? I think not.

When you hold the Universal Truth that, "We are love," you do not have to think about it, you just respond to it. But, if you start to think about the idea and analyze and assess it, you strip it of its essential nature. You have separated it from God's Truth. Saint Thomas Aquinas wrote, "Love takes up where knowledge leaves off."

Thinking is a substitute, and a rather poor one, for the loss of the God-connection. Thought functions through comparison; the God Space operates through unity. Rationality is cold and impersonal. Therefore, it is emotionally safe, which is one of the reasons the early scientists chose it. Walk the aisles of a modern supermarket – acres of tasteless, preservative-laden, scientifically developed processed paste, posing as food. Today our bodies are so filled with chemicals and preservatives that we would be rejected by an FDA meat inspection. This is what Ashley Montagu was referring to when he wrote, "An intelligence that is not humane is the most dangerous thing in the world."

Just to illustrate the point and demonstrate the limitations of rational thought: you can think about love and compassion all you want, read all the books you can find on the subject, go to every workshop you can attend, and although you will become very conversant in the theories about love, until you find the love and compassion that resides in your heart, nothing else will substitute, nothing else even matters. You cannot live life from a book. You cannot drink the description of a glass of milk. Sir James M. Barrie said:

If you have love, you don't need anything else.

And if you don't have it, it doesn't matter what else you have.

Science, medicine, economics and engineering all operate in the three-dimensional world and have a very difficult time functioning in or understanding, the spiritual realm above them. Consider the difficulty we have in encompassing the essence of The Creator in thought and words. It simply cannot be done. Science has tried to understand and research spirituality for years and failed. Three-dimensional thinking cannot understand the realms of other dimensions.

In that same way, who you are cannot be reduced into words or thoughts either. Eckhart Tolle wrote that, "Nothing you can know about you is you." What you call something or how much you understand about it does not change the essence of the thing. This is one of the confusions that people have about spirituality in general. You can't really talk or write about it! You can only experience it. Knowledge can certainly help guide us on the path, but we must also not lose sight of its limitations. Spirituality, like life, must be experienced.

Around 500 B.C. in India, Shakyamuni Buddha delivered his discourses on the profound subject of Emptiness. These teachings reside at the heart of Buddhist teachings on the nature of reality. In one of these discourses, the Buddha sat quietly for a time, saying nothing. Then he held up a flower to the assembled monks. The students were being very respectful and taking The Great Teacher very seriously and so they studied the flower intently.

At that moment, a monk named Kasyapa realized the deeper truth that is beyond words, and gently smiled. The Buddha, recognizing that Kasyapa had achieved the profound insight he was trying to encourage, praised the monk for his clarity and gave him the title Maha, which means "great" or "eminent." Mahakasyapa went on to become one of the great pillars of Buddhism.

Buddha then spoke to the assembled monks, telling them that they had come assuming that he possessed something – something that they did not. He pointed out that this presumption was not correct. He told them that the truth they sought could only be found within themselves and that no amount of learning or study could change that process. The inner path could be illumined by learning and the intellect, but never explored through them.

Several hundred years after Buddha's death, interpretations and recollections of his teachings (Sutras) were set in writing much as they were in the New Testament of the Christian Bible. In one of the Sutras, known as the Lotus Sutra, the Buddha points out that Nirvana isn't a state to be attained sometime in the future through long study and arduous effort. He says that Nirvana is simply a deep understanding of the essential nature of things, and that no method or study or technique is necessary for that. By teaching in this way the Buddha also reinforced his firm commitment to learning through experience rather than through study. "Simply" seeing a flower would be enough to evoke all teachings, all truths. Nothing more was necessary.

When Lao Tsu wrote the *Tao Te Ching* in 670 B.C., he begins text with, "The Tao that can be told is not the eternal Tao."[22] In *The Little Prince*, Antoine de Sainte-Exupéry wrote, "What is essential is invisible to the eye."[23] I have always enjoyed Isadora Duncan's comment, "If I could say it, I wouldn't have to dance it!" Referring to Mohammad's teachings on the subject of truth, Rumi wrote:

The Prophet said that truth has declared:
'I am not hidden in what is high or low
Nor in the earth nor in the skies nor throne.
This is certainty, o beloved:
I am hidden in the hearts of the faithful.
If you seek me, seek in these hearts.' [24]

Although there can be a number of intellectual truths about an issue, no thought or idea can encompass essential truth. The truth can only be known through the God consciousness. And that brings us to Principle Number Seven:

TRUTH MUST BE FELT

Fortunately, when it comes to spiritually based truth, we have an inner knowingness that goes well beyond our conscious awareness. Although it can be easily shut down and ignored, this gentle but fortunately persistent "still small voice" is the voice of the God Consciousness. Witness a sunrise, view the grandeur of a mountain or the delicacy of a snowflake, and you connect with something beyond what the rational mind can comprehend. You make a connection to the essential self. There are now seven principles to guide us to the God Space:

LOVE EVERYTHING

ANYTHING YOU DO NOT LOVE
WILL BECOME A LESSON

WHAT GETS YOU INTO TROUBLE ISN'T YOURS

YOUR LIFE IS PERFECT

THE EGO CANNOT LOVE

DO IT NOW

TRUTH MUST BE FELT

Knowledge isn't going to get you there. It has never been about knowledge, anyway. When the Buddha sought enlightenment, he did not cloister himself in a monastery to study and read; he meditated under the Bodhi tree and became a practicing shaman. He exorcised the demons that dwelt in his shadow. Certainly it is important to understand spiritual concepts, and share in the thoughts of spiritual thinkers, but knowledge is only a small part of the process.

Jiddu Krishnamurti provided an interesting insight into our views of life. Krishnamurti was born in 1895 in India. Many Buddhists believed that he was the Bodhisattva Maitreya, who was prophesied to achieve enlightenment and then teach the pure dharma to the world. Renouncing titles, Krishnamurti traveled for the next sixty years talking and teaching. His talks were published in more than fifty books. Krisnamurti summarized his teachings in 1980 with what he called "The Core of The Teachings." There is a great deal in this piece, I urge you to spend some time with it:

Truth is a pathless land. Man cannot come to it through any organization, through any creed, through any dogma, priest or ritual, not through any philosophic knowledge or psychological technique. He has to find it through the mirror of relationship, through the understanding of the contents of his own mind, through observation and not through intellectual analysis or introspective dissection. Man has built in himself images as a fence of security - religious, political, personal. These manifest as symbols, ideas, and beliefs. The burden of these images dominates man's thinking, his relationships and his daily life. These images are the causes of our problems for they divide man from man. His perception of life is shaped by the concepts already established in his mind. The content of his consciousness is his entire existence. This content is common to all humanity. The individuality is the name, the form and superficial culture he acquires from tradition and environment. The uniqueness of man does not lie in the superficial but in complete freedom from the content of his consciousness, which is common to all mankind. So he is not an individual.

Freedom is not a reaction; freedom is not a choice. It is man's pretence that because he has choice he is free. Freedom is pure observation without direction, without fear of punishment and reward. Freedom is without motive; freedom is not at the end of the evolution of man but lies in the first step of his existence. In observation one begins to discover the lack of freedom. Freedom is found in the choiceless awareness of our daily existence and activity. Thought is time. Thought is born of experience and knowledge which are inseparable from time and the past. Time is the psychological enemy of man. Our action is based on knowledge and therefore time, so man is always a slave to the past. Thought is ever-limited and so we live in constant conflict and struggle. There is no psychological evolution.

When man becomes aware of the movement of his own thoughts he will see the division between the thinker and thought, the observer and the observed, the experiencer and the experience. He will discover that this division is an illusion. Then only is there pure observation which is insight without any shadow of the past or of time. This timeless insight brings about a deep radical mutation in the mind.

Total negation is the essence of the positive. When there is negation of all those things that thought has brought about psychologically, only then is there love, which is compassion and intelligence.[25]

Zen Buddhism speaks of "true mind," i.e., mind without form, and "false mind," the mind of form. In India they have a concept called maya – the veil of delusion. It is their belief that the normal state of mind of most human beings contains a strong element of maya. Ramanah Marshi taught that, "The mind is maya."

There was recently a scientific brouhaha regarding whether or not Pluto was a planet. Some people treat these conflicts as important, but when the astronomers were all done, whatever they decided, Pluto still orbited the Sun. The planets had not changed one whit. Nothing the scientists decided would affect the solar system, just their rational understanding of it. Robert Bellah tells how one of his researchers, speaking at a conference, made the statement, "Some people believe that human life is priceless," and a scientific expert in all seriousness, stood up and challenged him. The scientist said, "We have no data on that."

The limitations of rationality can be further illustrated when we examine emotional processes. Telling a frightened child that there is no bogeyman under the bed does about as much good as making a scientific assessment of the situation. "But it's a scientific truth!" rationalists say, demonstrating their limited understanding of bogeymen. Anyway, tell that to the frightened child. Telling the child that it's all in her head isn't going to do much good either, no matter how much we learn about neurochemistry.

The search for a deeper reality is what drives many people around the world to become serious meditators. Meditation quiets the mind and allows deeper truths to emerge. Once they begin to resolve the wounds of their initial separation from the Creator, people find that they are not buffeted by the false images constantly created by normal conscious thought. Until then, they will be disturbed by that kind of calmness. We fear the deep quiet because without the constant chatter and noise of our daily existence, our deeper, darker unresolved feelings surface. In the past when we approached that state, things did not go well. We will discuss what happened, and the role our egos play in creating these problems in Chapter Nine, when we discuss the role of the past to affect the present.

> *Peace… comes within the souls of men when they realize their relationship, their oneness, with the universe and all its powers, and when they realize that at the center of the Universe dwells Wakan-Tanka, and that this center is really everywhere, it is within each of us.*

Black Elk (Hehaka Sapa) Oglala Sioux

"What exists in truth is the Self alone. The self is that where there is absolutely no "I" thought. That is called Silence. The Self itself is the world; the Self itself is "I"; the Self itself is God."

Ramana Maharshi

CHAPTER 4

Opportunity

The highest reward for a person's toil
is not what they get for it,
but what they become by it.

John Ruskin

When you are stuck in traffic and late for an appointment, when you are worried about not having enough money, when your kids upset you, or when you are mired in any one of a thousand other "problems," take a deep breath and recognize that this is not occurring as punishment, or because you are unworthy, or that you are messed-up. It is happening because you need to learn to open your heart. The situation has been created specifically so that you might learn to do that. It is an opportunity. That is how the system works. It is not a problem unless and until you choose to make it one.

Many people don't learn from their mistakes. They go through life repeating the same experiences over and over, learning little from these encounters. They can even go into therapy and work on their behaviors, but the changes they make will be intellectual and superficial as long as they ignore the core beliefs that drive them. They create pseudo-healing, which makes them feel better for the moment but does not require them to address their core beliefs. Later, when the body begins to fail, they will go to a physician and get a prescription for drugs to address their symptoms, once again ignoring the deeper issues The Universe is urging them to address.

The great equalizer in this situation is pain. By avoiding what life asks of them, avoiders entrench their resistance and increase the intensity of their future lessons. Each avoidance ratchets up a process that guarantees that if they continue to resist, they will be brought to their knees. We call this a crisis. Viktor Frankl hit the issue dead center when he wrote:

When we are no longer able to change a situation—just think of an incurable disease such as inoperable cancer—we are challenged to change ourselves.

A crisis comes only after there have been repeated requests for change which have been routinely refused. A critical situation is an invitation to change, with a heavy price for continued refusal. Some people hope that something magical will carry them past their fears and pain and make life peaceful so that they won't have to do anything. Needless to say, life doesn't work that way.

There is a limit to our ability to resist. After all, we only have so much strength. The Universe has no limitations. It has infinite power and endless stamina. It's not going to vanish, and it is not going to change its mind.

Making changes can be difficult. In life, much of our learning occurs in spite of ourselves. In our defensiveness, we either blame something or someone else, or in the alternative, turn things inward and beat the living daylights out of our already fragile psyches. In the moment, doing this seems easier than addressing the fear-driven beliefs that got us into trouble in the first place. Either way, we don't learn very much.

How is it then that we grow and change? How do we learn? We learn by failing. In the ideal, we try, fail, try again, get a bit better at it, try again and finally learn. That is the essence of life.

Think about a big fellow that the track coach has recruited to learn to throw the shot. He's never done it before, but standing there outside the ring, although he may be anxious, he is basically at peace. However, just standing there, even though he wants to throw that heavy thing, he's not going to learn much. He may have read the books and studied the training videos, but until he steps into the ring and tries to throw that 16-pound shot, stumbles all over himself, feels stupid and clumsy, falls in the dirt, scrapes himself up, gets sweaty, tries it again and again and again that he finally begins to get it– that he begins to learn. How? By trying and failing - and this is important– by learning from his failures.

If our young shot-putter tried a few times, didn't get it, and simply walked away, we would call him a quitter. If he tried and tried and tried, but never learned from his mistakes, we would call him foolish or worse. As President Truman once observed, "No learning takes place the second time you are kicked by a mule." The key is to learn from your experiences so that you are not doomed to repeat them.

If our budding shot-putter can find a way to hang in there and push the limits of what he knows and what he thinks he can do, he will find that he is capable of far more than he ever thought possible. If he is to succeed, he must move beyond the limitations of his beliefs and self-criticism.

If our young friend can step into the challenge and earnestly work at it, he can become the best he can be. Notice that I am not defining success by some external measure. He may not put up world-class numbers, but he can feel very proud of his accomplishments, and he will feel better about himself. This is true whether he is entering a relationship, learning to play the trombone, or simply being a good friend. Notice please, that the inherent qualitative difference here is his willingness to step into a situation, face his fear, put it on the line and risk failing. Remember the bungee jump?

And this is why good parents and good teachers and coaches (of all kinds) are so vital to young people. They don't just teach us skills, they teach us about ourselves and about life. You learn to get it right by trying and failing and learning not to quit, even when it hurts, even when you have plenty of reasons to hang up your cleats.

The real value of life, as in athletics, is in learning to pick up the pieces after a disaster and go on. In athletics, you have to really want to be good. You have to work very hard just to acquire the skills to be good. But the real challenge comes through competition. When somebody totally beats the pants off you and your ego is smashed and your pride is completely bent out of shape and you feel like they defined the word "failure" with you in mind, then the opportunity for really meaningful inner work begins.

Whether it's athletics or a divorce, a failed career or a broken friendship, when you have been chopped up in the grinder and fallen flat on your face, it is then that you have the opportunity to move beyond the pain and shame and your self-pity, and grow. Why? Because failure is ego stuff writ large. The opportunity is to look at your beliefs and to raise yourself beyond them. This is why Christ placed so much importance on "turning the other cheek."

Turning the other cheek means stepping back into the situation, opening your heart and possibly getting slapped again. It means not being controlled by your fear, getting back on the horse after you have been thrown and once again experienced the horse's power.

At the same time, there is also using your good judgment to get out of a situation when you have made unhealthy choices, or to keep yourself from being conned by someone who wants to use you for her own ends. That is important learning too.

If all that was at issue were athletic ability, you'd get back on the horse and try again. Harder and smarter to be sure but, and here's the key, your ego wouldn't be on the line. Life has created this situation so that you could examine what you do when your ego is threatened and you could fail. That is how life works. It is only when you are willing to let go of the image you hold of yourself that you begin to truly learn, grow and succeed.

You can learn a great deal about life by talking with successful people. By successful, I do not necessarily mean financially successful, nor do I mean well known. Fame can be more seductive and corrupting than money, especially in our society. Success has many dimensions, and many of the people that society deems successful are simply aggressive, but this has little to do with true success. It just means that you can make money and overcome obstacles by being self-confident. It is a measure of our society's veneration of aggressive behavior. That is why these people need

McMansions, expensive clothes and cars. They are constantly compensating for what's not happening for them on the inside.

Successful people are usually bright, but this is not always the case. Some are good-looking, some are not, but most of them do take good care of themselves as a matter of personal respect. Successful people don't set out to gain fame or notoriety. They recognized early on that people who did that invariably crashed and burned. They see that the glitterati like a face-lift. Things look OK on the outside, but on the inside it's hell.

Most successful people have good social skills, but that's not universal, either. For some of them, being social is just not a priority. I have met researchers, musicians and brilliant scientists who had a difficult time carrying on a simple conversation. Many, perhaps most, people in the arts carry a good deal of pain, and they have funneled their pain and their passion into their art. Their social adroitness can leave a great deal to be desired.

One generalization you can make is that many truly successful people are humble and compassionate, but beyond that, you cannot pigeonhole or categorize what makes a person a success, I think, with two exceptions.

Every successful person I have ever met was filled with gratitude. Some of them had enormous ego issues, but they were still grateful. Grateful for different things, but there is something about their gratitude that made them reach outside themselves, and this seems to be an important factor in success.

The other thing that each successful person had was a set of guiding principles by which they lived. Their principles were all over the map: some of them I disagreed with, but their lives were guided by this personal ideology and their gratitude. In some cases, you would call them bizarre or off-the-wall, but these people earnestly believed what they believed, and it gave them faith in something greater than themselves to persevere, in most cases, against odds that had already turned less successful people away.

These people's successes were a natural extension of their commitment to themselves and to their principles. Each person was dedicated to her own excellence, meaning that at critical junctures she didn't hold back or flinch.

She was not afraid of commitment or taking risks. She had learned that, as hockey legend Reggie Leach said, "Success is not the result of spontaneous combustion. You must set yourself on fire."

When Mohandas Gandhi, arguably the 20th century's most influential person, wrote his autobiography, he did not talk about his monumental achievements. His autobiography, which he titled *The Story of My Experiments With Truth*,[26] is a long discussion of his lifelong process of testing and refining the personal principles he held to be important. Whenever Gandhi found a flaw or a crack in his beliefs, or in his ability to adhere to them, he immediately set about making changes. He began with what were largely personal principles and refined and extended them to include all of humankind. His dedication to those principles, which he set out to bring as close to the God Space as he was able, and his remarkable commitment to them, even in the face of enormous pressure and incredible opposition, is what will inspire people for time immemorial.

It is this same refusal to compromise principles in people like Abraham Lincoln, Mother Theresa, St. Francis of Assisi, Anwar Sadat, Louis Pasteur, Nelson Mandela, Marie Curie, and Galileo that endears their spirits to us forever. These people were not only willing to suffer and fail for what they believed, they had the courage to put everything behind their convictions, almost always in the face of threats, ridicule and scorn.

America's 1846 "war" with Mexico was a trumped-up farce to steal land from that country, and one of the few public figures willing to stand up and say so was Illinois Congressman Abraham Lincoln. It cost Lincoln his seat in Congress, but you couldn't question his commitment to his principles.

I received an email a while ago from a woman who had undergone the scourge of bi-lateral breast removal. She wrote:

Do you have any insight on why I developed this disease? It's been very difficult for me to handle all the Unity Church beliefs and what they teach in "The Secret" that we create illness through negative thinking, because I worked so hard to heal my life and have lived a life of joy for the past two years.

I am asked about this sort of thing frequently and it comes from a part of the New Age community that has a rather fanciful understanding of how The Universe works. Their teaching that:

> . . . *you create in reality, in one way or another, whatever you focus your attention on. Your life is going to be an outcome of where you predominantly place your attention.*

. . . is misleading, and the woman who wrote me had fallen into the trap. First of all, the "The Secret" was mostly marketing hype. In order to sell it to the masses, the promoters left out some very important considerations that would have limited sales. "The Secret" relies on a "Law" of Attraction taught by some by New Age workshop leaders. The idea is a simple one: that what you place your attention on will manifest in reality. The assertion is not completely wrong, which is why it is confusing, but as presented, it is mental sleight of hand.

It is your beliefs, not your thoughts, determine what manifests in your life, and there are important differences between them:

> *If you believed that you deserved abundance, you would have it.*
> *If you believed that you deserved to be happy or successful, you would be.*
> *If you believed that you deserved a happy, loving relationship, you would have one.*
> *Otherwise, . . .*

If you want to see the real impact of the "Law" of Attraction, go to its opposite. The Universe is a place of infinite abundance. God has more love or gold or anything else you could desire in amounts beyond your wildest imagination. And He freely offers it all to you just like He does fresh air and sunshine. So the issue is not the availability of what you want, the question is, will you accept it?

Our beliefs push God's abundance away. God offers us love, peace and joy and we routinely refuse to accept these things because we do not believe we deserve them. And, our free will gives us the power to refuse. And most people do. Like so many needy children, we want what we want and want it now! We selfishly pollute the air and water, destroy the environment and at times act worse than a couple of kids fighting over a toy.

The only real consolation is that as you read this, The Universe is creating life experiences that will bring you to question your beliefs, especially the beliefs you hold about yourself. And no matter what else you desire, nothing is going to upset that process.

However, you can subvert the process for a time. You can postpone the inevitable by bulldozing your beliefs aside through force of will. And by committing your willfulness and your intellect, you can temporarily create what you desire by bending Universal Law.

Dale Carnegie has been teaching people to think successfully for almost a century. Norman Vincent Peale first published *The Power of Positive Thinking* in 1952. There is nothing new there. People achieve fame and fortune all the time by keeping a positive attitude and working hard. Every year, some people in corporate mergers, Wall Street brokerage firms, professional athletes and movie stars, work very hard and make a great deal of money. Western culture is built on the doctrines of positive thinking, overcoming obstacles and hard work. After all, America is the land of materialism and self-made billionaires (remember when it used to be millionaires?).

Americans are obsessed with money, private jets, expensive yachts, mansions and plastic surgery and trophy wives as they express a narcissistic obsession with the perfection of surface and ignore the pain and turmoil lying beneath it.

The problem with having money and notoriety are the reasons we usually seek them. Most of the time we are trying to compensate for what is not happening within us, and fame and money can be extraordinarily seductive to an empty and pain-filled soul. The periodic public self-destruction of some pop culture figures, politicians and athletes illustrates this phenomenon. People like Paris Hilton, Britney Spears, Rush Limbaugh, Congressman Larry Craig and Atlanta Falcons quarterback Michael Vick, to name just a very few, speak to the dangers of not doing one's inner work while seeking fame and notoriety. Their use of the bulldozer to achieve success only postpones the inevitable. These people will pay a severe price for their fame and financial successes until they deal with their unresolved emotional issues.

There is a considerable toll made on your physical and emotional well being for making a deal with the devil. It shortens your life, seriously degrades your sense of well being and dramatically reduces your peace of mind. Research tells us that angry people are three times more likely to have heart attacks, and that people who are optimistic and happy do better in life and live longer, so there is a good deal to be gained by doing your inner work. The issue is, can you come to peace with yourself so that you can let God's abundance manifest naturally?

If what you desire places you out of harmony with The Universe, your gains will disappear (painfully) as in the stories of the people who won the lottery or the public figures mentioned above. You cannot gain inner (or outer) peace through willfulness while ignoring your inner work.

You can do many things to improve your state of mind. And if what you do is superficial and without substance, then when a deep wave of pain or anguish roils up from the depths of your being, it will blow away anything that is not firmly anchored to the truth. Success motivation programs like "The Secret" are preoccupied with obtaining money and notoriety, neither of which can exist in the God Space. These programs have little to do with real spirituality. They speak to what can be accomplished through effort, intelligence and self-confidence, and although there is nothing intrinsically wrong with taking the bull by the horns, there is nothing inherently spiritual about it, either.

So if you ask, "Can I be rich or famous?" The answer is, "Sure, but don't confuse that with anything real." What God cares about is the love and compassion in your heart, especially the love you hold toward yourself. As long as you do not cause harm to yourself or to others, God doesn't really care what else you do. Earthly matters of wealth and fame are of little, if any concern to God. They have no place in the God Space. If you can be compassionate and rich at the same time, that is wonderful! But if you get lost in ego and ignore the love and compassion that God is interested in developing, there will be problems. Spiritual teachers have spoken about this dilemma for centuries. I think it is important to keep Morris Adler's words in mind:

> *Our prayers are answered*
> *not when we are given what we ask for,*
> *but when we are challenged to be what we can be.*

When I talk with successful people, I don't just ask them about their successes. I want to know about their failures, too. I don't ask about their failures to embarrass them, but I have learned that the most important and difficult part of learning to be successful is learning to accept and learn from failure as an essential part of the process. Most successful people are relatively free of the stigmas of the past because they know that what happened was a natural outcome of where they were at the time.

Although they certainly do not like to fail, these people see their failures as extensions of the way they saw themselves at the time. They can look back and see how their old beliefs, especially false pride and ego, held them down and limited their success. They didn't like giving up their old beliefs any more than you do, but they were able to see through their ego defenses and beliefs and use the situations of their lives – failed businesses, failed marriages, etc. - as mirrors, reflecting back to them where their ego-based beliefs were out of alignment.

Those who became successful coped with what happened, left the old beliefs behind and accepted a new, more expanded view of themselves and life that included significantly less ego than their previous version. They had both the willingness and the courage to grow from their experiences. They saw their failures as reflections of where they were, not of who they are. That is a lot of what separates them from not-so successful people. If they had not used their failures to refine and change their guiding principles, they could not have grown to be where they are today.

Professional athletes know that failure comes with the territory. You hate to lose, and you work like heck to prevent it, but when it comes, as it does, you accept it and learn from it (this is important!) and then you move on. Sometimes a better athlete defeats you, but most of the time you lose because your competitor was better prepared, had an emotional edge and just wanted to win more than you did that day. But however it comes, failure is something to learn from, it does not define who you are. In the villages of Africa they speak of a good cook as someone, "who has broken many pots."

And, by the way, most successful people have not yet "arrived." They continue to challenge themselves to be better. Their memories still carry pain, but it is not debilitating in the way that it can be for non-successful people, who tend to define themselves through their failures. Consider the life examples of Steve Jobs, founder and CEO of Apple Computer and Pixar Animation Studios as told in his commencement address to the graduates of Stanford University:

Stay Hungry, Stay Foolish

I am honored to be with you today at your commencement from one of the finest universities in the world. I never graduated from college. Truth be told, this is the closest I've ever gotten to a college graduation. Today I want to tell you three stories from my life. That's it. No big deal. Just three stories.

THE FIRST STORY IS ABOUT CONNECTING THE DOTS.

I dropped out of Reed College after the first 6 months, but then stayed around as a drop-in for another 18 months or so before I really quit. So why did I drop out?

It started before I was born. My biological mother was a young, unwed college graduate student, and she decided to put me up for adoption. She felt very strongly that I should be adopted by college graduates, so everything was all set for me to be adopted at birth by a lawyer and his wife. Except that when I popped out they decided at the last minute that they really wanted a girl. So my parents, who were on a waiting list, got a call in the middle of the night asking: "We have an unexpected baby boy; do you want him?" They said: "Of course." My biological mother later found out that my mother had never graduated from college and that my father had never graduated from high school. She refused to sign the final adoption papers. She only relented a few months later when my parents promised that I would someday go to college.

And 17 years later I did go to college. But I naively chose a college that was almost as expensive as Stanford, and all of my working-class parents' savings were being spent on my college tuition. After six months, I couldn't see the value in it. I had no idea what I wanted to do with my life and no idea how college was going to help me figure it out. And here I was spending all of the money my parents had saved their entire life. So I decided to drop out and trust that it would all work out OK. It was pretty scary at the time, but looking back it was one of the best decisions I ever made. The minute I dropped out I could stop taking the required classes that didn't interest me, and begin dropping in on the ones that looked interesting.

It wasn't all romantic. I didn't have a dorm room, so I slept on the floor in friends' rooms, I returned coke bottles for the 5¢ deposits to buy food with, and I would walk the 7 miles across town every Sunday night to get one good meal a week at the Hare Krishna temple. I loved it. And much of what I stumbled into by following my curiosity and intuition turned out to be priceless later on. Let me give you one example:

Reed College at that time offered perhaps the best calligraphy instruction in the country. Throughout the campus every poster, every label on every drawer, was beautifully hand calligraphed. Because I had dropped out and didn't have to take the normal classes, I decided to take a calligraphy class to learn how to do this. I learned about serif and san serif typefaces, about varying the amount of space between different letter combinations, about what makes great typography great. It was beautiful, historical, artistically subtle in a way that science can't capture, and I found it fascinating.

None of this had even a hope of any practical application in my life. But ten years later, when we were designing the first Macintosh computer, it all came back to me. And we designed it all into the Mac. It was the first computer with beautiful typography. If I had never dropped in on that single course in college, the Mac would have never had multiple typefaces or proportionally spaced fonts. And since Windows just copied the Mac, its likely that no personal computer would have them. If I had never dropped out, I would have never dropped in on this calligraphy class, and personal computers might not have the wonderful typography that they do. Of course it was impossible to connect the dots looking forward when I was in college. But it was very, very clear looking backwards ten years later. Again, you can't connect the dots looking forward; you can only connect them looking backwards. So you have to trust that the dots will somehow connect in your future. You have to trust in something - your gut, destiny, life, karma, whatever. This approach has never let me down, and it has made all the difference in my life.

MY SECOND STORY IS ABOUT LOVE AND LOSS.

I was lucky. I found what I loved to do early in life. Woz and I started Apple in my parents garage when I was 20. We worked hard, and in 10 years Apple had grown from just the two of us in a garage into a $2 billion company with over

4000 employees. We had just released our finest creation—the Macintosh—a year earlier, and I had just turned 30. And then I got fired. How can you get fired from a company you started? Well, as Apple grew we hired someone who I thought was very talented to run the company with me, and for the first year or so things went well. But then our visions of the future began to diverge and eventually we had a falling out. When we did, our Board of Directors sided with him. So at 30 I was out. And very publicly out. What had been the focus of my entire adult life was gone, and it was devastating.

I really didn't know what to do for a few months. I felt that I had let the previous generation of entrepreneurs down - that I had dropped the baton as it was being passed to me. I met with David Packard and Bob Noyce and tried to apologize for screwing up so badly. It was a very public failure, and I even thought about running away from the valley. But something slowly began to dawn on me - I still loved what I did. The turn of events at Apple had not changed that one bit. I had been rejected, but I was still in love. And so I decided to start over.

I didn't see it then, but it turned out that getting fired from Apple was the best thing that could have ever happened to me. The heaviness of being successful was replaced by the lightness of being a beginner again, less sure about everything. It freed me to enter one of the most creative periods of my life.

During the next five years, I started a company named NeXT, another company named Pixar, and fell in love with an amazing woman who would become my wife. Pixar went on to create the worlds first computer animated feature film, Toy Story, and is now the most successful animation studio in the world. In a remarkable turn of events, Apple bought NeXT, I retuned to Apple, and the technology we developed at NeXT is at the heart of Apple's current renaissance. And Laurene and I have a wonderful family together.

I'm pretty sure none of this would have happened if I hadn't been fired from Apple. It was awful tasting medicine, but I guess the patient needed it. Sometimes life hits you in the head with a brick. Don't lose faith. I'm convinced that the only thing that kept me going was that I loved what I did. You've got to find what you love. And that is as true for your work as it is for your lovers. Your work is going to fill a large part of your life, and the only way to be truly satisfied is to do what you believe is great work. And the only way to do great work is to love what you do. If you haven't found it yet, keep looking. Don't settle. As with all matters of the heart, you'll know when you find it. And, like any great relationship, it just gets better and better as the years roll on. So keep looking until you find it. Don't settle.

MY THIRD STORY IS ABOUT DEATH.

When I was 17, I read a quote that went something like: "If you live each day as if it was your last, someday you'll most certainly be right." It made an impression on me, and since then, for the past 33 years, I have looked in the mirror every morning and asked myself: "If today were the last day of my life, would I want to do what I am about to do today?"

And whenever the answer has been "No" for too many days in a row, I know I need to change something.

Remembering that I'll be dead soon is the most important tool I've ever encountered to help me make the big choices in life. Because almost everything; all external expectations, all pride, all fear of embarrassment or failure - these things just fall away in the face of death, leaving only what is truly important. Remembering that you are going to die is the best way I know to avoid the trap of thinking you have something to lose. You are already naked. There is no reason not to follow your heart.

About a year ago I was diagnosed with cancer. I had a scan at 7:30 in the morning, and it clearly showed a tumor on my pancreas. I didn't even know what a pancreas was. The doctors told me this was almost certainly a type of cancer that is incurable, and that I should expect to live no longer than three to six months. My doctor advised me to go home and get my affairs in order, which is doctor's code for prepare to die. It means to try to tell your kids everything you thought you'd have the next 10 years to tell them in just a few months. It means to make sure everything is buttoned up so that it will be as easy as possible for your family. It means to say your goodbyes.

I lived with that diagnosis all day. Later that evening I had a biopsy, where they stuck an endoscope down my throat, through my stomach and into my intestines, put a needle into my pancreas and got a few cells from the tumor. I was sedated, but my wife, who was there, told me that when they viewed the cells under a microscope the doctors started crying because it turned out to be a very rare form of pancreatic cancer that is curable with surgery. I had the surgery and I'm fine now.

This was the closest I've been to facing death, and I hope its the closest I get for a few more decades. Having lived through it, I can now say this to you with a bit more certainty than when death was a useful but purely intellectual concept:

No one wants to die. Even people who want to go to heaven don't want to die to get there. And yet death is the destination we all share. No one has ever escaped it. And that is as it should be, because Death is very likely the single best invention of Life. It is Life's change agent. It clears out the old to make way for the new. Right now the new is you, but someday not too long from now, you will gradually become the old and be cleared away. Sorry to be so dramatic, but it is quite true.

Your time is limited, so don't waste it living someone else's life. Don't be trapped by dogma – which is living with the results of other people's thinking. Don't let the noise of other's opinions drown out your own inner voice. And most important, have the courage to follow your heart and intuition. They somehow already know what you truly want to become. Everything else is secondary.

When I was young, there was an amazing publication called *The Whole Earth Catalog*, which was one of the bibles of my generation. It was created by a fellow named Stewart Brand not far from here in Menlo Park, and he brought it to life with his poetic touch. This was in the late 1960's, before personal computers and desktop publishing, so it was all made with typewriters, scissors, and Polaroid cameras. It was sort of like Google in paperback form, 35 years before Google came along: it was idealistic, and overflowing with neat tools and great notions.

Stewart and his team put out several issues of The Whole Earth Catalog, and then when it had run its course, they put out a final issue. It was the mid-1970s, and I was your age. On the back cover of their final issue was a photograph of an early morning country road, the kind you might find yourself hitchhiking on if you were so adventurous. Beneath it were the words: "Stay Hungry. Stay Foolish." It was their farewell message as they signed off. Stay Hungry. Stay Foolish. And I have always wished that for myself. And now, as you graduate to begin anew, I wish that for you.

Stay Hungry. Stay Foolish.[27]

So, in summary, the primary separation between successful and non-successful people are the beliefs that each carries and the gratitude they hold for life. Non-successful people become risk-averse because there is confusion between who they are and what they do. They seek to avoid failures that confirm their unworthiness and condemn themselves to mediocrity. This keeps them from being courageous and free. Whether it is a business or a personal relationship, it keeps them from stepping fully into life.

Where successful people learn and grow from their challenges, non-successful people carry their failures around as proof of their unworthiness. They are caught between what little success they will allow themselves and their envy of others. To get out from under their pain, non-successful people tend to blame external factors so that they do not have to look honestly at the role of their own ego-based beliefs in keeping them down.

One of the great hallmarks of Western civilization has been our attitude toward overcoming obstacles, no matter how difficult. Our ancestors prided themselves on their hardiness in the face of adversity. They willed themselves through obstacles. Our Roman ancestors built a culture through force and conquest. They had a motto: carpe diem, which translates to "seize the day." It expresses the Western attitude toward taking control of life. According to this philosophy, all you need do is reach out and seize life by the throat and bend it to your will in order to be successful. It's only a matter of genes, breeding, education, desire and determination.

This kind of thinking can be found in every aspect of society. The military is built around it. In the early 1600's, Sir Francis Bacon, one of the fathers of modern science wrote, "I come ... leading to you Nature and all her children to bind her to your service and make her your slave."

In either the ancient Roman or contemporary Marine Corps philosophy, there is no room for feelings. Emotion gets in the way. The military is built upon the concept of blind adherence to orders and doctrine, with no room for personal feelings or beliefs. In Iraq, soldiers bury their dead comrades and then go back out on patrol. That mindlessness is what has led to the killing and torture of civilians, massive posttraumatic stress disorder amongst returnees, the abuses at Abu Ghraib prison and the general failure of the effort in Iraq, just as it did in Viet Nam.

Westerners seek to conquer nature so that we can control our fate. We have tamed rivers, conquered diseases and walked on the moon. We have built great cities in hostile deserts and harnessed the vast power of nuclear energy. Everyone wants her piece of the pie regardless of the overall impact.

We can do almost anything except, it seems, to be happy and at peace. This is in large part because we have created a culture that in many ways runs almost completely counter to the Universal. It pays lip service to its religious heritage but is the most spiritually devoid culture in human history. You can will yourself across a river, but you cannot will yourself over God.

In one of my favorite cartoons, the setting is the foyer of a lecture hall with doors opening to two different lectures. At the first door, there is a large line of people waiting expectantly with pens and notebooks in hand. The sign over this lecture hall reads, "Lecture about God." There is no one at the second door. The sign over the empty second door simply reads, "God."

The cartoon illustrates to me the fundamental dilemma we face in reconnecting with the God-consciousness. It's easy to "do stuff" - read books and learn to meditate and go to workshops about spiritual growth, but actually facing God and living from these principles is a significantly different matter. It forces us out of the protection of our intellect into what feels like the less-secure realm of our feelings.

The Western belief system is built on false power, manipulation and a "win at any cost" mentality. This is because what we commonly call power is not true power at all. It is intimidation and manipulation, and these qualities are incompatible with the God Space. Westerners worship "false gods," as it were, as compensation for the truth they have forsaken. So do Islamic radicals. This is one of the core issues underlying the West's conflict with Islam today, but neither side wants to acknowledge the godlessness and heartlessness of its own belief system.

Unfortunately, Western values toward dealing with obstacles get in the way of people's healing and learning processes. If it is not happening, either you are not doing it right, you're not trying hard enough, or something else is wrong with you. Right? The shadow side of this version of achievement is that when people "fail," the emotional burden placed upon them can be very heavy. If you don't climb to the top of the heap, or if you don't want that kind of success, you are just not as good as the other people. You don't have "the right stuff." We build shame and feelings of inadequacy into the process as negative motivators.

The funny thing about life, though, is that whenever you act in contravention to the Universal, something always seeps through the cracks to upset the furniture. No matter how you create your life, if it's built on sand, things will eventually fall apart – they must. Families and societies are the same. People oppressed by social institutions will always create conflict with them as those in positions of power fight to maintain the social leverage they have achieved. What the establishment calls terrorism, repressed people see as patriotic heroism. But whatever you call it, it keeps tripping up and undermining the establishment. It has been said, "Those who you keep down will eventually bring you down."

Sufis are the mystics of the Muslim world, and even among Sufis, the great Sufi mystic Mansur al-Hallaj was an anomaly. Many Sufi masters feel it is inappropriate to share mysticism with the masses, yet al-Hallaj openly did so in his writings and teachings. The Mullahs saw him as a threat, as the Pharisees did with Christ.

Mansur al-Hallaj would fall into trances, which he attributed to being in the presence of God. During his trances he would utter "Ana al-Haqq," meaning, "Truth is me" or "I am God" and also, "In my turban is wrapped nothing but God," which his deriders took to mean that he was claiming to be God. He would also point to his cloak and say, "Maa Fil Jubbati Illa-Allah" meaning, "There is nothing inside/underneath the cloak except God."

His fanaticism led to a long trial and eleven years in a Baghdad prison. In the end, he was tortured and publicly crucified in 922 AD. As Mansur al-Hallaj was about to be tortured and crucified, he is said to have spoken this prayer:

> *O Lord, if you had revealed to them*
> *what you have revealed to me,*
> *they would not be doing this to me.*
> *If you had not revealed to me what you have,*
> *this would not be happening to me.*
> *O Lord, praise thee and thy works!*

Mansur al-Hallaj

CHAPTER 5

The Misunderstanding

One day, as I was asleep on the floor of this halfway house, I woke up like I had all my life, I opened my eyes like every human being does, but this morning the depression was gone, the suffering was gone, the pain was gone. I felt free and alive. I saw how the mind worked; it was all so simple, so clear. When I believed my thoughts, I suffered. When I questioned them, I didn't.

Byron Katie

Having spent nine months in the warm nurturance of the womb, when a child emerges, her world changes rapidly and abruptly. Life on the "outside" is confusing and chaotic. Lost in this bewildering chaos, the child struggles to make sense of it all. One of the ways she does this is to create a sense of "I am" and "you are" as differentiating concepts. These are the beginning steps in the creation of her ego.

Psychologists tell us we need a healthy ego. This is not entirely true. A growing child certainly needs a strong and healthy self-image in order to have a meaningful and productive life. And during the process of maturation if she is fortunate enough to be supported in a way that encourages her to love herself, she will find that elusive human quality–a healthy ego. As she develops spiritually, her sense of self will eventually become an encumbrance, and she will discard it.

This is another of those places where our language (or Freud) fails us. Because what we call a "healthy ego" is really the absence of a protective or compensating ego. A healthy ego is simply being who we naturally are. It allows, where the protective ego compensates for our feelings of unworthiness. Note that the compensating ego is internally focused and externally expressed. A healthy ego just is.

However, when we do not learn to love ourselves, and believe ourselves to be damaged or defective and see the world as emotionally unsafe; the defenses of the compensating ego become essential for our survival. Consciously or unconsciously, we can cling to our fears and egos like rats to a floating log. We will be reluctant to challenge them, even in the face of mountains of evidence to the contrary. This other part of us feels inadequate and does not want to muck around in her feelings of insecurity and unworthiness. She has been convinced that if it lets go of its protection, as dysfunctional as it may be, she will be left with nothing – naked and alone in a world that has been unsafe in the past. This repeats the cold and abandoned feeling she had at the Original Separation from The Creator. It is powerful opposition, and it can be very frustrating.

The compensating ego helps us to get through the impossible minefield of securing at least some love from the world while exposing as little of ourselves as possible, minimizing the inevitable damage. In that frame of mind and needing protection, the jump from the ego space to the God Space can seem like an impossible leap. We fear disappearing into the abyss, even though the jump itself is really quite small. And this creates a conflict within us. Part of us wants peace, it sincerely wants to heal, while at the same time, another part of us fears the change that this represents. And that is why it is difficult for us to make changes.

We hold on to our ego-based behaviors because we do not feel prepared to deal with the "opportunities" The Universe is presenting. Since we do not have a conscious connection to the God Space, it feels as though there is a hole in us. So rather than take the chance of being hurt, we say no to life. We become emotional, we rationalize and deny. Most likely we shut down, contract physically and close off our hearts. Sometimes we express our emotions outward by becoming aggressive and blowing situations up. Or instead of outright refusal, we step in only partway, also guaranteeing failure, but limiting our exposure to blame and criticism.

At a talk in his later years, Krishnamurti froze an audience to complete attention by asking them, "Do you want to know my secret?" You could have heard a pin drop in the theater. After many years, the Master was going to reveal one of his most sacred teachings. "This is my secret," he told them, "I don't mind what happens."

Krishnamurti knew the truth. He had a healthy relationship with himself and although he cared deeply about people and the world, he didn't have to be overly concerned about what it thought of him.

The difficulties you are experiencing, if you will look at them, all focus attention on the places you do not hold the God Space, and they can be set off by external triggers. As a result, most of your attention will be external, and unlike Krishnamurti, "You care what happens."

Most people are caught up in the issues and the drama created by their shadow (their dark side), and we would be crazy not to pay attention to what was happening in our lives. Yet if you simply stop there, you lock yourself into a struggle that you cannot possibly win. Even more importantly, you miss the opportunity to go to the place of learning contained in every situation.

The purpose of the ego and its attendant dramas is to provide a sense of isolation from a situation your inner child feels inadequate to deal with. And her perception is accurate. Alone, she cannot adequately address what is happening. When she tried to do that in the past, she got run over. But together, the two of you can face anything. Separately, it is impossible. She needs the security of your love and the resources you bring.

Whatever the situation is, by its very existence, your soul is telling you that you are capable to deal with it, irrespective of how you feel. So the guidance I would offer you is: DON'T MOVE! Don't get into the self-recrimination, shame, denial or the hundred other diversions the ego can easily create to allow you to avoid and run. Hold center, even though it will be uncomfortable. Welcome the waves of life as they break over you, because this is the place from which you will grow. Find the courage to receive your deepest pain. Know that you are eternal and cannot be harmed. Don't become aggressive. Don't run away, don't get distracted. Stay present with your feelings. Don't stay if you are being abused, but sometimes we confuse life's external pressures with abuse.

> *Do you have the patience to wait*
> *until the mud settles and the water is clear?*
> *Can you remain unmoving*
> *until right action arises by itself?*
>
> *The Master does not seek fulfillment,*
> *and by not seeking, by not expecting, is present,*
> *and can therefore welcome all things.*
>
> Lao Tsu, The Tao Te Ching

In assessing any situation, first identify the core issues, because they stand on their own. Core issues are factual. They contain no emotion. You either need to replace the water heater or you don't. If you don't put gas in your car, you're going to run out. Core issues are like that. There may be legitimate reasons for you to hold back from another person (although they are few). Maybe the other person is deranged and violent, or a Klan member. Maybe she is a sociopath or wants you to enroll in a multi-level marketing scheme. Under those circumstances, prudence says that you need to take care of yourself, although you still can open your heart (be kind) to her, while not agreeing with the values or choices she has made.

The same principle holds for the things other people say. Mostly we make their words important when they lend support to our own feelings of inadequacy. Certainly, no one likes being judged or feeling rejected. No matter how emotionally healthy you are, being pushed on is not going to feel good. But there is a big difference between not liking something and being "sticky" to it.

If you were to focus solely on the content of what others say (the core issues), you would either accept their advice or criticism and make changes to your life, or disagree with them and let it drop. That would be the end of it.

But when someone says something that hurts, you feel pain because your focus is on the perceived insult, not on the core. So if you are "sticky" to their message (or to what you hear them saying), some part of you believes that either what was said was true or that you deserved to be treated badly.

The problem is that it replays the old wounding. You do not yet know the truth about who you are, and the rejection or criticism takes you back to a time when you felt helpless and vulnerable. This is what makes the present interaction both significant and difficult. Your internal process gives the perceived insult an importance that it cannot sustain on its own. Eleanor Roosevelt said, "No one can make you feel inferior without your consent."

When someone takes a shot at you and it sticks, try and step out of the moment and recognize that an important learning opportunity is at hand. Your pain isn't about the present situation. That tug you feel isn't coming from the outside. It may feel like it is external, but it's not. What you are mostly feeling is your unresolved inner woundedness being triggered. Your feelings really have little to do with what is going on in the moment. Deal with the situation, but keep in mind, as The Course In Miracles points out, "You are never upset for the reasons you think."

After you finish nuking your partner, friend or coworker for hurting your feelings, recognize that you are being asked to look at a place where you do not love yourself. And here's the key: if you did love yourself, you wouldn't react to the situation! You might have feelings, but not emotions. Remember Krishnamurti's words, "I don't mind what happens."

If you knew the truth about who you truly were, the criticism would roll off you like water off a duck. As it stands today, you choose to accept what is said or done and give it meaning. This brings us to Principle Number Eight:

IF YOU DIDN'T BELIEVE IT, IT WOULDN'T MATTER

Look at your present situation. How much of what you are currently fussing with has anything to do with core issues and how much of it is about the drama and protective cloak (your woundedness) that is being triggered? Remember, this experience has been specifically created to give you the opportunity to work on your feelings of woundedness.

So, here are our Principles so far:

LOVE EVERYTHING

ANYTHING YOU DO NOT LOVE WILL BECOME A LESSON

WHAT GETS YOU INTO TROUBLE ISN'T YOURS

YOUR LIFE IS PERFECT

THE EGO CANNOT LOVE

DO IT NOW

TRUTH MUST BE FELT

IF YOU DIDN'T BELIEVE IT, IT WOULDN'T MATTER

Let's assume that I have a fear of intimacy. I need to be loved, but I am afraid to venture out to make a real connection with others because I am convinced that I am unworthy. Therefore if I take a risk, I believe that I will be rejected. My standard mode of operation then, will be to withhold. "I am just shy," I tell myself.

You and I meet, and in that moment I have to make some choices. In truth, as you will see, there ultimately is only one choice, and that is for me to open my heart to you. But that is a long-term consideration. In the moment, my beliefs rule, and I am afraid to be exposed. So I hold back, I meet you only partway.

You will feel my reticence and in all likelihood, that will make you wary and you will hold back in response. That is The Universal Mirror in operation. I am not creating a welcoming space. You feel that, and then respond to it, making our connection tenuous and shallow. Completing the circuit, I will in turn, feel your wariness, and be affected by it. I feared rejection, held back and got exactly what I was afraid of! I will walk away from this exchange feeling worse about myself. Our meeting has resurrected old pain and exacerbated the feelings of unworthiness I carried into the situation. But I also did not get humiliated which is the big fear I carry.

My choices now are to either feel badly and sit in self-pity or recognize that these old feelings are being dredged up so that I can become aware of the power they still have to affect my life. Since I have been unable (although it is a choice) to open my heart, the only possible outcome will be for me to experience disappointment (pain). If I do not listen to the pain and make changes, my discomfort will grow with each situation. I will eventually experience a breakdown i.e., a physical or emotional crisis (or both) that will bring me to confront what I have been avoiding all along - the way I see myself. Notice then, that although my reluctance to open to you took me on a circuitous route, I ended up face-to-face with the same issue of unworthiness that I began with. Only now, things are more intense.

There is really only one choice – to open my heart in every situation. To Love Everything. This is "the secret" that Abraham Lincoln knew about the pig in the mud. Had he walked away from that situation and allowed that small piece of disharmony to persist, it would have cost him. He had learned from his other life experiences that the price for ignoring the discomfort of another would be to disturb his own peace of mind. And he had come to love himself too much to allow that. This is important!

This is a very self-centric (not selfish) perspective. We refer to this as living from principle, and although this is true, the deeper truth is that living otherwise creates pain for us! Many people tune it out, but that does not make its impact disappear. As we learn to love ourselves, our tolerance for disharmony drops because we become unwilling to be held prisoner by it.

Notice also, that in the example of our meeting, when you reacted to my withholding, you may have added your own insecurity to the situation. Our meeting will have triggered your fear, giving you the opportunity to work on your issues as well. That is the perfection of the process.

In the alternative, if you had not been affected by my reluctance, and met me openly and sincerely with an open heart, even though you might disagree with my behavior, you would give me the message that I was OK. It would conflict with my belief, and I might not have let it in very far, but acceptance is something we all hunger for. Your loving response would draw me out, even if only a little. And, your acceptance of me brings me at least a little closer to questioning my self-limiting beliefs!

Developing a healthy ego (allowing a child to be herself), can be a tricky process. As a child grows and her consciousness evolves, she realizes she is powerless. Everything in her life is regulated and controlled by adults. They tell her when to get up, when to go to bed, what to eat, what to wear, what to think and what to feel. At some point she will naturally want to establish at least a modicum of control over her life. To do this, she will have to wrest power from her parents. The way most children do this is to say "NO!" to parental authority. And she will do this over virtually everything.

Making things confusing, the child will not behave consistently. One moment she will be a dependent child, needing love from Mommy or Daddy, and the next moment she will turn into a three-foot-tall tyrant, demanding to have her own way. She really doesn't want much of anything except to push on parental boundaries in order to learn about her power.

In a non-nurturing environment, the child will be caught between her desire for freedom and the competing fear of alienating her parents. Alienating her parents threatens her vital source of love and support. A child instinctively knows that she will die if she is not cared for. So in a non-nurturing situation the child walks a thin line between dependency and freedom.

In a healthy environment, parental love cannot be threatened and she will know it. She knows that her parents will be there, that she is loved and that she can depend upon their love unconditionally, even when she pushes their buttons.

And with children, if things are going to go badly, this is where it usually happens. Parents are certainly entitled to set limits, but under the circumstances, it can be a tricky proposition. As you know if you have children, this can be a very trying time. In even the most healthy and loving environments, the parent is often going to be "wrong" as the child grapples for leverage. That is why this time is called the "Terrible Twos." Yet, if a child is to progress through this period successfully, she needs to learn to love herself and not be made wrong for these endeavors while she also learns the value of living within limits.

To begin with, most parents don't feel very secure themselves. Most parents have not addressed the pain from their own childhoods, and every adult is naturally insecure about their ability to parent. As a result, defiance from a child presents a threat to the emotional well being of even the most normal adult.

And if the parent is emotionally challenged, disputations with her children can become totally overwhelming. In "low-nurturance" families, this time can be a special hell for both parents and children. Although most parents love their children, in a low-nurturance environment, the parent's insecure response to the child's challenges will be to close down and withhold love. The parent will shut the child out and pull a classic power trip (or in the opposite, please or disappear).

The message that comes across to the child is, "Who you are is not acceptable, but things will be better for you if you do as I want." Or in the alternative, "You are too much, I can't deal with you." A child in a low nurturance family, by the age of three, will have accumulated enough negative messages in her hopper to last for the rest of her life.

A note: I want to be clear that most parents are good, well-meaning people. But they may also be marginally competent as parents. Raising children can be difficult for anyone, but in addition to loving the child, being a good parent also requires skills that can be, but are rarely, taught. As an aside, I have always found it incomprehensible that schools taught subjects few people would ever use like chemistry or algebra, while vitally important life skills like relationship and parenting - things people will need every day for the rest of their lives, and which will profoundly affect the future of society - are never even attempted. But, returning to the subject at hand:

Compounding the situation, when a parent acts precipitously or irrationally, a child does not have the capacity to understand what is driving the parent's behavior. Children have few coping skills to help them deal with or understand parental dysfunction. A small child cannot understand alcoholism or repressed sexuality. Plus, powerful negative emotions are overwhelming to children. All she will know is that something is very wrong, and this puts her already-fragile sense of emotional security at even greater risk. This is an important, and easily overlooked, point: as an adult, you can walk away from a difficult encounter, but a child cannot. She is trapped. Without guidance from a loving adult, trapped by the situation, children will lock their feelings up inside themselves.

Another situation that creates a good deal of confusion for children is to be told that they are loved and to have their material needs provided for, while meaningful emotional connection is withheld. The child will have great difficulty reconciling what she has been told with what she is feeling. On the surface, everything appears fine, yet inside she feels empty. She will have yearnings for what she does not have while she is being told she is loved, and this is crazy making! And, she may not be able to recognize what is wrong for years afterwards because it will be all she has ever known.

In a healthy environment, the child will evolve out of dependency on her parents to a healthy interdependence, sustained by the knowledge that she is loved and lovable. Her love of self will allow her to grow into a functional, self-loving adult. It will allow her to release her need for ego protection and live closer to the God Space. She will know The Truth. But if she is not able to do this, she will have to create a substitute system, i.e., beliefs, that allow her to get by, as she remains in an emotionally dependent state.

In a low-nurturance environment, the child will learn to cope with difficult situations by sacrificing her needs and desires in order to placate her parents' anxieties. The pain of her discomfort must go somewhere, and since she does not have the power to hold her parents accountable for their behavior, and is further hampered by her inability to understand her parents' dysfunction, she will compensate by caving in to their demands, effectively side-tracking the development of her natural self. She will collapse her feelings inward and create a set of false "I am not worthy" beliefs that will allow her to get through these difficult and trying circumstances. She will become convinced that she is not only unloved but more importantly, unlovable. Truthfully, she has little choice.

Her process will go something like this: "The love that I need is not here," and then she takes a fatal step. She says to herself, "There must be something wrong with me." And in that moment, she decides that she is part, if not the cause, of the problem.

She will take what had been external conditions created by her parents and internalize them into a set of personal defects and failings. She will rationalize the family situation by seeing herself as inadequate or at fault (shame or guilt). She will decide that she does not deserve to be loved. Whatever the reason – and she will not know what it is! She will conclude that something must be wrong with her. This is The Misunderstanding, and it will drive the creation of her beliefs. From that time forward, The Misunderstanding will powerfully influence everything that she does, thinks and feels. Until she heals The Misunderstanding, she will go through life crippled as though she had lost the use of one of her limbs.

Maybe she is too exuberant or too shy. Perhaps she isn't pretty enough or smart enough. She may even see herself as bad. However the issues coalesce, she will feel that somehow she just doesn't measure up, and this will be reinforced by a host of direct or indirect messages from her parents. God probably doesn't love her either, otherwise why would He allow this whole mess to happen in the first place?

Instead of learning to love herself as she might in a healthy environment, she will remain dependent upon her parents or other external sources for love, approval and acceptance because of her "personal inadequacies." She will believe that she needs to be dependent upon other people's beliefs and ideas rather than her own.

Her dependency creates an impossible situation. She needs love and support, but since she has not learned to love herself (remember, she doesn't deserve it), the only place she can get at least some of what she needs is from the same sources that she fears will reject her. This puts her in a terrible bind, and she will be inwardly angry about her predicament, although she may not be aware of that.

So long as she feels defective, she will remain in a dependent state, unable to stand freely and confidently on her own. Notice that I said dependent. We all like approval, but because the development of her natural love of self has been hindered, she will now need a substitute source. This is not a want, it is a need.

Remember, the ego exists to do one thing. It creates a sense of self, separate from the world and the God Space. When we are threatened, we have separated from the God Space and lost its guidance. The ego's function is to manage the separation. Its task is to insulate us from being hurt in the moment.

The ego shuts us down, makes us unaware, rationalizes, denies and in a hundred other ways creates psychological distance between ourselves and perceived emotional threats. The "I am" part of us that helped us when we were young to create order out of chaos, now serves to compensate for the growing belief that "I am not enough."

This is how the ego "protects" us from situations that our inner child thinks could be threatening. It acts as a risk manager, only allowing in what the inner child believes to be safe, or in the alternative, what she thinks she deserves. She will create beliefs to support that structure. The ego maintains a careful balance between external threats and her need to interact with the world.

Notice that in order to do this, she will have to limit and reinterpret input from the outside and shape her own thoughts and perceptions. She will have to edit her memories, manage and edit what she hears, and let in only that which does not conflict with her preconceptions. The truth of a situation will be bent before her need to survive. She will not have access to reality. Her reality will be an artificial one. Her decisions and her decision-making processes will be based upon heavily edited information. She will also have to distort her thinking. She may be in the same room as other people, but she will be in a very different world.

We treat our perceptions as real, but we know that this is not true. The mind sifts out a few fragments from millions of pieces of input and weaves a "reality" for us that is largely based upon our past experiences, biases and beliefs. Otherwise, the brain would overload and have to shut down.

Have you ever noticed how tired you get when you are traveling in an unfamiliar place? Your mind is constantly working overtime, absorbing a great deal of new information because it has little in its "library" to fall back on. That is the same principle behind "the outsider" who plays such an important role in scientific discovery and invention. The outsider's mind is not cluttered, and therefore obstructed, by what everyone else "knows" to be true.

We have problems when the mind's creations are brought into conflict with reality or someone else's reality. Puzzles and optical illusions take advantage of this phenomenon by giving the mind clues that lead it to miss a larger truth. These puzzles take advantage of the way the mind creates reality based on a few clues. There are many of these "puzzles," but consider a couple of examples:

Count every " F" in the following text:

> FINISHED FILES ARE THE RE
> SULT OF YEARS OF SCIENTI
> FIC STUDY COMBINED WITH
> THE EXPERIENCE OF YEARS...

How many did you find? You are probably wrong. There are 6 F's. Read it again, perhaps backwards. The brain has difficulty processing "OF" as an "F." Its reality does not conform to a more studied approach to the text. Then read this:

> I cdnuolt blveiee taht I cluod aulaclty uesdnatnrd waht I was rdanieg The phaonmneal pweor of the hmuan mnid! Aoccdrnig to a rscheearch at Cmabrigde Uinervtisy, it deosn't mttaer inwaht oredr the ltteers in a wrod are, the olny iprmoatnt tihng is taht the frist and lsat ltteer be in the rghit pclae. The rset can be a taotl mses and you can sitll raed it wouthit a porbelm. Tihs is bcuseae the huamn mnid deos not raed ervey lteter by istlef, but the wrod as a wlohe. Amzanig huh? Yaeh, and I awlyas thought slpeling was ipmorantt.

Even though the language is garbled, the mind draws clues and creates a reasonable interpretation. The conscious mind creates an artificial reality. The conscious mind cannot grasp reality. The mind's process gets us by under "normal" circumstances, but what happens to "reality" when we add emotions and the tumult, fear and pain of life? How "accurate" will our perceptions be then?

Researchers at Harvard showed people videos of basketball players passing a ball and assigned them the task of counting the number of passes made by one team or the other. Then either a gorilla or a woman with an umbrella would walk right through the middle of the action for about five seconds. Sixty percent of the people were so focused on counting passes that they never even saw the gorilla or the woman. They saw what their minds had predisposed them to see. It is this sort of mental deception that explains how magic tricks "work" and how people witnessing the same accident can see very different events, or viewing the same social problem can come to vastly differing conclusions.

We do not like to accept this truth, but the mind does not always give us a reliable reading on reality. The mind is pulled by fear, anxiety and the complex aspects of ego to create a reality that may have different ends than the simple conveyance of information. The conscious mind gives us a contrived reality that has significant differences from the truth. Most of our disagreements with others originate from a difference in perception, usually driven by fear. In the extreme, this is one of the forms of mental illness. In some mental illnesses the individual must create an altered reality for themselves because "normal" reality is too painful or threatening for her to live in.

The image the ego presents to the world will not be of her true self. It will be a false protective shell to keep the world at bay and to not expose her "flaws." This is how The Misunderstanding comes to dominate and control our lives and how we end up avoiding (for the moment) the learning that The Universe has proffered us.

Probably the most effective part of the ego's system is the way it gets us to avoid threatening situations before they even appear. It does this through self-degradation and self-condemnation. Have you ever wondered why you criticize yourself so forcefully? Notice that you do it today for events that happened years ago. It is one thing to have memories, but why is it necessary to literally beat the dickens out of yourself for things that happened years ago? The answer is that self-criticism keeps you from putting your fragile psyche at risk, and that is its purpose. The ego makes you gun-shy. You become conditioned to not even show up. The other thing the ego does is to get you to retreat into your mind. Thinking replaces feeling because thoughts are easier to manage than emotions.

To reiterate the core concepts: becoming dependent upon externalities and surviving through the use of ego sets her into an inevitable conflict with The Universe. The ego is an expression of separation, which is antithetical to Universal Law. In the God Space everything is connected, energy flows. Separation cannot exist, although we can convince ourselves that this is not true.

Yet, although the process of individuation as a healthy, self-loving being must reach completion, a person who believes that she is unworthy can derail the process for a time. But her beliefs will continue to cause problems as life pushes on her to change.

The ego's resistance, although it creates pain, is a way to manage the amount of change we can absorb. Consider the brakes on your car. They limit your forward progress by creating friction and a good deal of heat. Brake too much, and you get lots of heat and little forward movement. You do not progress; you are stuck in stasis and will feel frustrated. On the other hand, brake too little and you will rush headlong into life and are likely to crash. I find that to be an apt analogy.

Think of your beliefs as training wheels to use until you are ready to ride the big bike. The little bike is safe, but you don't go far, and you can't go very fast on it. Although training wheels are necessary, making graceful maneuvers with them is difficult. On the big bike, you learn to maneuver the challenges that life presents with grace and speed. It is the same thing with the ego and your beliefs. The ego just does not work well at speed. In order to fully and freely navigate life, you must be free of the constraints and fear-based beliefs that run your ego-based behaviors and keep you separated from the God Space. In the God Space you can go as far as you want and as fast as you desire without restriction or limitation.

The difficulty with dysfunctional childhood beliefs is that they become portable. Instead of being able to leave the dysfunction in the relationship with her parents where it belongs, the dysfunction becomes internalized as her inadequacy. It will then be with her wherever she goes.

This begins her descent down a dark passageway. It does not matter that her beliefs are not based in truth. She will wall off her own feelings and create compensating behaviors. Feeling that she is not lovable to her own parents, she will internalize their conditional love as proof of her own unworthiness; and she will cripple her evolving sense of self in the process.

Her fears and beliefs will cause her to hold back, to withdraw, and to not engage fully in life. By limiting risk in the moment, she will avoid immediate pain, but insulating herself in this way closes her to the real joys of life. She will accept half-measures and compromise what she really desires. She will learn to survive on dry crumbs and moldy bread.

After her experiences with her parents, she will leave the nest and go to school, carrying her beliefs with her. She cannot allow herself to be vulnerable because she has learned that if her flaws are exposed, she will be emotionally abandoned and rejected. And yet, her dependency demands some sort of external emotional connection. She will interact with teachers and other children, holding her "I am damaged and defective" posture. Guess how other people will respond? Their reactions will further confirm her beliefs, which, we must remember, are built on The Misunderstanding.

Later will come high school and dating, adding additional reinforcement to her already low self-image and frustration with life. Later, she will replace her parents with other parent figures – partners, bosses, teachers, ministers, politicians, etc.

Once established, the shame and guilt held by her wounded inner child will dominate her behavior. On the surface she might be aggressive, or in the opposite, she might cling to other people for approval and affection. She might appear to be doing fine on the outside, while imploding inside. She will learn to be scared, to avoid taking risks, to avoid commitments and to hide both literally and emotionally. She will adopt a hundred other compensating behaviors or their opposites. Her threshold of anxiety will be lower than average and her day-to-day stress levels will be high. Other people will react to her attitudes and behavior and respond accordingly, further reinforcing her negative self-beliefs.

Perhaps she learned to be a "good girl" (or a "nice boy") to avoid criticism and gain approval. In the alternative, she may become rebellious and antisocial, but this is only the same pain in contrary clothing. She may also bury her pain and pretend that it doesn't exist, or she may get high to numb her feelings. It is like going through life wearing very dark sunglasses. You don't see much, but at least you can hide your eyes from the paparazzi.

She will become a pleaser or a shrew. She will live on the surface, being overly concerned with superficial matters like appearance and immediate gratification. She will have fears of abandonment, overwhelm easily and will fear taking risks. She will either trust too easily, and be used and feel hurt, or trust too little and live alone in anxiety and suspicion. Her sense of reality will be distorted, making it difficult for her to see her own dysfunction and to see the motives of others. She will live in denial, depression, repression, and fantasy or perhaps even paranoia.

She will learn to accept failure at work, friendships and relationships as the regrettable consequence of getting through immediate dilemmas without having to expose herself and confront the core attributes that she believes mark her as unworthy. She will stifle her passion, project her failures onto others, or perform any manner of other emotional gyrations to avoid judgment and rejection. Or in the opposite, she will collapse the whole thing in on herself in a painful, self-defeating exercise of self-destruction. The system is that effective.

She will have difficulty having legitimate feelings. (Remember Principle Number Three: The Ego Cannot Love.) Focused on herself, even if she is in a position of caretaking, she will not be able to really care about other people. Since real bonding with others will be difficult, she will make "deals" with other "false-self people" to obtain at least a semblance of what she needs.

We see this dynamic played out often in the choices people make regarding partners. People will actually turn away from relationships that offer a meaningful heart connection in favor of a co-dependent connection with another damaged soul that can be built on mutual need swapping. People will sometimes even seek out others who are being controlled by their false selves so they can create low-level ongoing conflict. This provides stimulation and allows the person to avoid real intimacy. This also permits them to sustain their beliefs of personal unworthiness.

Most people who claim to be "in love" do have legitimate feelings, but few of them are really in love at all. In the first place, most people have never experienced real unconditional love, do not know what it feels like and are afraid to be that vulnerable in order to find out. Instead, they live in a self-created distortion of reality. As I pointed our before, most couples connect through mutual neediness and a desire to salve personal loneliness and pain. They hope that having a partner will make them feel accepted and fill the holes they feel in themselves.

These people would like their relationships to go deeper, but the vulnerability required frightens them. It is simply too great an exposure. Most of these relationships will fail. Some couples will learn real love over time, but this is uncommon. Consider your present relationship. Do you handle your conflicts and disagreements with love and compassion?

Wounded people engage in serial shallow relationships that end up in an ongoing series of tragedies. This keeps everyone off balance, without the hope of ever really enjoying life. After each breakup, these people move into blame (of either themselves or others), shut themselves down emotionally and then move into the next dysfunctional relationship. Life will be a succession of failed relationships, jobs and friendships that fell apart for a host of reasons, none of which had anything to do with them. This will guarantee that they will ultimately remain alone and unhappy, whether in a relationship or not. As I pointed out in Chapter Two, and as Faust learned, there is always a price for making a deal with the devil.

Sometimes a person will go into limbo, clinging to a dead relationship for years because it is safe. Under these conditions, real relationship is impossible, leaving her to endure an emotionally numbing, robot-like, half-life existence. Yet, this is all that she feels she deserves, and the relationship will not be threatening. It will not ask her to go deeper emotionally or to look at her pain or fear. Unable to surrender, she dooms herself to a life of emptiness, stress, sadness and frustration.

The dynamics of this situation are very much like the dynamics of a drug dependency. Drug addicts will put themselves in awful and degrading situations just to keep their addictions going. This same pattern holds true for a child who is unable to develop a healthy sense of self and remains dependent on external sources for love and support. She will pay a very high price to feel desired. She will put herself through hell trying to fill a hole in herself that cannot be filled, because it does not exist! In the shamanic world, we speak of this disconnection from the natural self as "soul loss."

In some relationships, there comes a time when one partner rises above the frustration and pain and seeks to heal herself. As she begins to gain emotional strength, the resulting imbalance stresses an already fragile relationship, often to the breaking point. There are some instances when her growth will invite, perhaps pressure, her partner to address his beliefs. This provides an opportunity for the couple to grow together, but unfortunately few couples are able to make that step. It requires both partners to be willing to look inward, face their fears and make changes.

Journalist Leroy Sievers does a monthly program on NPR where he shares his cancer experiences. He talks about how having cancer breaks down the walls of pride that usually separate people. Something he said hit me hard. He said, "My cancer has freed me to do the things that I should have been doing all along." Sievers' insight brings us to Principle Number Nine:

YOU DETERMINE YOUR EXPERIENCE

The quality of your life experience is not determined by what happens, but by how you respond to it. Events don't come with a script that says, "You must react in this way." In fact, your reactions are determined by your past conditioning and really do not have much at all to do with what is happening in the moment. That is why different people have such widely ranging reactions to similar circumstances.

You cannot control the events of your life, but having free will means that you do get to decide how you feel about what happens, and this is no small matter. This, as Krishnamurti pointed out, is the great secret to living a spiritual life. Life does not change; but we can change our relationship to life. The trick is to choose compassion in every instance. To paraphrase Aldous Huxley, "Experience is not what happens to a person; it is what a person does with what happens to them."

Even though you may not directly control events, your reaction to what occurs does influence what happens in the future. Here is how it works: As you begin to move from a place of greater compassion and self-love, your soul alters the intensity and direction of your future experiences. So you do have an effect on what is going to happen, but it is not as direct a relationship as you might have thought (or desired). Complicating this is the residue of your unresolved (painful) past-life experiences that will also get in the way until they are resolved. We will speak at length about them in Chapter Nine.

You don't have to like what's going on. Much of the time you are not going to like what is happening at all. Life can be difficult. But no one ever said that this was an easy process. The challenge is to learn to remain openhearted and at peace, regardless of what comes your way.

There is no proof for the next Principle other than your inner knowingness and a thousand separate bits of information that buttress your faith, but just in case you have not garnered this Principle on your own, allow me to say it:

NOTHING CAN BE WRONG WITH YOU

You may feel inadequate or unworthy, but you cannot be these things. You are a child of God, and it is simply not possible for you to be anything other than divine. How does that fit with how you see yourself? Yes, you are sometimes angry, crabby, or scared, but that is not who you are. It is just how you sometimes act, interestingly enough, when driven by your fear-based beliefs. So, now we have ten Principles:

LOVE EVERYTHING

ANYTHING YOU DO NOT LOVE WILL BECOME A LESSON

WHAT GETS YOU INTO TROUBLE ISN'T YOURS

YOUR LIFE IS PERFECT

THE EGO CANNOT LOVE

DO IT NOW

TRUTH MUST BE FELT

IF YOU DIDN'T BELIEVE IT, IT WOULDN'T MATTER

YOU DETERMINE YOUR EXPERIENCE

NOTHING CAN BE WRONG WITH YOU

So now that you understand what is going on, what do you do about the sticky places within you? First, recognize that the emotional charge comes because these situations open old unresolved wounds. The events of life resonate with what used to happen when you were a powerless and helpless child, subjected to the emotional whims of your parents.

When someone cuts you off in traffic, you probably focus on your hurt feelings and on the insult to your designated driving space. That is an old wound. It is being replayed to give you the opportunity to heal it. You do not have to like what they did, and it is perfectly acceptable to hold them responsible for their actions. They have something to learn from this exchange too, and that is the perfection of the process.

But to see the incident as an insult to your dignity and an offense to your right to use the road and remain angry at her instead of making the necessary adjustments for your safety and then going on about your business, is only to get lost in your ego and gain nothing from the experience. This is how many people spend their entire lives! They are like the proverbial hamster on its treadmill, spinning their wheels, burning up personal energy and getting absolutely nowhere in the process. No wonder they feel frustrated!

Now, think about how you respond to your partner.

Some people, instead of being aggressive and expressing their feelings, become submissive, and allow others to emotionally trample all over them. This response is obviously not healthy, either. It is simply the polar opposite of the anger response, but it is still an expression of not deserving to be valued. This is a good example of opposite-seeming behaviors both stemming from the same root. They are merely polar expressions of feeling unworthy.

Your task is not to seek for love,
but merely to seek and find all the barriers within yourself
that you have built against it.

Jalal ad-Din Rumi

*"When all the self-identifications are thrown away,
what remains is all-embracing Love."*

Nisargadatta Maharaj

CHAPTER 6

The Inner Child

While we try to teach our children all about life,
Our children teach us what life is all about.

Angela Schwindt

Our ancestors used fables, ballads and fairy tales to explain life. Those stories contain the cumulative knowledge of thousands of years of the culture's experience in dealing with life. They are the legacy of our pre-scientific culture. Because life principles appear simple, librarians secrete these stories away in the children's section. Find them. Read them. Study the symbolism contained in these stories. They have been developed and refined over thousands of years of experience. They can teach you more about life than anything else I know of. What follows is hardly a classic story, but hopefully it will help you see the process you are participating in:

A MODERN FABLE

In this story, you are an infant. One of your parents, let's say your mother, is holding you. Mom is struggling with her personal issues, and although she is doing the best she can, she cannot give you the attention you need. As a result, she is unable to hold you as securely as you would like. Feeling insecure, you naturally wonder if she is doing this because there is something undesirable about you. After all, if you were really valued, she would treat you with greater consideration. (Note: When the love a child needs is withheld, the child will naturally question her worthiness. We all do this. Love and support, although desirable for you, are essential to a child's survival.)

As your mother's struggle with her issues intensifies, the relationship between you becomes difficult. She is distracted, perhaps distraught and scared. She doesn't mean to hurt you, but she lets you slip out of her grasp, and you fall. Unfortunately, you land in a fresh cow pie.

Your initial feelings of not being good enough have just been strongly reinforced. Your mother picks you up, but her preoccupation with her own issues prevents her from cleaning all the manure off you. You look around for help from Dad, but he's not there. He's mostly at work and when he's home he is not emotionally available anyway.

So there you are, soiled and smelly. Something is obviously wrong. Not only are you feeling unloved and unworthy, you now have the stink to prove it. The other people in your family aren't able to clean you up either. They don't know how to get rid of their own manure. No one in the family does.

Your grandparents try to help, because grandparents are immune to the odor of manure, but it's just not enough. Because of all of the non-nurturing aspects of the family, your feelings of unworthiness become significantly reinforced.

The manure dries, you start to grow up, and having little choice, you become resigned to living with it. Who you are has become tainted with the aromatic flavor of something potent that does not belong to you. You do not deserve it, but the circumstances of your life have caused you to believe otherwise. You become convinced you are unlovable, and there isn't much in your environment to contradict that belief. Actually, there's quite a bit of negative reinforcement regarding your various imperfections and failings. When you play with the other kids you quickly learn they don't want to play with a smelly kid. You make friends with the other smelly kids. This leads you to conclude that this must be what you deserve. You resign yourself to the belief that this is what life has in store for you.

In order to get by, you start applying perfume to mask the smell of your "imperfections." Although this temporarily helps, you know you are living a lie, and are in constant fear someone will pick up the telltale scent and you will be exposed. Some people sense something funny, and shy away from you, making you feel worse.

You, of course, must act as if the perfumed you is the normal you, while hiding your "real" self away. You treat your real self as though she has leprosy, hiding her from exposure and criticism. You live on a tightrope, alone, cursed and unable to risk getting close to anyone who is "clean" for fear they will detect the smell and reject you.

So, you seek out manure-wearing others to have relationships with. You make an unspoken deal: "I will ignore your manure if you will ignore mine." However, when the other person feels scared or hurt, they will break the agreement and point to your manure as the source of the problem. You, of course, respond in kind. Soon you are engaged in a "manure war" with all sorts of manure flying around. Each of you becomes entrenched, busily defending your own position. Little that is constructive is accomplished.

Wounded and despondent, you pull back from life and start looking for answers to your dilemma. The church tells you the manure is your fault and you should be repentant for your sinful nature. Your boss says you are just not trying hard enough to overcome it. A therapist shows you how to behave as though the manure didn't exist. A yoga teacher encourages you to achieve calmness in spite of the smell. New Age books and CD's tell you that beautiful flowers grow in manure, and you need to surrender to your bliss and make lemonade from lemons. Some of what you learn is helpful, but you still stink and you don't like it. You know it interferes with your relationships with other people, but you seem unable to shake it loose.

Unable to get real answers about what is going on, and beset by a continuing series of problems, you pray to God for help. To your surprise, there is an answer. God says, "Take off your soiled clothing and bathe yourself in love. That which is causing you pain is not yours. It does not belong to you, it never has."

Conditioned by years of experience, the thought of giving up your soiled clothing seems impossible. "But," you reply, "I can't. This soiled state is all I know. It's who I am. It's what I deserve."

After all, what would happen if you gave up your soiled clothing and there was nothing else for you to put on? You would be left naked and alone out in the cold! It has felt this way in your previous lives, and that is how it felt when you separated from the Creator to come here. And there is little reason to believe the present will be any different. Feeling like a failure, you turn away from your feelings and God's advice, and you persevere, doing the best you can with your smelly rags.

Clinging steadfastly to your beliefs of unworthiness, life continues to create pain for you, but you persist. The lessons intensify. Eventually you are confronted with a crisis. Perhaps it is the painful end of a relationship or a business failure. Maybe it is a physical crisis, with the prospect of death or a considerably worsened physical condition. Each pushes on you to make serious changes to the way you see yourself.

Whatever the obstacle, you are pushed to the point you can no longer sustain your old beliefs and behaviors. The façade will simply no longer hold. Pushed over the limit, your resistance breaks. Bruised and beaten, and finally really willing to surrender, you cry once more to God for help.

He says, "I understand." And then He repeats, "Take off your soiled clothing and bathe yourself in love. That which is causing you pain is not yours. It does not belong to you, it never has."

With nowhere else to turn, a crack in the darkness appears and you begin to see that it is really not you. It never has been! The manure you have been carrying all this time has been the source of your pain, and it's not even yours!

God continues, "You left here with little self-awareness. The process you have experienced has been created so you would come to see the truth about who you are. In the process, you will heal the vulnerability that allowed the manure to stick to you in the first place. Your vulnerability gave the beliefs a place to stick."

He then tells you, "This is all part of the process we have created together called Life," and that learning to accept the truth about who you are is an important step in your spiritual development. Since you have free will, it was necessary for you to come to this realization by yourself. He could not give it to you.

Okay, it's just a story. But it illustrates what happens when a child comes up against her parents' dysfunctionality. No matter how egregious the parents' behavior, the child will still assume at least some responsibility for the problem. Either she created it, or her parents acted as they did because she was defective and deserved to be treated that way.

As we saw in the last chapter, this is The Misunderstanding, and it is the obstacle every child must confront. The Misunderstanding is not accidental. It is how the energy disharmony within us plays out in human reality. This is the place where our energies do not move well. The Misunderstanding sets in motion the driving forces (your pain) that will lead inevitably to its destruction because it is built on untruth and cannot be sustained. Your pain will drive you to resolve the disharmony that disrupts your life.

Your beliefs, created out of The Misunderstanding, cause you feel vulnerable, and life brings that vulnerability to the surface through your interactions with other people. Your feelings of vulnerability around the disharmony are what led to the creation of your beliefs and your problems/opportunities in the first place. These are the issues you came to Earth to resolve.

If you study humanity, you will see that everyone is "dancing" with everyone else. The loci of all these "dances" are our mutual disharmonies. In the story, you danced with your parents, each of you causing pain for the other around your mutual vulnerabilities. This is the gift for growth we bring to each other. You give to them, they give to you, and it can hurt like hell.

Today, if you look at your various relationships, you will find that each of them is built around a shared opportunity for personal growth.

When you were young, the family situation overwhelmed your limited coping abilities. The inner child's fear is that if she is forced go there again, she will be overwhelmed and helpless as before. She created strong prohibitions against going there once, and those prohibitions remain formidable. Her anxieties are not unfounded. Without a significant change in your attitude, it is likely that you will shun her again. You will act as though she does not exist. You will leave her by the side of the road, hurting and in pain, just as "they" used to. When you shut her out, you become the same kind of a threat "they" once were.

In addition to being cut off from an important part of yourself, ignoring your inner child's pain presents an enormous problem. She controls your power. You have your wit, your wisdom and your intellect, but emotional situations are her domain. You have undoubtedly had experiences where you felt "out of control," "not yourself," etc. that's her and her fear taking over. If I asked you to fill the room with anger or laughter or joy, it would be an effort. A three year old can do it in a heartbeat. It's her territory.

And when she feels threatened, she will take control. And as long as she sees herself as flawed and unworthy, she will approach life defensively. She will do whatever is necessary to survive. If she needs to shut you down, she will. If she needs to lie, cheat, manipulate or steal in order to survive, she will make you do so.

You have virtually no control over her decisions. If she needs to make you scared in order to withdraw from life and not expose her to rejection, that is what will happen. If she has to make you anxious, obnoxious, put you into denial or make you afraid of intimacy, she will do it. She can cause you to be abrasive, angry, domineering, controlling, seductive or manipulative in order to get what she needs or to create safe distance from a threat. Or, if she needs affection, she can push you into an unhealthy relationship (remember that she is starved for love). She will push for chocolate or ice cream in order to feel nourished, or for new clothes or shoes in order to feel powerful or attractive. And, like it or not, she has the power to totally control your life.

She is not trying to be contrary or difficult. Her view of life and the world is probably negative, and most likely very different from yours. She operates under the assumption that the world is as threatening as it was when she was young. In her world, you need to remember, she was powerless, and the environment was overwhelming. That hasn't changed and it is therefore necessary for her to sabotage anything she feels might put her at risk.

Until you build a bridge to her, so she can receive your love and protection, she has no alternative but to shut you down. If you will not address her fears and protect her, then she is forced to take control of the situation. When she does, then you both suffer because what takes over is a powerless, helpless, vulnerable, scared and emotionally challenged four year old. That can make life a living hell. And, by the way, the view you hold of yourself may not be helping things either.

While all this is going on, you become something of a spectator, powerless as your life unravels around you. When we feel "out of control," we often respond by using our willfulness to try and regain control of things. Instead of working with her fear and anxiety, we push through situations, shoving her aside so we can do what we "think" we should. After all, emotions are risky and unreliable, and they make us feel vulnerable. In order to avoid our emotions, we must live from our conscious minds, since in separating from the God Space, we lose the guidance of our natural internal compass. How do you think that will play out? Can you say "stress?"

Calling what often happens between adults and their inner children at a time like this "an adversarial relationship" is being polite. It is more like an all-out war. You want to take a risk, and she is frightened. You want to become intimate with someone, and she is afraid of being rejected. You want to be successful, and she cannot permit that kind of exposure. Or, in the opposite, she is emotionally starved and desperate for love and affection, and she will sell your soul to get it. It feels like you try to run your life, and she keeps pulling the rug out. That, by the way, is exactly how she feels when you try to run things.

Shutting down her feelings also consumes an extraordinary amount of your personal energy. In order to control her, you must rigidly constrain your own power. You literally become the proverbial dog chasing its tail. Only, this tail can bite back. That's why you're tired so much of the time! The result of this conflict is stress. When chronic, the condition will lead to exhaustion and eventually disease. In over twenty-five years of healing people, I have yet to see a case of chronic fatigue, for example, that did not involve a pitched battle between the inner child and the adult.

It is difficult for some people to accept that the inner child does not trust them to keep her safe. If a loving and trusting relationship had existed, the inner child would have become an important part of your life long ago. So, the most important task in cleaning out your inner closet will be to create a relationship of love and trust with her, and this is where many people have trouble.

She is probably holding a good deal of old pain. You haven't been comfortable dealing with it in the past, and you probably aren't very anxious to deal with it today. So, your tendency when going to your inner child is to say, "I love you, but don't bring your pain into our relationship." How would you feel if I told you I was willing to have a relationship with you as long as you did not bring any hurt and pain? I suspect you would not like it. You would probably feel disrespected. You would also not trust our connection. This is what your parents probably did to you!

The primary tool she uses is emotion. Emotions are different from feelings, and the difference is important. Feelings emanate from the God Space. They come, you hold them for a short time, and then they pass on. All you are left with is a memory of having the feeling. But with an emotion, a feeling comes and you make a connection through the present experience to a previous event, which is usually, but not necessarily, an unresolved hurt.

For example, let's say one of your parents was critical of you. Thirty or forty years afterward, until that wound is healed, the emotion (shame) when criticized will be very much alive in you. We would describe you as "sensitive to criticism." Here is how it works: orchestrated by your protective ego, when you are criticized, an alarm goes off and says, "Danger, Will Robinson." Your ego will then take the feelings from the present moment and pull you back into the unresolved pain of your parent's criticism and the vulnerability and helplessness you felt at that time. Your present feeling will get buried under an avalanche of old unresolved pain. That is an emotion.

The hurt is real, but it is also based upon The Misunderstanding. So although the present pain exists, what you feel is going to have more to do with resurrecting an old hurt than with whatever is going on in the moment.

An emotion is a protective energy mechanism designed to shut your feelings down in order to insulate you from insult. In the God Space, energy flows. Emotions block the movement of energy. This can be confusing because it can look otherwise.

When you are criticized, the first thing you do is to contract energetically. Contraction itself requires a good deal of energy. If pushed beyond your personal threshold, you then use additional energy to react. In reaction, you either collapse the energy further inward or push back against the insult, perhaps even attacking back, to create emotional distance.

If you think of someone becoming emotionally explosive, it seems as though she is moving a great deal of energy. But this is an apples-to-oranges comparison. We must look to the core contraction of the person. The outer display is a shell, created for diversion. The surface reaction is real because it is driven by real fear, but it is also a diversion to prevent a deeper devastation.

In reaction you will do one of two things: you will either lock the contraction down even further (the fortress), or you will defend yourself by becoming aggressive (the dragon). Whatever your response, the original contraction (the hurt, the insult) is there. The difference is if you explode, you will release some of the initial contraction. But it is a very high price to pay just to release some of your tension.

Emotions speak to the separation from the God Space created by The Misunderstanding. If I am a failure, if I am inadequate, I cannot allow you to see who I really am. I must protect myself from being exposed. Shaman refer to this as soul loss. It is also important to keep in mind that emotions do not resolve issues; they only create psychological distance from them.

Emotional reactions come in polar opposites. They do not have a middle place. We either contract or strike - fortress or dragon. Fight/flight, love/hate and passive/aggressive, for example, are polar-opposite reactions originating from the same source. The fight or flight responses both originate from the fear-based belief of "not safe." Love/hate (which is comprised of neither real love nor real hate) originates from the part of the self that feels unlovable.

When you mix black paint with white paint, you get a blend, something in-between; you get gray. But emotions are not like that. A light switch is either on or off, a bucket either overflows or it does not. In the emotional state, you will either confront the aggressor or retreat and shut down.

There is no middle position (at this level of consciousness) because a middle position would make you feel vulnerable – the very thing the emotion is seeking to avoid. For example, although there are degrees of intensity, mixing a little love with a little hate does not create a feeling of safety. Reducing rage until there is nothing left might cool the situation down, but its absence will not create compassion, only emptiness. To create a "middle way," you must transcend emotionality and move to another level where you realize that you cannot be harmed. When you know you are safe, then you mitigate the need for an emotional response.

Interesting also with emotions, we often see pendulum swings – people will sometimes flip between the two polarities as quickly as you can turn a pancake. They go from one pole to the other because, as I said, there is no middle position to emotions. Each person has a different threshold determining when she will switch from internal compression (fortress), to outward "emotional" expression (the dragon).

A person's reaction is not always obvious from the outside. A repressed person will compact energy in until she either completely collapses or explodes. When the tectonic plates of the earth collide, they can accumulate enormous amounts of energy, which is eventually released through violent outbreaks such as earthquakes, or over centuries more quietly, through the creation of mountain ranges.

If you have ever driven a stick shift car, you may have tried to drive with the emergency brake on. That is like having emotions. If you killed the engine, that is like the contracted response. It keeps you from moving. If, however, you were able to drive off, the car would be sluggish. So, yes, you would move, but not freely. The emotional response is like driving around with your emergency brake on. You can move, but it takes a great deal more energy!

There was a time when feelings ran your life. Watch any child, and this will be obvious. Your parents, the school and the church had a difficult time with your natural, expressive self. To accommodate them, you disconnected from a part of that natural self. You had little choice. Some kids rebelled, but this was only the externalization of their inner pain. What you probably did was internalize your feelings. Those feelings, by the way, are still there, you have just lost your connection to them. That is what rushes to the surface in an emotional response.

Unless you have children of your own, it can be easy to forget how psychologically fragile and vulnerable children can be. I encourage clients who do not have small children to spend time around little ones to observe. It is always an eye-opening experience. It is best to observe them at a time other than play, because children are fairly natural and uninhibited then. I urge people to observe children when they are in unfamiliar circumstances, like in school or around adults, in order to see how fragile and vulnerable they themselves once were.

When you witness a child's fragility, you see how easily The Misunderstanding can occur. Children's tools for comprehending adult motives are very limited. It is impossible for a child to understand that Daddy does not know how to give love or that Mommy has never dealt with her issues around intimacy.

If you had known who you really were when you were a child, you might not have liked what was happening some of the time, but the things that caused you so much pain then would just be difficult memories today. The situation would have been unsatisfactory, but you would not have taken things personally. If you had known who you were then, you would have been able to hold the truth, and the dilemma would have remained with them (where it belonged), instead of lodging within you. You would have looked at your parents and wondered what was going on with them. You would simply have said to yourself, "I wonder why they are acting so strangely?" In our fable, the manure would not have stuck.

Without the awareness of who you truly were, you internalized the situation into being your problem. You concluded that things did not go well because you were defective or inadequate. This is The Misunderstanding, and its effects can be devastating.

Turning your perceptions around is one of the secrets to healing, and in Chapter Eight we are going to use the Shamanic Journey process to give your inner child a way to see what really happened. Until today, she has believed she was at least partly responsible for what happened. We will revisit those events to see things as they really were. We will show her that she was not responsible for her parents' behavior. What occurred was the result of their fears and anxieties, not her inadequacy. This gives you the opportunity to free yourself from the emotional burden you have carried your entire life.

You cannot change what happened; that is history. But you can change the interpretation you hold regarding those events because those misinterpretations are active in the present. Your Misunderstanding has been the source of your trouble all these years. But, before you can address it, there is something important you need to do first.

In order for you to heal, you need to establish a loving relationship between yourself and your inner child. You must become her friend and ally. In concept, it is not difficult, but many people have a poor relationship with their inner selves, so what is simple in concept can be problematic in practice. She did what she had to do in order to survive. You need to appreciate where she was emotionally at that time. This may not be easy, because many factors influence our relationship with our parents. After all, they were also your source of love and sustenance!

The process is not complicated. Simply find a quiet place where you can sit or lie down undisturbed for about fifteen minutes. Dim the lights or draw the curtains. I like to light a candle or an oil lamp when I am doing inner work, but it is not essential. When you are comfortable, simply ask her to come and be with you. You may mostly feel her instead of actually seeing her, and this is fine. Work with what you get.

Let her know you are here to be her friend, that you care about her, and you are trying to learn how to be with her. You might also want to apologize for not being with her in the past. You will get one of several responses:

When she comes, she will probably be sad or hurting. She has been in a good deal of pain all these years, and her feelings are understandable. Open your heart to her. Think how you would react if one of your own children (or grandchildren) came to you hurting like that. What would you do? It is astonishing how people will freely give love to other people or their pets, and yet withhold love from their own inner children.

If she will permit it, hold her. Love her. Be with her. Let her know in whatever way you can, that she will never have to face the world alone again. This is a big commitment, by the way, so do not make it casually. Make a connection from your heart chakra to hers. After the two of you connect, she may want to go play. By all means do so. It is probably something you have not done in a while.

If when she emerges she is angry, there are a couple of possible explanations. Either she is legitimately upset with you for ignoring her for so long, or we are dealing with the additional presence of a negative entity. If the latter is true, it is likely that the entity is throwing up emotional stuff as a screen to protect her.

If she is simply angry, deal with her feelings. In addition to your holding her pain, this is also going to involve your making some life changes. Up to this time, when life got difficult, your choice has been to exclude her and her feelings. So if you mean what you say, you will have to begin making feelings the primary consideration in your decision-making. This means respecting her in everything you do.

What I am going to say next cannot be sufficiently emphasized in words:

MAKE HER THE MOST IMPORTANT THING IN YOUR LIFE

Think about what that will mean. Today you probably run your life largely from your head, ignoring her. For good or ill, that approach has brought you this far. In an important sense, I am asking you to turn your life on its head. I am asking you to make the feelings of an angry, scared, neglected four year old, paramount in your considerations. Here's the secret – if you don't include her consciously, she will take control anyway when she feels threatened. So, you really haven't been accomplishing much by what you are presently doing. Respecting her feelings includes her in the process and provides space for negotiation and healing–two things you probably could use a healthy dose of.

I urge you to take this commitment with the greatest earnestness. It is one of the most important things you will ever do. Include her in everything. For a short time, you will probably need to do this through the use of your conscious intention, but the new habit will develop quickly. We will call this Principle Number Eleven. Here are our eleven principles:

LOVE EVERYTHING

ANYTHING YOU DO NOT LOVE
WILL BECOME A LESSON

WHAT GETS YOU INTO TROUBLE ISN'T YOURS

YOUR LIFE IS PERFECT

THE EGO CANNOT LOVE

DO IT NOW

TRUTH MUST BE FELT

IF YOU DIDN'T BELIEVE IT, IT WOULDN'T MATTER

YOU DETERMINE YOUR EXPERIENCE

NOTHING CAN BE WRONG WITH YOU

MAKE HER THE MOST IMPORTANT THING
IN YOUR LIFE

I suggest people contact their inner children no fewer than 675 times each day. It's a simple matter. There are hundreds of moments in each day, between your other thoughts or when you are shifting attention from one thing to another, when you can contact her. It only takes a few seconds. Ask her how she is feeling. Let her know you are there and that you love her. If she is doing well, then offer her your love and go on about your day. But if she is anxious or concerned, then as soon as is humanly possible (and you can excuse yourself from almost any situation to go to the bathroom), take a minute to sit with her and find out what is troubling her.

Another good way to remind yourself to stay in contact with her is through your breath. With your in-breath, connect to her, tell her that you love her and ask her how she is doing. Then, on your exhale, listen for her answer. If you practice this, you eventually become sensitized to her feelings so that your awareness of her feelings is constant.

If she is feeling anxious or afraid, she is most likely concerned about a future event. She may also have feelings about certain people. Whatever the problem, she needs to know you will be there to love and support her. You cannot guarantee what other people will do, and of course, do not put her into harm's way, but interestingly enough, this isn't what she is really concerned about. She needs to know that no matter what happens, you will be there to love and support her. This may not seem logical, but that is how it works.

When the inner child comes to you if her anger is excessive, if she is aggressive, if she seems "off," if she rants, or is abusive, it is likely you are dealing with an entity. This is not something to ignore, but entities in our world are actually rather common. I will devote a significant part of Chapter Nine to the subject, and you will learn how to successfully deal with entities. So if you see or sense a dark energy around her, you have some extra baggage to deal with.

There is a more advanced stage that is not common, but we do find from time-to-time. If her behavior is fanatical, if her eyes flash, or are hollow or if she seems unworldly, she has become what people used to call "possessed." It is an important condition, not something to be ignored, but it is also something you can manage. You will need to read through the next two chapters before addressing either of the above situations. And after a few attempts, if you are not successful in ridding yourself of the entity, locate a good shaman. In the meantime, extend love from your heart chakra to her heart chakra. This effectively cuts out the entity. It won't resolve the situation, but it is an important first step in the work you will do later.

For many people, making the inner child's needs important is a considerable departure from their old behaviors. After all, we are taught not to be self-centered. But this has nothing to do with narcissistic selfishness.

Truthfully, it's what you would have been doing all along had you learned to love yourself when you were young. For many people, it means simply giving the same love to themselves they give to others. Loving yourself does not mean you don't consider the feelings or needs of other people. True self-love actually opens us more to the needs and pain of other people, the animals and the planet. But you will need to stop putting others' needs before yours. It is an issue with deep roots, and you may want to use the Shamanic Journey process to address it.

Some people have trouble making a connection with their inner child. It's new and alien, and there is no standard against which you can measure whether or not you are doing it correctly. It can feel like you are making it all up. That is just your mind fussing. She is probably trying to distract you because she is afraid of the exposure. You can safely assume she is there, even if she won't come out. She may not feel comfortable connecting with you, but she is there. What will save both of you is that she needs this connection more than you do.

Her unwillingness to come out speaks to a lack of trust on her part. People don't like hearing this, but the problem isn't going to be on her end, it's on yours. She may be lost, angry and confused, but she wants to heal. The problem is, she needs a safe and nurturing environment for that to happen, and your life choices have not always provided a safe and loving space for her. Actually, quite often the opposite has been true. You have probably ignored her fear and her pain as you plowed forward to get what you wanted.

If the trust between the two of you has been damaged to the point that she is unwilling to come out and meet you, you need to accept this as an important message that your behavior and attitudes need serious realignment. This is fixable. It is always fixable. It is just that waiting until later makes it more difficult.

If you are having trouble, begin by opening your heart to her. Assume the fault is yours. Inner children do not do irrational or irresponsible things. If she is holding back, she has good reason. When you finish Chapter Eight, then begin to work with the part of you that is reluctant to feel.

Continue to open your heart to her, even if there is no response. You can also try going to her. See yourself as taking the initiative and moving toward her. If your intent is sincere, you will eventually make contact with her.

No matter how well intentioned you are, in these early stages you will forget her from time to time. It happens to everyone. You are changing long-established patterns, and it takes a little while for new behavior to sink in. If your intention is sincere, she will understand. When you realize you have fallen back into your old ways, simply stop, reconnect to her, apologize and go on. If it becomes a chronic situation, then there is something deeper you need to address. Some other part of you is afraid of this connection and the change it represents. After learning the journey process in Chapter Eight, work on this issue.

Do not ignore her concerns and simply go on with life. Otherwise, you treat her as unimportant just as "they" once did. It may be necessary for you to deal with touchy situations and people she has concerns about, but do not simply barge ahead, disconnected from her/your feelings.

Your newfound awareness of her/your feelings can help you formulate different strategies toward other people and the events of your life. Inner children do not come to their feelings arbitrarily. Perhaps there is something about the other person you need to consider more carefully. More likely, perhaps the person or the situation touches something painful from the past or speaks to a deep-seated unfulfilled need or wound she carries. This means there is an important issue for you to address.

People in our culture are particularly skilled at living from their heads. Although it is a conscious choice, many people retreat into their minds to avoid having to address their emotional issues. We get a lot of good training and encouragement for our mental prowess. But, when you live in your head, you isolate yourself from your feelings. It is a short-term strategy, but it gets people by.

Unfortunately, as you realize by now, The Universe will not be denied. It will persistently push through your intellectual resistance. "Persistently" is the operative word here. We see many people in personal crises (relationship problems, disease, etc.) as they are literally brought to their knees in order to break them out of the fortresses of their rational minds. If this is happening for you, you have an important challenge awaiting you.

I was recently asked to help a 92-year old man who had steadfastly refused to open his heart his entire life. He had recently been stricken with a serious heart attack. Even at his advanced age, The Universe wasn't going to let him off the hook. It was insisting he look at what he had been doing. I learned from him that it is never too late to change. Don't wait until you are 92. Why waste your life being scared, angry and upset?

I am frequently asked what the inner child is. First and foremost, until she is healed, she represents an arrested stage of your early development. There will likely be more than one of her, representing critical stages in your process. She will be afraid of being exposed and criticized. She will feel powerless, hurt and probably unworthy. She is also very likely to feel unlovable.

In addition to being the repository of your childhood experiences, you will also find an archetypical child who is the gateway to your past lives. She carries a recollection in detail of everything that has ever happened to you, especially the unresolved pain from your past life experiences. Healing those old wounds is an important part of your healing process, and we will address them in Chapter Nine.

You have several ways of connecting to the other realms, and a few of those run through her. This is especially true regarding your connection to the God Space. Think about the qualities of the God Space – compassion, kindness, gentleness, openness, caring, etc. Now think about the innate qualities of an innocent child. They are identical. You have a connection to the Creator through your chakras, and she has a different, but equally important, connection to Him as well.

If you will permit a short digression, I wish to talk about a particular aspect of the inner child as it relates to spiritual work. Her position is central to your spiritual connection, and her feelings and fears can easily contaminate an otherworldly spiritual connection. If she is angry, scared, frustrated, etc., the communication can be tainted by her emotions and fear.

Thus if someone seeks to channel, read the Tarot or do astrology, for example, even with the best intentions, if her personal inner issues are not fairly-well resolved, it is almost impossible for the information to come through cleanly. The inner child's fear, anxiety, rationalization and, in some cases, paranoia, will interfere with and distort the information being channeled. In most cases, the aberrations will be minor, but in others, important distortions and misunderstandings can occur.

This is not just a problem for New Age channelers, spiritual teachers and Tarot readers, however. Spiritual leaders and mystics throughout history have written about sacred transmissions from God. As a result, the holy books of every major religion contain ego-based misinterpretations of the truth.

I mentioned The Doctrine of Original Sin in Chapter Two and its questionable connection to God's Truth. There are also significant passages in the Christian Bible, the Torah and the Koran that express ego-based misunderstandings.

There is confusion in the Old Testament about God because many years ago a manipulative entity called Gurumpara would play upon spiritual men's vanity and ego, and masquerade as God. One of his favorite "stunts" was to play the vengeful God, creating no end of confusion about who God really was. It is a confusion that has occupied religious scholars for centuries.

When John of Patmos wrote Revelations, his unresolved personal emotional issues seriously compromised his vision of Armageddon. Muhammad told us the Koran was given to him by the Archangel Gabriel. I do not mean to impugn Muhammad's veracity or his credibility, but we know this kind of channeling is easily influenced by contamination under even the most ideal circumstances, and Muhammad, by his own admission, was a conflicted and troubled man.

To see how this happens, we need look no further than to the leaders of today's fundamentalist faiths of any religion to see how bigotry, bias, prejudice and fear can corrupt God's truth and be propagandized as His teachings. Consider just a few examples:

And when we destroy 40 million little innocent babies, we make God mad. (Speaking of 9/11): I really believe that the pagans, and the abortionists, and the feminists, and the gays and the lesbians who are actively trying to make that an alternative lifestyle, the ACLU, People For the American Way, all of them who have tried to secularize America. I point the finger in their face and say, "you helped this happen." —Rev. Jerry Falwell

The feminist agenda is not about equal rights for women. It is about a socialist, anti-family political movement that encourages women to leave their husbands, kill their children, practice witchcraft, destroy capitalism, and become lesbians. —Pat Robertson

But when the forbidden months are past, then fight and slay the pagans wherever ye find them, and seize them, beleaguer them, and lie in wait for them in every stratagem (of war); but if they repent, and establish regular prayers and pay Zakat, then open the way for them: for Allah is Oft- forgiving, Most Merciful.[28] —Muhammad

The Jews of Temple Beth Sholom are sinful, greedy, Hell-bound, money-grubbing sodomites; and they have dedicated their synagogue to be a gay and lesbian propaganda mill and recruiting depot, soliciting young people to sodomy. —Rev. Fred Phelps

Some Zanadiqa (atheists) were brought to Ali and he burnt them. The news of this event reached Ibn 'Abbas who said, "If I had been in his place, I would not have burnt them, as Allah's Apostle forbade it, saying, 'Do not punish anybody with Allah's punishment (fire).' I would have killed them according to the statement of Allah's Apostle, 'Whoever changed his Islamic religion, then kill him."[29] —Ibn 'Abbas

. . . kill any Jew who comes under your power.[30] *—Muhammad*

And as I looked at those demolished towers in Lebanon, it entered my mind that we should punish the oppressor in kind and that we should destroy towers in America in order that they taste some of what we tasted and so that they be deterred from killing our women and children.

And that day, it was confirmed to me that oppression and the intentional killing of innocent women and children is a deliberate American policy. [To them] Destruction is freedom and democracy, while resistance is terrorism and intolerance. —Osama bin Laden

What should do we do about these pronouncements? This is where it is essential that you learn to listen to your own inner guidance. There are many reasons to heal your inner child's pain, but a very important additional one is to allow your built-in truth detector to function. Your "still small voice" is your "truth detector." When you hear something that is "off," you will know it. You can feel it. It probably will not come as a voice, but the feelings will be there. You may need to learn to slow yourself down so you can listen more discriminately, however. Without your inner guidance, you are vulnerable to the influences of people who seek to manipulate you through your fear, and the world has many such people.

Returning for a moment to the story that opened this chapter, if you are carrying manure around, it's because you believe you deserve it. Smelly or not, the manure provides a certain amount of protection from a world that has been unsafe. It makes giving up the manure even more difficult. Fortunately, there is a way out. The secret lies in coming to know the truth about who you are underneath your fear. You see, you are a child of God, and God does not create good children and defective children. God creates children. All children carry burdens for their own and for others' learning, but never as punishment and never because there is something wrong with them. I would like to share one man's story with you:

BRUCE'S STORY

When I first met Bruce he was a half step away from living in the street. His health was in chronic jeopardy and he was in constant, often agonizing, pain. He could eat few foods and could barely take in enough nourishment to remain alive. He looked like a death camp survivor. His refusal to address his inner pain was so profound that his soul had brought him near death on several occasions, trying to break the stranglehold fear had on him. His case is extreme, but you will probably recognize his feelings. I suggested he do some stream-of-consciousness writing, and he returned with these notes:

My God, I haven't accomplished anything! My future looks dim. There is no way I can be secure and safe. I am frantic and terrified that I won't have a home or food. This world is going crazy. There is no one out there I can depend on. I am fed up with this world! I want to leave it. Death is the only escape. Where is the comforter? I am so angry, I want to lash out but it doesn't do any good. I don't have a voice. I fear being reprimanded or harmed. No one hears my cries of plight.

My mind doesn't have the answers. It only creates more problems and more dilemmas. I wait in silence. Something has to come in and guide me through this awful, painful maze of existence. Where is Love? All I want is love, intimacy, connectedness with someone but I am afraid to trust another for fear of being hurt. Why am I so afraid to give up control to the unknown?

I am exhausted from not sleeping, of not being able to fall into sleep and from the pain. I feel displaced. Nothing on the outside will fulfill me. I feel so disconnected from everything - so distanced from the world. There is no security and a lot of anxiety. Where are the angels people talk about? I can't feel them. I can't even feel me.

Almost magically in the middle of his agony, Bruce's inner child burst through his writing and said to him with eternal wisdom:

When will you pay attention to me? When will you listen to me? When will you face me squarely and see me for what I am? I bring you the gift of pain to awaken you. I am underneath all your pain. When will you give me your time, your attention? You make a big deal out of suffering and then miss me. Please acknowledge me. Please find me before it is too late. Accept what comes fully and then you will locate me. Do not cover up the pain. I will only magnify it, and then you will feel tortured by your body even more. Be in the silence with love and wait with inner ears open to receive what I am. Give up the search for a solution to your dilemmas. It will only cause more pain. Bear witness to simplicity for it will guide you home. Your mind cannot take you home to peace. The mind must be a disciple of the heart to know peace. Your concerns are getting in the way of your being at peace. I wish to emerge and be free again - to just Be.

Ignore your mind and all of its stories and judgments. Be not afraid of the pains you carry on the surface of your heart. They are the shields that keep you from coming home. Arise with courage and determination to finish the journey. Feel your heart. Open your heart. When it closes, it is because of fear. Sit with that fear and love it with all of your heart. And then once again, you will be open and be filled again with love.

Nothing I could have said to Bruce would have had the force of his inner child's message. By going out as far as he did, Bruce now has knowledge and experience that will allow him to help other troubled souls in a way few others are able to. He paid a great price for his gift, but that was the path his soul had chosen for him.

> *What exists in truth is the Self alone.*
> *The self is that where there is absolutely no "I" thought.*
> *That is called Silence.*
> *The Self itself is the world;*
> *the Self itself is "I";*
> *the Self itself is God.*
>
> Ramana Maharshi

CHAPTER 7

Gratitude

To speak gratitude is courteous and pleasant,
to enact gratitude is generous and noble,
but to live gratitude is to touch Heaven.

Johannes A. Gaertner

We have discussed a number of concepts thus far in the book, but before we proceed to address your personal issues, there is another important topic we need to cover.

If I were to ask you what the single most important thing you could do to improve your emotional well-being, enhance your health and actually add years to your life, what would you choose? Meditation? Yoga? Diet? Psychotherapy? Meditation is great, and yoga improves your emotional state, but interestingly enough, the one thing you could do to improve just about every aspect of your life - your emotional health, your physical well being and your lifespan – would be to move into a daily practice of gratitude.

In fact, "Practicing Gratitude" may be the most powerful words in the English language. Gratitude is the most effective spiritual resource we have. It is unlike anything else. People are moved, opened and humbled through experiences and expressions of gratitude. Feeling grateful generates a ripple effect through every aspect of life, potentially satisfying some of our deepest yearnings - for happiness, healthier relationships and inner peace. A practice of gratitude is the one thing that can quite literally maximize the enjoyment of life and significantly reduce the impact of your difficulties. Without gratitude, life can seem lonely, depressing and impoverished.

Want to be more compassionate? Work on gratitude. Want more inner peace? Work on gratitude. Want more patience? Work on gratitude. Want to reduce your stress? Want to live longer? Want to heal more quickly? You get the point. Gratitude does this by creating new contexts through which we process the occurrences of our lives. And it is our perspective on life that determines the ability to experience gratitude.

Dr. Robert Emmons has both studied and researched the subject of gratitude at length. Much of the material in this chapter is based on his work, and I am most grateful to him for what he generously gives to all of us. He writes in his book *Thanks! How the New Science of Gratitude Can Make You Happier*:

> . . . *grateful people experience higher levels of positive emotions such as joy, enthusiasm, love, happiness and optimism, and the practice of gratitude as a discipline protects a person from the destructive impulses of envy, resentment, greed and bitterness. We have discovered that a person who experiences gratitude is able to cope more effectively with everyday stress, may show increased resilience in the face of trauma-induced stress, may recover more quickly from illness and benefit from greater physical health.*[31]

Gratitude is much more than just a feeling. It is a state of being. Our language confuses issues because it lumps everything related to gratitude, such as appreciation or thankfulness together, making the state of gratitude indistinguishable from its aspects.

At its core, gratitude is a deep feeling of appreciation for everything - for the gifts we have been given, for nature and the Earth, for each other, for life, for humankind and also for those who are closest to us – our parents, partners, children and animal friends. Expressing gratitude creates a feeling of expansiveness. We reach out and touch other people, nature, God, the universe. . . Receiving gratitude is also unlike anything we experience. It melts the doubt and uncertainty that dogs us. It soothes our pain.

It has been said that, "Gratitude is the heart's memory." Or, "Gratitude is like holding the door knob to the gates of heaven." Centuries ago, Cicero argued that among virtues, gratitude was, "the parent of all the others. He called it, "a virtue that begets other virtues." Albert Schweitzer called gratitude, "The secret to life." There is a great deal of truth in these assertions.

Gratitude is personal. It is centered in us, but not in an egocentric way. It is an expansive feeling of thanks for all that we have been given and for all the things we appreciate. Words simply cannot express the grandeur of gratitude. It is an essential, perhaps the essential, aspect of the God Space.

Some people have a difficult time receiving and expressing gratitude. Their resistance to their life experiences has left them feeling bruised and beaten. The Universe, in its never-ending quest to help us, pushes us to change in places we feel insecure, and we naturally resist, some of us more than we need to. As a result, it is impossible to go through life without feeling a bit roughed up by the process.

For resistant people, life has not been a journey of learning, but rather a wounding process filled with difficult and painful experiences. They are obliged to defend themselves against further harm. They (understandably) approach life as victims rather than students of it. And it is difficult to be grateful for, or even acknowledge, the potential for learning contained in life experiences when they create pain. These people fear the return of the awful pain of their past. After all, they came into the world wide-eyed, vulnerable and emotionally open, and got run over by a cement truck! That makes them question their worthiness.

So long as a person remains vulnerable and feels victimized, she will also need her anger, shame and other defenses. These emotions provide insulation from feelings that could otherwise overwhelm. This tells us that The Misunderstanding is still very active, making this person vulnerable to outside influences and making it difficult for her to receive or express heartfelt gratitude.

"But," you say, "I am grateful for my lessons." But it is usually not real gratitude. It is only half a loaf. So long as you live in ego-driven fear, it will be difficult for you to allow gratitude to flow freely, even if you do appreciate the lessons The Universe has brought. Your life experience has also brought with it scars – resentment, jealousy, envy and greed, which are the natural enemies of gratitude. These emotions inhibit your ability to freely express what is in your heart or to receive it freely from others. These emotions cause you to judge, condemn and dislike. And until you heal the wounds underneath them and come to see everything in life as a gift, you will be on a slippery slope.

One of the most powerful aspects of gratitude is a feeling of appreciation for the many gifts the Creator gives us, but it is difficult to acknowledge those gifts if we are feeling beaten up by life (by Him). We may be unhappy with our parents, but we are also probably upset with God for putting us in this fix, or allowing it to happen!

Feeling gratitude does help to heal the emotional bruises we receive as we journey towards enlightenment. It is much easier for a student, even though the lessons may be stressful, to be grateful for the opportunity to grow. This stands in stark contrast to the victim's perspective. Once the student has accepted life as teacher, she can begin to trust the process. And that is a very big key – learning to trust the process, which is difficult for someone who feels victimized. An attendee at one of Dr. Emmons talks commented:

It is a good thing we humans do not get what we (feel that) we deserve. Otherwise we would have a difficult time explaining why so many fortunate things come into our lives.[32]

Experiencing gratitude gives us a vote of confidence that we really are OK. It connects us with both God's love for us and other people's appreciation for our being here. It pulls us out of the limited myopic view of our personal struggles and reminds us that we are not alone and that we are loved. We are left with the feeling that, "I guess I'm not such a loser after all."[33]

Psychiatrist Viktor Frankl survived Nazi concentration camps and wrote about what he witnessed in *Man's Search for Meaning*. The Library of Congress lists Man's Search For Meaning amongst the ten most influential books in

America. It is a book that I recommend highly. Based on his camp experiences, Frankl concluded that the basic human drive was to find meaning in life. He called it "the will to meaning" as opposed to Adler's Nietzschian doctrine of "will to power" or Freud's "will to pleasure."

Frankl concluded that our greatest gift was our ability to choose our reactions, even in the face of extreme suffering. He saw the conditions of life as influencing us, but placed far greater importance upon our freedom to choose our responses, irrespective of the conditions we find ourselves in. To Frankl, everything could be taken from us but the freedom to choose how we relate to our experiences. He wrote:

> We who lived in concentration camps can remember the men who walked through the huts comforting others, giving away their last piece of bread. They may have been few in number, but they offer sufficient proof that everything can be taken from a man but one thing: the last of the human freedoms—to choose one's attitude in any given set of circumstances, to choose one's own way.[34]

In 1953, Japanese businessman Yoshimoto Ishina developed a meditation technique he called Naikan. Naikan means "looking inside," or "introspection." A more poetic translation is "seeing oneself with the mind's eye." Naikan practice consists of reflecting on three questions regarding the various people in your life. In one of 20 Naikan retreat centers in Japan, people sit in meditation for a week before a blank screen and reflect on their relationships with significant people, in their lives (especially their parents). They meditate on:

What have I received from _____.

What I have given to _____.

What troubles and difficulty I have caused _____.

The First Step involves straight-up gratitude, i.e., recognizing the gifts we have received from a certain person. A good way to do this is to explore the good events in our lives. This helps us appreciate what we have received from others. We know that when you move into gratitude, you increase your positive emotions and happiness.

Step Two brings into conscious awareness the gifts that we bring to others. This step takes us into acknowledging our expressed gratitude – something we do not usually do because it conflicts with our self-image.

Step Three is an interesting departure. It asks us to look introspectively at our behavior by considering the pain we cause. Not only does this require us to honestly acknowledge what we have done, it also encourages us to look at and take responsibility for our motives and insensitivity, driven by our fears and anxieties. In looking into our drives, we free ourselves from the guilt and shame we usually beat ourselves up with regarding these occurrences. Otherwise it is too easy to see ourselves as "bad" or defective. Naikan adherents are urged to spend 60% of their meditation time on this third step. I found this piece from the Naikan web site to be appropriate:

> It is rare to meet a person whose life is full of gratitude. Even though the course of a single day may bring innumerable blessings to us, the few moments of genuine gratitude we experience is(sic) often overshadowed by our complaints, disappointments, sorrow and frustration. We may not truly appreciate what we have until it is gone. And having lost the opportunity to be grateful, we simply find a new opportunity to be disappointed. Gratitude requires attention and reflection. If we don't pay attention, the countless and constant ways we are supported go unnoticed. If we don't reflect, we fail to acquire the wisdom that comes with perspective. . . . Many people are struck by how much they have taken for granted. And too often we miss what is being done for us because our attention is caught up in feelings of selfishness, resentment or self-pity.[35]

We all have done foolish and hurtful things. I certainly have. I have been angry, used bad judgment, hurt friends and family – we are all capable of acting and reacting out of fear and anger. Does that make us "bad people?" No. It only makes us human for not having resolved our Misunderstandings.

Certainly I am not condoning or making excuses for hurtful behavior – these are things we should never condone or ignore. But the simple truth is that at this stage in our evolution, we are all capable of such behavior. When we look into our motives and see the fear, the need to be loved and the pain underneath them, it is much more difficult to judge and condemn ourselves. You may repress your emotions and try to keep them in the freezer, but they are there, nonetheless.

Most people's focus is on themselves, but not in a healthy way. They are being protective. They spend their time fearing rejection and feeling that they are not worthwhile or lovable. Those fears shape everything they do. They take and take, giving little in return or lash out at the world that has hurt them when they are not collapsing internally. These people cannot help it. Because of the issues they are confronting, their focus of necessity must be on themselves.

Heinous acts do not start on the outside. Narcissism and these other behaviors are coping strategies designed to create insulation from a world that devastated an innocent child. They are driven by severe inner turmoil. The desire for retribution plays a role as well, because there can be a great deal of repressed rage. External events just trigger what is already boiling over inside the person. Many of these people are not even conscious of the pain they leave in their wake.

One of the things that often confounds spiritual seekers is what to do about the few "bad" apples who take and abuse without real regard for the harm they cause. Criminal and anti-social behavior, drug and alcohol abuse and many mental illnesses are coping and sometimes retribution mechanisms. They express personal overwhelm and the inability to deal with significant inner turmoil. Criminals, angry and confused people and self-centered narcissists can be devastating to the people around them.

Certainly we must protect ourselves from being harmed, but if God does not judge these people, who are we to? How can we set ourselves above God to determine who is and is not acceptable? Christ said, "Let him who is without sin cast the first stone."[36] Our judgment denies the perfection of the Creator's plan. Everything here, even the bad stuff, is purposeful! Perhaps these people are here to help us learn compassion! We do not have to like or condone their behavior, but that is a different matter, and generally not what our judgments are about anyway.

It doesn't matter what the situation is, and you do not have to like what others do, but try to hold compassion for them regardless. Love who they are, not their actions, not their fear, not their rage, not the foolish and stupid things we all sometimes do. This is especially true if you are motivated to oppose them. Do it from a place of heartfelt compassion.

I think that Gandhi's most endearing quality was that even when he was in opposition to someone, he treated his opponent's views with the utmost respect. He might totally disagree with them, but he honored their right to their beliefs. His attitude as an attorney was, "How can we come together and resolve this situation without compromising the truth?" I think that this automatically garnered respect from the other party and opened space for resolution that otherwise might have been very difficult to find.

We end up in conflicts because we move into fear and must justify our lack of compassion to protect our egos. We do and say unkind things as protection because we are afraid to be hurt. If people would ever stop and think about what they were doing in these situations they would, if nothing else, simply walk away. But, their pain is so great that they cannot. They must react in order to protect their sense of personal integrity. Some couples use arguments to "clear the air" and then get to issues they are reluctant to discuss otherwise, but this is a very costly process. For other people, conflict is a way to keep things off balance without being vulnerable.

Remember also that you may have feelings about a situation, but your emotions will be only remotely connected to what is going on. You may dislike what someone does, for instance, but your emotion, as we discussed earlier, comes from both The Misunderstanding in this lifetime and your unresolved past life woundedness. Your emotion has been triggered by the present, but your reaction really has little to do with it.

We were all moved by the expressions of compassion and forgiveness expressed by the Amish of Nickel Mines, Pennsylvania toward the man who cruelly murdered five innocent Amish schoolgirls and seriously wounded five others in the autumn of 2006.

The Pennsylvania Amish spoke of the need to forgive the killer of their children. The family of one of the murdered children visited the killer's family just hours after the incident. The Amish family came to the door and said, "We forgive you." I found myself wondering, "How many of us could do that?"

The spokesman for the killer's family talked at a community prayer service a few days after the murders. He said he was at the home of the assailant's father when an Amish neighbor came to comfort the family. The spokesman said, "The Amish man stood there for an hour, and he held that man in his arms, and he said, 'We will forgive you.' He extended the hope of forgiveness that we all need these days."

One Amish man said, "I don't think there's anybody here that wants to do anything but forgive and not only reach out to those who have suffered a loss in that way, but to reach out to the family of the man who committed these acts also." An area resident (who is not Amish) said, "This is imitation of Christ at its most naked. If anybody is going to turn the other cheek in our society, it's going to be the Amish." He continued, "I don't want to denigrate anybody else who says they're imitating Christ, but the Amish walk the walk as much as they talk the talk."

I could not help contrasting the reaction of the Amish Christians with the reaction of the Conservative Christians in Washington D.C. after the attacks of September 11, 2001. After the 9/11 attacks, there were no expressions of compassion in Washington. There was no desire to reach out to the terrorists or their families and understand what had driven them to do such terrible acts. There were no thoughts of compassion. The establishment had been challenged, and there was only the desire for punishment and retribution. The Conservative Christian God, it seemed, was an angry and vengeful God. I wonder what our world would be like today if we had an Amish Christian as President when 9/11 happened? Maybe 9/11 would never have needed to happen at all!

The next Principle is really an extension of the LOVE EVERYTHING Principle, but it is so important that it needs special emphasis. As I said in Chapter One, every life situation comes down to a simple choice: You either choose to be compassionate or not. It is that simple, and it is a choice. You either open your heart to the other person or turn away. Our Principle Number Twelve will be then:

CHOOSE COMPASSION

We fear choosing compassion because opening up to another person brings up the vulnerability we felt in the past, and we fear being in that situation again. This tells us that The Misunderstanding is still functioning.

There is another, and perhaps even more important, consideration to moving to compassion. The God Space operates through compassion. Every time you are given the opportunity to love and you choose otherwise, The Universe must respond to the disharmony you create by pushing you to change. And as I said previously, saying no to The Universe's invitation, sets in motion forces guaranteeing the opportunity to make changes will return, only with greater intensity. So if you want your life to be easier, start by loving everyone, especially yourself!

We are going to address the deeper issues connected to the fear of being open and being hurt, but for now I would like to encourage you to practice opening your heart however you are able. There is a secret here, and it is important: Do not do it for THEM. Do it for YOU. Do it because it will make YOU feel better. And it will make you feel much better. Take your focus off them, and look at what is happening for you. As Vincent van Gogh said, "The best way to know God is to love many things."

Opening your heart makes you feel better, and where you cannot, you become aware of the places where you need to work. This is a valuable gift, because you get to see your resistance without shame or blame. This is one of gratitude's most important contributions.

Today, if you have to push yourself to be compassionate, do it. Set aside your resentment and pain and find compassion if you possibly can. By the way, you do not have to subject yourself to hurtful behavior. Take care of yourself, but be compassionate toward their fear, toward their pain, toward whatever is driving them. Perhaps you will have to do this at a distance, and that is fine, just open your heart. Love them because they, too, are children of God. As Bartholomew said, "When you choose love when you have every reason to choose other, then you truly become the Master." Choose Compassion. And in addition, if you can extend some of that compassion to yourself, that would be especially wonderful.

Choosing compassion can be difficult. The ego screams that we could be hurt. And, yes, sometimes the other person responds to compassion with ingratitude or by getting scared and escalating the situation. After all, they crucified Christ rather than heed his message of love and compassion. People may try to take advantage of your compassion – if you let them. But short of physical violence, even though it may be temporarily uncomfortable if they react, or yell at you, you will still feel better for having made the effort to stand in your heart space. And in addition, you are going to learn by doing this that you cannot really be hurt! And that is a very valuable lesson for people who have felt victimized by life! If you are ever unclear as to how to respond to another person, I suggest you use Bernie Siegel's approach. Ask yourself, "What would Lassie do?"[37]

Our fear to be open is one of the things that bog us down in "discussions" with our partners and friends. We feel too vulnerable to admit our underlying anxieties. This is why couples almost never fight over the real issues. There are always elephants in the room that no one will acknowledge. They end up arguing over their limitations. This is also why so many of our conversations are smokescreens. We do not deal with what is really going on. We intuitively know that what we feel is not about the situation, and we are reluctant to get into the truth because it makes us feel weak and vulnerable.

We used to believe that humans created language in order to share information, but this is only a small part of the reason. Years ago, believing in the information theory, computer scientists fed the rules of grammar and dictionaries into computers hoping to make the machines speak intelligently. The results were disappointing, to say the least. You can see this in the ridiculous suggestion's your computer's grammar check program sometimes makes. The scientists learned that language isn't a "thing" with fixed boundaries. It is part of the flexible, changeable glue that binds our relationships together. Language is contextual. Its rules change to fit the situation. We alter our communication and our behavior to fit each situation. And interestingly enough, one of the fundamental reasons we have relationships (and therefore language) is to help ameliorate our personal feelings of inadequacy.

We use our interactions to feel accepted, to buttress our need for support and to create leverage to feel more secure. The subject of our conversations may be about partners, friends, relatives, children, dieting or clothes, but the unspoken part of most of these communications is "recognize me," "support me" "please help me feel worthwhile."

If our "discussions" involve differences, we know that to admit to fear, uncertainty, anxiety, in other words, what is going on for us, would cause the posture we have taken to lose traction. It "weakens" our position. And we are already feeling uncomfortable without further undermining our stance. To admit that we felt depressed or hurt would give the appearance of weakness, and you don't want to be the weak one in the shark tank. After all, you can't let them see you sweat.

One of the interesting things about dealing with cancer patients is the honesty and frankness in their interactions. These people don't have time for posturing. They are dying. Of course, we are all dying, but they have been put on notice. Cancer patients have little interest or time for the trivialities that most people clutter their lives and their conversations with.

As an observer, it is fascinating to see the Creator seriously encourage people to change when a major shift is required. These people are testimony that the process works. But it is a high price to pay from the human perspective.

Try this experiment: the next time you are in a situation when strangers are being introduced to one another, stand aside and pay attention to what is said, to the tensions, the interaction, the body language, etc. It can be a most interesting exercise.

Some time ago, as a personal exercise, I began to pay close attention to how much people's interactions were motivated by their need to be loved and accepted. I was fairly certain what I would find, but seeing it clearly was an eye-opening experience. Our process of social interaction is dominated by our insecurities. Although the possibility for free, unfettered love (and communication) exists in all of us, most of our marriages, friendships and business relationships are built around both our need to feel accepted and the defenses we create because of our fears of rejection.

We want to be liked, in many cases need to be liked, or at least not disliked. Since we need to feel accepted, we manipulate and manage our relationships. We want to create an image (or at least not be embarrassed), so we tell people what they want to hear, or what we want them to hear. We do share information in our conversations, and although it varies from person to person, we often do not speak the truth. Someone asks you, "How are you?" and you say, "Fine" even though you may be dying inside. A waitress asks us how our shoddy meal is and we say, "Fine." This is partly because we know that they really don't want to hear it but also, because we are not prepared to deal with how they might respond. We do not want to let down the façade and appear vulnerable or weak or "make" someone else upset.

Unspoken in most of our exchanges is the trade that, "If you support me, I will support you." It helps mitigate the fear of rejection and the painful and powerful negative internal self-dialogue that most people carry around hidden (so they think!) within themselves. This is also the primary source of pain we feel when our relationships fail, because we have lost a vital and necessary codependent resource.

Most "civilized" cultures can be determined by the extent to which the society relies upon secrets. Economic and political power comes from the manipulation of information. Because when it can be withheld, information is power. When it is out in the open, it is just the truth. Western culture would experience massive culture shock if information were to become openly available.

Secrecy was what we grew up with. Hiding personal pain and failure receives a great deal of reinforcement in our culture. We tell one person this, the next person that. We don't actually lie, we withhold. We carefully manage who is told what. Withholding is a violation of trust and the impact on a relationship or a friendship can be devastating. But when you feel that the truth about who you are is awful, you cannot allow yourself to be exposed. And when people withhold from you, it also confirms your feelings of unworthiness.

Certainly there are times that social courtesy demands discretion, but if the other person is open to hearing the truth, then you simply find another time or another way. That purpose is quite different from the intention to manipulate. The other side of this issue are the people who use "honesty" to commit social felonies. They toss aside their compassion in a misguided attempt to be accepted, overcome their insecurity and give them social leverage. Note again the polar opposite behaviors (withholding and "honesty"). Each is based in the fear to be vulnerable. To hold the truth, you must feel secure enough to transcend the fear of being exposed.

Tribal life can be very different from the "civilized societies" most of us grew up in. My tribal friends have few secrets. Just about everything is out in the open and when you live with them, they want to know everything about you - not to pry, but to understand you so as to better integrate you into the fabric of the community. Even though I considered myself fairly open, I was struck by how much I had to change. I felt quite naked and exposed at first, because I was accustomed to personal information, once disclosed, eventually being used against me.

But once I got the hang of it, being open is a remarkable way to live. It is astonishingly freeing. My native friends taught me just how powerful the truth and honesty can be in a loving and non-judgmental environment. When the truth is available for everyone to see, it is very difficult to do something selfish or dishonest. There isn't a lot of "wiggle room" for a person to manipulate or deceive.

In the village, if two people weren't getting along, the community brought its insight and a multiplicity of resources and experience to bear on the problem, and the conflict either got resolved or the group would split. If someone was having trouble with parenting or a relationship, there was a wealth of experience available. And when done in a loving way, this focuses the group (not just the individual) on what needs to change both in the person and, if necessary, in the community. The native lifestyle is not free of problems by any means, but living in an open and heartfelt space after the private hell that is so common in our society can be a most remarkable experience.

One of the most important things our partners, friends and parents do for us is to provide someone to lean on during difficult times. To put it simply, if I have doubts about myself, and I feel that you love and accept me, even with all my baggage, it is easier for me to face life. Until I begin to accept myself, it can be very difficult for me to heal my wounds. Much of our concept of friendship is related to "being there" for each other. And that is a good thing, so long as we keep our agendas clean and do not make the relationship codependent.

Consider religion. More than anything else, what religion gives us is acceptance of who we are and faith in something greater than ourselves. Think about the purpose of a hymn or prayer. They connect us to God's love for us and help us to find our "faith." Faith is simply connecting to God's love. Having faith in a king used to giver people something similar. Today democracy urges us to have faith in each other.

And although we do love each other, unfortunately far too often we keep our love under wraps. We love our partners, our children and our friends, but we mask that love and often only let it out on special occasions. When pushed, for instance if someone is ill or injured, our love is freely given. We set aside resentments and petty differences and our fear to be rejected, and we open our hearts. But the rest of the time, we are inhibited by our unwillingness to be hurt if rejected.

Our withholding is not without substance. People important to us (translation: people to whom we have felt vulnerable) have hurt us in the past, and we do not want to repeat the experience! At the present stage of our evolution, feelings of fear, inadequacy and anxiety dominate our behavior.

Christ and Buddha stand as examples of what is possible for us. Our other heroes used to do the same. They were people just like us, who reached inside themselves and found the courage and wherewithal to do great things. If they could do that, we could, at very least, try. Unfortunately our heroes are smaller today. Too often they are hollow people whose accomplishments are media manipulated and driven by performance enhancing drugs.

Our need for support goes well beyond friends, family and religion. The primary role of many organizations is to provide group support and approval for the individual. They do share information, but their primary role is to provide a collective nod of acceptance. Organizations as diverse as political parties, garden clubs, Alcoholics Anonymous, veterans' organizations, environmental groups, street gangs, animal rights groups, the Ku Klux Klan and the NRA all primarily exist to guide, support and mold the beliefs of their memberships. Interviewed gang members frequently speak of the value of family-like relationships in the gang that they are unable to find elsewhere.

It is through struggle that we grow. This is the foundation for the Principle that urges us to LOVE EVERYTHING. It comes out of the feeling of gratitude for the process that is pushing us toward enlightenment. I will sometimes ask a group "What would you pay for this day?" I know that we have all had days we would gratefully give back, but seriously, what is this day worth to you? How much would you pay for it? It is an interesting question.

While the need to protect my woundedness interferes with my ability to express gratitude, experiencing a trying life experience, can actually deepen it. It gives me an appreciation for life. We see this universally amongst survivors of catastrophes or serious illnesses. Disaster and loss (or its possibility) jerks us out of our daily routine and reawakens us to what we otherwise take for granted.

The value of the evening news is that we touch the misfortune of others and feel for a moment our own good fortune - "There but for the grace of God, go I." Elie Wiesel, another Holocaust survivor and Noble Peace prize recipient, spoke of "the kingdom of night." He said, "No one is as capable of gratitude as one who has emerged from the kingdom of night." A 9/11 survivor said, "Each day that I stay as a guest on this green earth suddenly seems like outrageous good fortune." One hurricane Katrina survivor said, "We stopped taking our ordinary lives (and each other) for granted." One father commented, "I had this overwhelming joy to be alive. . . that's what was important. . . that elation that we were alive; that really stuck with us."[38]

As painful and necessary as the events of life can be, they are also gifts - gifts we would usually rather avoid, but important and necessary gifts, nonetheless. The Universe is going to a great deal of trouble to help our healing. As we leave feeling victimized, we will be able to see more clearly the perfection of our lessons. We will also begin to see how hard everyone around us (like it or not) has worked to help us grow and evolve. It is a wonderfully humbling time. It is then that we truly move into gratitude. After all, The Universe could have just turned away. So, even though life has been painful, there is a great deal to be thankful for.

I want to ask you to try something. As you read these words, get in touch with who or what you are not loving right now. Perhaps list them. Then take a moment and allow yourself to feel compassion for the other, especially if it is you. As you do this, notice the changes that occur within you. This isn't about them, and it isn't about the relationship. It's about you feeling better about yourself.

As you think about opening your heart, look at your reluctance. What holds you back? Maybe they won't respond the way you would like them to. But that is just your need to be loved getting in the way. There is more to it than that.

If opening to people close to you is difficult, start by being kind to someone less threatening, perhaps a stranger or a casual friend. Then work your way back up to the people you are close to. Eventually, get to yourself.

"But what if my advances are rejected?" you might ask. BIG DEAL! What do you really lose? Okay, so maybe your pride could get dinged, but in truth, you lose nothing. You will go on. You will survive. The truth is that you really risk NOTHING, and you might actually feel better about yourself for having made the effort. And you never know what might happen. It might really mean something to the other person! That's one of the best deals you will ever get.

That's the truth. The reality, however, is different from that. Your resistance to expressing gratitude is because their reaction might bring up the parts of yourself that feel inadequate. If their reaction is in any way negative, it could painfully throw you back into a place you do not want to go. This brings you to the crux of the victim/student of life idea. If you see your anxiety as an opportunity, as a gift to illumine and work with a part of you that does not feel loved or lovable, then the other person's reaction provides valuable input for your process.

How different our world would be if we could find the courage and take the time to express our gratitude! How joyful life on earth would become if we could tell others how much we loved them and how grateful we are that they are in our lives! When I go out and about, I observe people to see how many of them seem happy. It saddens me to report that there aren't many. Most people are sort of in neutral and just OK. I think about how much difference just a few of us could make if we made a dedicated effort to thank just a few of the people who love us and make our lives safer and easier.

The next time you have contact with someone who helped you – a store clerk or a colleague, hold eye contact (this is important!) and tell them "thank you" – and really mean it. One of my personal goals in life is to make everyone I come in contact with feel richer for the experience. I don't always succeed, but I try. You never know what they will do, but the real secret is, you will feel much better. And if it makes you feel foolish or embarrasses you, then you have rich fodder for your healing process.

It is simply not worth being invested in the tension, stress and anxiety we create for ourselves. It makes us miserable, shortens our life spans and pulls the energy of the whole planet down. But, as I have pointed out, with all human endeavors that are commonly experienced, what is really important always lies deeper. We do not express gratitude for svery important reasons.

Dr. Fredrick Luskin, in his book *Forgive For Good*, offers a very simple, but surprisingly effective technique for developing gratitude. He calls it "The Breath of Thanks."[39] Luskin suggests:

1. Two or three times every day when you are not fully occupied, slow down and bring your attention to your breathing.
2. Notice how your breath flows in and out without your having to do anything... continue breathing this way.
3. For each of the next five to eight exhalations, say the words, "thank you" silently to remind yourself of the gift of your breath and how lucky you are to be alive.

Luskin suggests practicing this technique at least three times a week. To begin, I would suggest that you practice it several times each day anytime you get a quiet moment. Do it, when you wake up, before you go to sleep, while doing the dishes, during television commercials, etc. It is a surprisingly powerful process!

As you do this practice, does your mind wander? Can you make eight breaths before you stop, start thinking or find some other distraction? On first try, most people make it through about three exhalations before their mind starts to move off.

Look into your resistance. What is she trying to say to you? Why does she feel the need to distract you? If you stay with it, this can be a very useful learning. Maintaining a gratitude practice can be difficult because it brings up our fears of inadequacy. Let us turn our attention to the development of gratitude and look at what gets in our way.

Dr. Emmons and his colleagues have researched the subject at length and tell us that the best way to develop gratitude is to keep a daily "Gratitude Journal." In the Journal, you log at least five blessings each day and why you are grateful for each. Doing it on the computer will work, but it is more effective if done longhand. And as you do this, make a conscious association with each blessing as a gift.

Be aware of the depth of your gratitude. When starting the process, doing the Journal every day is essential. Some items on your list will be there every day and others will change.

I cannot urge you strongly enough to do the Journal. It will change the lens through which you view your life. You will feel better, be happier, more connected to others, improve your relationships, be less depressed and actually live longer!

Developing gratitude is a most important and powerful transformational tool. And in sort of an interesting turn-about, the Gratitude Journal also presents a wonderful opportunity for you to look at the parts of yourself that frankly, you'd rather ignore. One of gratitude's many gifts is that it gently, but powerfully, offers us awareness of the wounds that we carry.

What happens is that as you begin to express your gratitude for other people and suddenly your mind will "flip," and BAM! a voice will pop up saying something like, "What, those jerks!" or, "Who could be successful working with those idiots?" Pay particular attention to every thought that comes up as you do your daily entries.

Sometimes the thoughts that come will be downright vile. Even the most pure of hearts seem to be not above "cusswords" when it comes to the Gratitude Journal. The process takes us to where our dark feelings reside. In one class, a woman wrote about her gratitude for her children, and immediately the thought came to her, "Those noisy little bastards!" That's what I mean about these thoughts sometimes being nasty. In my Journal, I put these negative thoughts in brackets in order to segregate them.

As unpleasant as it is for us to see our own dark side, that is part of what comes out in these moments. Inside you is a little girl who has had the emotional stuffing beaten out of her. She's angry, frustrated, alone and powerless to change things. She is hurting big time, and you want to sit there and get all giddy about your kids, your mom and that jerk you live with who couldn't show emotion if he was dipped in it! WHAT ABOUT HER? What about her pain? How come you aren't there for her when she is frightened and anxious? And let's not even get into how angry she is at God for making her endure all this! So, when this woman wrote about her gratitude for her children, her hurting inner child needed to express her resentment at being excluded from that same love.

The process of doing the Journal will bring up your frustrations with life, show you the beliefs you are hanging on to that limit your happiness, and it will bring up the places where you hold resentment in a wonderfully non-confrontive way. The person that confronts you will typically be older than the child who holds the pain behind these feelings. So, you probably won't surface the underlying issues themselves, but the reactions that surface as you do your Journal will provide important signposts directing you to them. Underneath those signposts will be your unresolved aspects of The Misunderstanding.

I am giving away a secret here, but in 20 years of getting groups to list the things they were grateful for, NO ONE has ever listed gratitude for their inner child, or for the pain and anguish that the child has had to endure. It's like trying to be grateful for a bratty kid – it doesn't compute. The need to protect our fragile egos makes it difficult to feel and express gratitude. That "failure" is also a warning that something is amiss. This is how The Universal Mirror works.

We are going to address the inner child's pain at length in the next chapter, but I would ask you to recognize that The Universe has provided you with an easy and non-threatening way to access your inner pain. When you attempt to feel gratitude and experience interference, The Misunderstanding is active. If you have trouble doing the Journal or if you start a Journal and quit after a few days, know that your unresolved issues are interfering (and winning)! This is why it is important for you to get all your thoughts on the page. In the next chapter you will learn to use the shamanic journey process to revisit the issues raised by your resistance to doing the Journal.

When you do get the Journal process going, pay attention to the changes that occur in your life. Watch how your feelings shift. Although the process will probably be bumpy because it brings up issues, it has also been deeply rewarding for those who have been able to stick with it.

As you learn to feel your gratitude, you will also want to begin to express it, and the two will bootstrap together to create a positive upward spiral, improving your feelings about life. You will find yourself wanting to thank a friend, or a special waitress or customer service person, and each time you do, the whole structure of your life will ratchet up a notch. The other person will feel better, but what is really important is how much better it will make you feel. What a wonderful win–win situation!

I tell clients and students that the next time they are feeling depressed and blue, do something nice for someone else – not to manipulate them, so don't go on a fishing expedition, but as a sincere gesture of appreciation. I tell them to watch what happens to their depression as they go through the process.

And I will say this to you: If you are feeling down, get out in the sun and take a walk. Try and feel at least some appreciation for having the day, for the gift of the sun and the sky, even though your life may be tough at the moment. Get your eyes up off the sidewalk and into the trees and the birds and the clouds.

So many people in our world stand on the sidelines. They read books and do spiritual exercises, but when it comes to getting their feet wet, they won't get in the pool. Sometimes they'll make it look like they do - they get into relationships, make friendships, etc., but their hearts aren't really in it. They hold back and then when things fail, are quick to blame something or someone other than themselves. Or, in the alternative, they will take it all on themselves as proof of their inadequacy. We will give you a way out of that morass in the chapters that follow.

I walk by gyms and see people busily working out, doing yoga or running outdoors in order to improve their health and look better, and I want to say to them, "If you really want to live longer and improve the quality of your life, pay attention to all those self-condemning and self-critical inner thoughts you beat yourself up with all the time! Those are far more deadly than being overweight or out of shape!" And actually, it is what led to the weight being put there in the first place! But, it is not an either/or situation. We need to learn to love ourselves both emotionally and physically.

When you know the truth, there is no damaged self to occupy you. There is no inadequate self to compensate for. So instead of being a victim, holding a loving space allows and encourages you to be aware of the pain and fear of others. No other single act could heal the wounds of the world as this one might, if we were to practice it. As Rumi said, "It is only from the heart that you can touch the sky."

Here are the twelve Principles. Spiritual concepts are always simple, but that does not mean that they are easy to do:

LOVE EVERYTHING

**ANYTHING YOU DO NOT LOVE
WILL BECOME A LESSON**

WHAT GETS YOU INTO TROUBLE ISN'T YOURS

YOUR LIFE IS PERFECT

THE EGO CANNOT LOVE

DO IT NOW

TRUTH MUST BE FELT

IF YOU DIDN'T BELIEVE IT, IT WOULDN'T MATTER

YOU DETERMINE YOUR EXPERIENCE

NOTHING CAN BE WRONG WITH YOU

**MAKE HER THE MOST IMPORTANT THING IN
YOUR LIFE**

CHOOSE COMPASSION

CHAPTER 8

The Journey Process

He who looks outside, dreams.
He who looks inside, awakens.

Carl Jung

If you lived in a traditional society and presented your tribal shaman with a case of cancer, arthritis, heart disease, snakebite or the breakup of a relationship, the shaman would address the immediate problem and then search for the emotional or psychic disturbance that was causing your dilemma. In traditional societies, the healing process requires that the cause of the failure be addressed as well as the immediate difficulty. If only the presenting or symptomatic cause is addressed, the shaman knows the disturbance will either recur or manifest elsewhere in the person's system. He or she knows that until the originating problem is resolved the client will only get temporary relief.

Your blood pressure may be high, your cholesterol count may be off the charts, your joints may be stiff and your arteries may be weak, but to traditional healers, the heart disease, arthritis, stroke or cancer that can develop from these systemic problems, although regrettable, are natural progressions from unhealed psychic or emotional disturbances. Moving away from the purely physical, your personal relationships may be a mess and you may be having a difficult time fitting into the world, but unless you address the deeper causes to these difficulties, you only address the manifestation without attending to the core problem.

Allow me to be clear: if an organ or a body system becomes dysfunctional, it is essential to intervene and bring the system to a more normal state, but in addressing the systemic failure, we must not be confused about this being healing, for it is not. It is restoration of the highest order, and it is vitally important!

Restoration usually entails adding something to the body such as drugs, or a physical intervention such as heart surgery or splints to a broken bone. This is extremely important work, but it is not the same as healing. To heal we must address the deeper disturbance that cased these manifestations. We must release the beliefs that drive them. Healing, then, is letting go.

In tribal belief systems, the body experiences problems because of an underlying emotional or psychic cause referred to as "soul loss." Soul loss can occur as the result of a shock or trauma, but more typically it is the result of habitually refusing to listen to the guidance of the gods or spirits.

The misalignment of spiritual nature as the source of a person's physical or emotional difficulties is a theme found frequently in the precepts of indigenous cultures. The Iroquois, for example, speak of disease as resulting from the conflict created when the soul's needs are not met. They believe the soul becomes "resentful" when ignored and then creates difficulties for the individual. The soul's perspective is, of course, God's perspective. So to the Iroquois, disease is the result of turning away from the God Space.

The Mayans would agree. They see disease as the result of a disturbance to the relationship between people and the gods, created by an individual's disharmonious behaviors and attitudes. Healing requires that individuals make changes not only in their behaviors but also to their beliefs.

Navaho medicine woman Annie Kahn describes illness as "the habit of excluding," which disturbs the natural harmony. She says, "To heal, one must...accept. This very act causes healing." People who know nothing of shamanic practices often speak of feeling a hole in their spirit. If this separated part is not "retrieved," the person is then vulnerable to emotional and physical problems.

We get romantic about tribal cultures holding these truths, without realizing that these beliefs were once a very important part of our own culture as well. When Christ healed the sick, it was through blessing and forgiveness, not through the manipulation of the body. When he put his hands on someone, it was "to reawaken," "to remind," the tissues of the body of their normal state. He was rebalancing the natural order. In Christian theology, the Holy Spirit, the third and frequently neglected part of the Trinity, is described as the creative, healing and renewing presence of God. In shamanic practice, a disharmonious system must be brought back into a resonant state in order for it to heal.

Carl Jung wrote, "When the God is not acknowledged, egomania develops, and out of this mania comes sickness."[40] Once regarded as a "quaint" and "primitive" idea by Western intellectuals, some physicians are beginning to recognize and accept the wisdom of these ancient and time-tested concepts. Jean Achterberg, a professor of psychology and physical medicine writes, "It is becoming increasingly clear, that what the shamans refer to as soul loss - injury to the inviolate core which is the essence of a person's being - does manifest as despair, immunological damage, cancer, and a host of other very serious disorders."

To heal means to find your true self. It means to strip away and release the contrary beliefs and attitudes that keep the real self hidden. In the shaman's view, it is soul loss that leads to the creation of pain and physical and/or emotional disease. When we heal, we eliminate the things we have identified with which are "not us." Healing does not involve adding anything to the system, whether that is pharmaceuticals or knowledge. Rather, healing is a process of releasing, of letting go. Remember the lesson of the Lotus Sutra and Buddha's flower. This brings us to Principle Number Thirteen, our final Principle:

HEALING MEANS LETTING GO

Healing means letting go of the beliefs, fear and anxieties that keep you out of the God Space. It is not about learning anything, taking drugs, surgery or acquiring some esoteric meditation technique. Consider this poem by someone who is learning the truth:

You realize that what is supposed to be yours
no one can take away, delay, or stop from coming to you.

You know that your success does not depend on certain individuals or circumstances,
but on the ever-generous pouring forth from the
cornucopia of Universal abundance.

You know that destiny is your servant as well as your master.

You perform your duty in harmony with the Divine will,
and therefore you can disregard the state of the moment-to-moment results.

You know that everything you have done will eventually and inevitably lead
toward the ultimate completeness of your material and spiritual rewards.

You surrender, and therefore you win.

(author unknown to me)

Here is our list of thirteen Principles:

LOVE EVERYTHING

ANYTHING YOU DO NOT LOVE
WILL BECOME A LESSON

WHAT GETS YOU INTO TROUBLE ISN'T YOURS

YOUR LIFE IS PERFECT

THE EGO CANNOT LOVE

DO IT NOW

TRUTH MUST BE FELT

IF YOU DIDN'T BELIEVE IT, IT WOULDN'T MATTER

CHOOSE COMPASSION

NOTHING CAN BE WRONG WITH YOU

YOU DETERMINE YOUR EXPERIENCE

MAKE HER THE MOST IMPORTANT THING IN YOUR LIFE

HEALING MEANS LETTING GO

You cannot alter the aspects of yourself that are part of The Universal. This is a safety mechanism built into the process. But our fears and beliefs can and do present significant impediments to our holding that space. This is an important point, because as you deal with your pain, or if you are involved with helping others to heal, you need to be mindful of the powerful and primal forces that can oppose the healing process.

This is not a small matter. One of the biggest obstacles in counseling is getting a client to let go of the life structures she has created, no matter how dysfunctional they may be, in order to make room for new behaviors and attitudes. When people come for healing, it is because they are hurting and frustrated. If they felt their old way of doing things would still work, they wouldn't be asking for help. The challenge is helping them feel safe enough to risk finding a different way of life. Some of them try to get the world to change so they don't have to, or blame other people and circumstances, but it usually doesn't take long for them to see through their own resistance.

Bringing our pain to the surface is messy and disruptive to the structure we have created, no matter how dysfunctional it may be. Nisargadatta Maharaj said, "The search for reality is the most dangerous of all undertakings for it destroys the world in which you live." In the moment, it is easier to avoid the inner child's fears and pain and simply push through a challenging situation.

And until you are ready, really ready, to give up your fears and limiting beliefs, they will interfere with your ability to be whole. What you need to do in concept is very simple. But you have to be ready to go there. You must really want it!

There is an old Chinese story about a famous healer who lived near the top of a mountain. He had a great gift, but the climb to reach him was difficult, especially for people with afflictions. Someone asked him once why he did not move lower so people who needed his healing could reach him more easily. His answer was most interesting. He said, "Those who really want to heal will get here." His answer may seem callous, but there is a great deal of truth in what he said. Healing isn't about acquiring something; it is about giving things up. So long as you see yourself as unworthy and in need of protection, you will not be ready to relinquish the fears and limiting beliefs that allow you to hide from life. Until you are ready, really ready, your beliefs will interfere with your ability to be whole.

When a person comes for healing I know we are dealing with at least two personality parts. One part of them sincerely wants to heal or they would not be in my healing room, but the other part of them is afraid. Otherwise the client would have already healed herself and would not need help.

The dilemma for the therapy process is that in order for someone to heal, she needs to confront pain she has been avoiding all these years. She must come to terms with the beliefs she holds about herself. So by asking her to address what she has been avoiding, the initial healing work actually stirs the pot and makes her feel worse than when she came in! Fortunately, this pain is short-lived, and after a little work, she begins to feel the powerful benefit of living from a new and healthier place.

Sometimes people come wanting a miracle in order to avoid dealing with the pain of having to change themselves, but it doesn't work that way. That would be just about the worst thing that could happen for them.

Our ancestors recognized that deeper spiritual-level changes were required for healing. As part of the healing process, they encouraged individuals to make fundamental changes to their beliefs and behaviors. A significant part of their commitment involved the making of a sacrifice.

Our word sacrifice is from the Latin word "sacer" meaning "to make sacred, to consecrate, to make holy." Our understanding of the process of sacrifice has been grossly distorted, sensationalized and misunderstood, but in its true form, sacrifice serves a vital role in the healing process. The Greek word for "healing" originally meant, "sacrifice to the gods."[41]

To the ancients, disease and mental problems in either a person or a community were brought about by profanity, i.e., the misalignment of an individual or group to The Universe. To our ancestors, profanity was that which could not be brought into the temple. To cure a disease was to heal the spiritual body that had lost its connection to the God Space; in other words, one that had become profaned. To heal a community was to bring the group back into harmony, releasing the toxicity of dissention. This is the purpose of sacrifice. So in its true form, the act of sacrifice makes sacred that which has been profaned. And anything we do not love, we profane, whether it be in ourselves or in others.

We usually think of sacrifice as an act of contrition, because we see the visible manifestation – the act of making amends or restitution, such as righting a wrong. But we must also learn to see the intention that lies beneath the form. To sacrifice is to give up the short-term benefit that comes from ego-based behavior, in favor of the longer-term, more positive benefit of living in the God Space.

When we question our beliefs and leave our ego-driven behaviors behind, we make a sacrifice. We give up the immediate gratification of our anger or a second helping of dessert because we realize we no longer "need" them. And this is very important – most religious leaders, psychologists and diet programs put the cart before the horse. They want you to change your behavior before you have addressed your need for "the fix."

The act of sacrifice, kept to its strict meaning, is a powerful part of the healing process. In order to illustrate how sacrifice works, consider an example: Assume a person's ego has been driving her and she has been sexually promiscuous. The sacrifice this person would be asked to make would be to look inside and deal with the needy part of herself that has been driving her behavior. She would be asked to forgo illicit (ego-driven) sexual pleasure for the deeper pleasure of real intimacy. And this is where sacrifice becomes difficult because real sacrifice means giving up the "heroin" that has sustained her wounded self. From the outside, this looks like returning either to monogamous sexuality or, if the dysfunction was more serious, to withdraw from sexual activity altogether as she addresses her emotional issues. The true nature of sacrifice is not just a change in behavior, nor is it punishment. It is rather a process to facilitate deeper change.

It is true, you really do not need that second piece of pie. You do not need to be unkind, either. Yet the problem is that in that moment your inner child does! It is vital to her. You can white-knuckle through the change until she learns she really will survive without it, but this entails hog-tying her down until she gives up. Doing this can ultimately help us to feel better about ourselves, but it's one hell of a way to heal. This is the Marine Corps approach to life, and it is how we used to "cure" drug addicts and drunks. We would put them in a segregated hospital ward, dry them out, maybe give them a little counseling, introduce them to AA and hope for change. Since the Marine Corps approach worked for a few of them, and since we didn't know what else to do, we stayed with it.

Sacrifice is toward the back end of the process. It is what we do as we address our dysfunctional attitudes and beliefs. A sacrifice is made to reconnect us with the aspects of the God Space we have turned away from because of our ego and our fear.

Making a sacrifice is not simply about giving something up. It is about healing the need driving dysfunctional behavior. Sacrifice allows us to reconnect with our true self. Yet many people are simply not ready or willing to accept the truth about who they are, making real sacrifice difficult.

In making each act, every moment, sacred, life itself becomes sacred. In doing this, the toxicity of human hubris (defiance of the gods) is drawn out from people as they heal the wounds created by their ego-driven fear. People are then naturally brought back to their essential, divine connection to The Universe. The origin of our word "gift" comes from a Germanic word meaning "that which is toxic to the profane."

The idea of sacrifice lends itself readily to distortion and manipulation. Within the fundamentalist sects of some religions, sacrifice has come to mean doing without comforts or even enduring pain. This only pays homage to the outer shell of sacrifice. Mortification and penance were common medieval church practices which sometimes approached masochism. Rev. Michael Geisler, spiritual director of Opus Dei in St. Louis, attempted to explain the theological purpose behind the practice of "corporal mortification." He reminds me of a Marine Corps drill instructor when he writes:

> *Self-denial helps a person overcome both psychological and physical weakness, gives him energy, helps him grow in virtue and ultimately leads to salvation. It conquers the insidious demons of softness, pessimism and lukewarm faith that dominate the lives of so many today.*[42]

There is nothing wrong with discipline, and our society could use a good dose of it, but the connection between denial and salvation is fraught with problems, not the least of which is that abuse has nothing to do with spirituality. True spirituality can only be found through compassion.

Like everything else, the concept of individual sacrifice has been corrupted through time. People don't like having to make changes to themselves, and they do not like having to give up the things they get from their egos. So, the unscrupulous have found ways to corrupt the process of sacrifice. Churches, always in need of money, began to accept monetary payment, "sacrificial offerings," as substitutes for individual sacrifice. Of course, when you allow the individual to avoid accepting real responsibility for her actions and remain separated from the God Space, the real value of sacrifice is lost.

Going back in human history, animals have often been allowed to substitute for individual sacrifice, and have been used in various ways to "appease" the gods. Rabbis used to place all the community's misdeeds on a goat. The goat was then "mercifully" allowed to escape into the wilderness where it was almost certain to be killed. This was the origin of our concept of the "scapegoat."

The idea of human sacrifice gets everyone's attention, and for good reason. When we consider the mass human sacrifices attributed to the Incas and Aztecs, we all feel, "but for the grace of God," we could have been up there getting our hearts cut out too!

But this is not sacrifice. The idea of sacrifice has been twisted and manipulated by rulers for political and egotistical ends throughout history. Unrestricted power over other people's lives seems to be the ultimate political aphrodisiac. Megalomaniacal rulers have ritually killed captured warriors to thank the gods for victories. They have slaughtered people to appease the gods for poor harvests or to thank them for good ones and as testaments to their own divinity. These are barbaric practices, and they give Hollywood a lifetime supply of material to sensationalize, but it is not sacrifice. It is what sacrifice can be prostituted into for political or narcissistic ends.

I do wish to point out that much of what has been written into the historical record about human sacrifice came from people with real axes to grind. These Christians had enormous prejudices and fabricated stories to curry support from other European Christians for the destruction of indigenous cultures and beliefs. Today, we know a great deal of what they wrote was not true. Nonetheless, human sacrifice did occur, and it can only be described as heinous.

As a political act, a ritual suicide is a powerful weapon. It is the ultimate statement of commitment to a cause or an idea. Buddhist monks have immolated themselves to protest social concerns, and their sacrifices have made powerful political statements. But is this a powerful political statement, or is it personal sacrifice writ large? It can be considered to be the ultimate sacrifice for the spiritual well being of the community.

In the same vein, return to your own culture for a moment. Over 620,000 young American men sacrificed their lives over the issues of slavery and the preservation of the Union in the American Civil War. Although many of them were conscripts and could be hanged or shot for desertion, most of these men gave their lives willingly because they were fighting for something they believed in. So did the 900,000 U.S and British and 8,000,000 Russian soldiers who died in WWII to prevent the spread of fascism. We accept these sacrifices because they fit into our cultural ethic. Whether or not you agree with war, we honor these deaths as sacrifices to the perpetuation of the values we hold essential.

Tribal societies use ritual and ceremony to help an individual or group make both a public and personal recommitment to living closer to the God Space. Ritual and ceremony are the vital cores of their culture. Our tribal ancestors took ceremonial work very seriously. They knew that ceremony, done with integrity and with the support of the community, was the most powerful way to re-focus and re-commit a person's intention to living more closely to the God Space.

We have little understanding of real ceremony and legitimate sacrifice today, because these practices have been expunged from our cultural ethic and drained of their traditional vitality. The ceremonies we do practice, like marriage or baptism, are often empty shells with little real spiritual significance.

The original idea of a "penitentiary" was as a place of deep silence where sinners would pray and meditate (be penitent) about their wrongdoings. Guards wrapped rags around their boots to muffle their footsteps, and the wheels of carts were similarly covered so there would be no noise to interrupt the penitent's meditations. Unfortunately they found that being faced without guidance or support, made most of the inmates insanse and therefore penitentiaries fell out of favor in Europe and were eventually turned into the noisy, overcrowded warehouses we have today.

. You are about to undertake a process that will undoubtedly ask you to make a sacrifice of some of your ego-driven behaviors.

THE SHAMANIC JOURNEY

We are going to use an ancient shamanic healing ritual adapted to fit our culture and our values. The core process has demonstrated effectiveness for more than 20,000 years of continuous use. I find it fascinating that one can go to almost any culture on the planet and find that shamanic practices which have been developed independently are virtually identical. These tribal shaman were separated by thousands of miles, thousands of years and massive cultural differences. It speaks I think, to the universality of the process to address essential human issues. After all, we may speak differently, believe differently and even look different, but underneath it all, we really are the same.

In most tribal societies the Shaman goes on the journey you are about to take for you, and then returns and talks to you about the changes you need to make in your life. Since we no longer have clan Shaman, and since you and I are not in the same place, we need to find a workable substitute.

Also, I have found it valuable to teach people how to do this work for themselves so they would be empowered to manage their own healing. This is particularly helpful in Western society, which devalues people and looks down on emotional problems as defects of character.

There is another reason I do not take the journey for people. In tribal societies, there is great respect for the shaman. When the shaman tells you to do something, you do it. Not listening to the shaman's guidance is considered extremely foolish, because people know that if they don't make changes, their problems will get worse.

Unfortunately for shaman, Westerners are not good about taking spiritual or psychological advice. It is, I believe, the legacy of our spiritually empty culture, our fierce individualism and our "damn the torpedoes, full speed ahead" approach to just about everything as we ignore our emotional and spiritual needs. It is also a convenient way to avoid making emotional changes few people really want to make anyway.

I have learned that if people learn to do this work themselves, they find they are creating their own difficulties. When this bothers them sufficiently, they will make the changes The Universe has been asking them to make all along.

The Shamanic Journey Process can be used, as we shall see, for many things. In addition to working with your inner child, you can visit past lives, explore the origins of physical problems, deal with entities, visit with the spirits of the deceased, connect with beings in other realms and call on your spirit guides. It is rich territory. I encourage you to explore it!

In regard to your inner child, the first thing we will want to do is to explore the pivotal and painful times of your childhood that created The Misunderstanding you still practice. We will give her the opportunity to see, perhaps for the first time, the truth about what was going on so she can change the beliefs that were created at that time, beliefs you/she has carried ever since.

It would be useful at this point to share a few things about the world you are about to enter because it is different from the one with which you are familiar. There is no time or space in this dimension. You can travel freely to your past and past lives to learn what formed and shaped your present beliefs and attitudes. (We will explore past lives in Chapter Nine.) You will be able to deal with people from your past, and settle things that remain unfinished or, as you will see, heal old pain.

In this realm, you can occupy more than one space at the same time and can observe yourself as you re-experience events. As far as space is concerned, the density of your present physical reality binds you to a tangible existence. In the other realm, you can fly, move around, take other shapes and sizes, pass through objects and do all manner of things not possible in the waking world.

A general rule about this space: if you are not sure about something, you can always ask. You do not have to ask anyone special; in fact, it is better if you do not. The answers will just come. We tend to get caught up in the moment and forget that we can do that, but asking can be a very valuable resource. If you ever have doubts about what you are being told, just continue to ask. The truth never wavers. In this realm, the truth is so crystal clear and obvious, there will be no question as to its veracity.

It is best not to do a lot of asking, however, until the major negative energies are cleared from your system. If, as you observe your inner child you see a dark cloud or something that looks like tar around her, you will want to read the next chapter and then address this beforehand. This helps insure that what you hear will be accurate and uncontaminated. Entities can distort and manipulate, so dialoging with them is never a good idea.

Things in this new realm operate according to your will. If you want something to happen, it will. For example, if the inner child wants an entity to leave, it must. The entity may try to talk you or her out of it, but if your inner child persists, her wishes must be respected. The corollary to this is that if something is not happening, some part of you is resisting. This is often the case when we tell an entity to leave and it does not, or when it returns after a short time. Driving the situation will be a wounded child, probably different from the one you have been working with, who is not ready to give up the protection of the entity.

Most people are dominantly visual, so you will probably (mostly) see your inner child and what she shows you. Other people operate more easily from feelings. Work with what you get. Don't be too concerned about it. Both are fine. When I describe a particular experience, use all of your senses to relate to it. Whichever one(s) you lead with will be fine.

The first step in preparation is to be clear in your intention. Be as specific as you can about what you want to address. If you are uncertain, then set your intention to address your uncertainty. We are going to deal initially with your inner child's pain, so she will set the agenda for your first few journeys.

So, set healing her pain as your intention. Later, when you have moved past this first set of issues, you can progress to other issues – perhaps something you are afraid of, a relationship issue, issues raised in doing your Gratitude Journal or perhaps a physical problem.

We are going to go through a process that will provide good protection from outside interference. This is why we use particular steps. Each step has a purpose. As you become familiar with the process, then feel free to simply focus your intention and connect to your inner child. But for now, I encourage you to use the longer form.

First, find a quiet place where you will not be interrupted for about a half hour. You might want some soft meditative music, or perhaps you prefer quiet. Other people prefer shamanic drumming (which is the traditional way). Shaman describe this drumming as "God's heartbeat." Listening to drumming or having someone drum for you can be quite powerful and very helpful to the experience. (Several suggestions for recordings of shamanic drumming are noted at the end of the chapter.)

I like to use candles or an oil lamp, but some people are sensitive to the fumes. True beeswax candles have great energy and little odor. Be aware that candles can be sold as beeswax that contain little real beeswax. I advise against using scented candles, they are just too artificial. This is also a very good place to use aromatherapy oils. At the end of this chapter is a simple test you can use to determine which oil is appropriate for your journey.

Most people find it easier to do this work lying down, but a comfortable chair will also serve. You will want your head to be well supported, and you may want to cover your eyes. Relax your mind and decide to leave the day-to-day world behind.

BEGINNING YOUR JOURNEY

Close your eyes and imagine yourself alone at a special place where the land meets the water. It can be a lake, stream, waterfall or ocean. This place may be familiar to you, or imaginary, but what is important is that you are alone and the place is completely safe.

Dawn is just breaking. Feel a gentle, warm breeze blowing through your hair. Feel the incredible energy in the water. Feel the sun on your face. Listen to the sounds. Smell the smells. Feel the earth or sand under your feet. Feel the sunlight as it reflects off the water into your eyes.

Walk along the shore or riverbank until you come to a crystalline pool. There should be no other creature or being there. If any other beings or distractions appear at this stage, you are dealing with interference from an entity. Proceed through the next chapter; come back to this point and then deal with the entity.

Enter the pool and cleanse yourself of the energies of this world. As you leave the pool, there may be a robe for you to wear.

It is not unusual to feel some anxiety at this point in your journey. We are going to travel to a realm you are not familiar with and a certain amount of anxiety is not only normal, it is healthy. Your inner child separated from her world for good reasons some time ago, and you are asking her to re-open old wounds. It is perfectly normal for her to be anxious about returning there. Try to remember that nothing can happen unless your higher self has already accepted it. If your conscious mind interferes, put it on a shelf with a promise to attend to it later.

After cleansing in the pool, if you look up, you will see a temple or other sacred place. It may just be a sacred clearing or a special cloud. Some people see a sacred waterfall. Most people find a temple. Do not be concerned by its condition. Go to the door of the temple or the perimeter of the sacred space and ask permission to enter. Once you are inside, you may find an altar. Spend a moment there and dedicate this journey to dealing with your inner child's pain.

Ask your inner child to come and be with you. In addition to comforting her and offering her your friendship, get clear on what she is feeling – ask her to tell you.

With your intention in mind, tell her to take you back and show you what it was that caused her to feel as she did. (This will be a troubling place for her, and it may take you several journeys.) In all likelihood, she will take you back to a childhood scene. Perhaps it will be a single traumatic occurrence, or she may show you a typical situation that repeated many times.

We want to connect with what caused her pain. Perhaps these were overt acts on the part of your parents. Maybe your mother was withholding love or was taking her frustrations out on you. Perhaps your father was being distant or unkind. But most often we find the emotional abandonment children feel when parents are struggling with their own emotional issues and are unable to give the child the love she needs.

Once you have grasped what she felt, there is a very important additional step. You know how she feels/felt. Now urge her to tell you how the situation made her feel about herself. Notice the distinction. The answer to how it made her feel about herself is an indication of how deeply The Misunderstanding cut into her developing sense of self-worth. This is the core of what you came to address. Certainly she felt badly, but what is even more important is what these events made her feel about herself.

The child may not be eager to open this old wound. She might throw up interference or want to distract you. If in the middle of the journey you find yourself wondering about your to-do list, or taking some kind of a fantasy trip, recognize what is going on and talk with her about her fear. She will be anxious and in need of reassurance. It is essential you make a commitment to be there for her. Hold her, nurture her, and comfort her. Let her know you are there for her. You cannot change what happened, but you can deal with the charge it carries and the self-condemnation she took from it.

Sometimes the emotion of these recollected memories can be quite powerful, and it is easy to slip into the trauma of the events and relive the old pain. If that happens, bring both of you back into the temple. Her pain may have been overwhelming, and although it is essential you be there for her, do not become her. If you do this, you are likely to become caught up in the pain (again), and it will be very difficult for you to move forward. Some people get caught in the cycle of pain and remain there most of their lives. Feeling the pain is merely one step in the process. You must not get lost in her emotions while at the same time being compassionate.

A useful technique to help stay clear of the emotionality of the situation is to go back into the family environment as a fly on the wall. This allows you to observe what happened from a place of detachment. If the encounter with your family was difficult, once you have a grasp on what the situation was, feel free to get her out of there. Create an absolutely wonderful place for the two of you to go.

She may take you to a time immediately after a painful occurrence. Ask to be shown what took place. If you get fragments, ask for more until what you have been shown makes sense. You want to clearly know what happened. The scene may seem innocuous at first, but pay attention to what she is feeling. Keep asking to be shown more until you get what you need.

If the event is particularly traumatic, as in sexual abuse situations, she may show you something like her room – but it will be empty, or maybe she will just be sitting in it. Be gentle but firm, and encourage her to tell you about what happened. Take your time. This is likely to be very difficult for her, and it may take several journeys to get most of the story. Be patient. If the trauma was great, don't be too proud to get professional help. You don't have to deal with this by yourself.

In that same light, if you find yourself stuck, if your problems continue and you just do not seem to be getting anywhere, get competent professional help. Find a good shaman. The reason you got locked in your head in the first place was to protect you from things that were painful and overwhelming, otherwise you would not have done it! If you are familiar with your childhood and cannot make sense of the inner child's reaction, remember, inner children do not act irresponsibly. Whatever took place was important to her, and her behavior will always be a measured and accurate response to the threat she perceived.

It cannot be repeated too often: all these beliefs come from The Misunderstanding, and none of them can possibly be true. Your role in helping her see this is critical. Your perspective about what happened is a far more accurate one than the view she presently holds. We are going to make good use of your perspective in order to help her heal.

People are sometimes concerned that they may not be able to take care of their inner child. They are having a difficult enough time keeping their lives from unraveling, and the idea of caring for this hurting child seems like it will be too great a responsibility. This is subterfuge. In the first place, the problems you are experiencing are because you have not dealt with her and her feelings. Change that, and your life will change.

Secondly, all she really needs is your love, and you can give that to her even in the middle of even the most challenging situations. Third, you cannot guarantee anyone's safety. No one can. Your obligation to her and to yourself is not to put yourself at unreasonable risk.

People who have been abused sometimes have important issues about physical safety, but mostly this is not what she is asking for. She wants to know you will be there to love and support her, no matter what happens. She is looking for the unconditional love and support she needed years ago and did not receive.

If she knows that regardless of circumstance, you will be there to love and support her, it makes a huge difference. Fortunately, there is no limit to the amount of love you can give, and you can love her no matter what else is going on. I cannot overemphasize how important this is. Let God take care of the details.

She may have some reluctance to either share her truth or to admit things were as bad as they really were. She was caught between her parent's dysfunction and her own need to be loved. Her need for care and affection may have outweighed her other needs. Now it gets tied up by shame. These dynamics caused her to rationalize what was happening and possibly deny how painful things were. This was a way for her to get at least a modicum of love and support from your parents so she could survive. If she had honestly owned her feelings back then, the family situation would have likely gone into meltdown and things would have been even worse for her. Where would she have been then? She did the only reasonable thing she could, and you might want to thank her for that.

Considering the situation, she made reasonable decisions. But this is now, not then. However, she is still operating under the old rules. It will help your situation tremendously if you can show her that life with you will be a lot different, and much better, than things were then. This is where the relationship you created with her in the Chapter Six will begin to pay real dividends. If she knows your love is really there, and that you will be there for her, she will feel free to bring her hurt and pain to the surface where it can be addressed. (Remember The Misunderstanding.) She will be able to share, perhaps for the first time, what she really felt about what happened.

You may already have a good idea of what was going on for your parents or caretakers. One of the important issues here is that she does not have that perspective, and one of the gifts you bring her is the opportunity to see things through your eyes. This new view is essential to her healing. You can look back at what your parents did and at your life experience with a clearer perspective than she had at the time. Use what you know to help her see the fears and anxieties that others brought into the situation. If you aren't sure, or have doubts for any reason, simply have her take you back and show you what happened. What was going on will be obvious.

Most often, the other people were not being cruel, they were just unable or afraid to give her the love she needed. She will have assumed their withholding was because she did not deserve to be loved. The truth is, their behavior had nothing to do with her at all. They were locked into their own struggles. What your inner child felt, thought or did, had almost no impact on their behavior or choices at all! Give her the opportunity, perhaps for the first time, to see this truth. Explain things to her. Remind her that she was just a child and had done nothing to deserve the treatment she received. This begins to unwind The Misunderstanding, which will, in turn, begin to unravel the ways she views herself. You may need to go back to other occurrences and make more journeys before her beliefs unravel. But stay with it until she is clear on the truth.

It was not possible for her to express her feelings back then. It was not safe. It rarely is. Prepare yourself to feel some emotion. You are going back to a painful time, and the feelings, mostly sadness and some anger, that have been bottled up for a long time are likely to surface. They will continue to surface for the next few days. You have already been through the experience and survived it. Remembering may be painful, but memories cannot harm you.

Give her what you would give any child under these circumstances: love, comfort and safety. Provide any healing she needs. You have the power to do that. Hold her and talk with her. Continue to demonstrate to her that the situation was not of her creation, it was not her fault, and although it happened, she did not deserve to be treated like that. We are not seeking to blame your parents or anyone else. They did what they could, yet they were also unable to give her the love she needed, and it is perfectly appropriate for you to address that truth. This is not about blame, but about placing responsibility for what occurred where it belongs.

She may move into fear because of the replay of frightening events. She will need your support. Later, as she becomes clearer about what happened, she may feel anger at her mistreatment. There is a technique later in the chapter that will help you deal with this anger. Don't rush to go there. Let the experience of her reawakened feelings sink in.

A caution: I will say again, if what she brings forward overwhelms you for any reason, get professional help. When you go into a state of shock, which is what overwhelm is, it can be very difficult for you to heal. Get someone competent to guide you through the process. An objective view and advice from someone who has dealt with her own issues can be very helpful. The

helping professions exist because at some point these issues were too much
for just about everyone else, and this process isn't about heroics. I could not
have done my work on my own. Get a good shaman, or if one is not available,
find the best therapist you can, only find one who has dealt with his or her
own emotional issues. Other therapists know who is good. Call around and
ask them who, beside themselves, they would recommend. When you find
the same names repeated on your list, you will know who to call. You are
worth it. Consider it an investment in your life.

ENDING YOUR JOURNEY

When you have gone as far as you wish on this journey, gather your inner
child (or children) you have worked with, and either leave them in a safe
place or bring them back to the temple with you. Spend a moment at the
altar and give thanks for your journey.

Go to the temple door or to the perimeter of the sacred space, and ask
permission to leave. Bring the children with you if they want to come,
sometimes they prefer to remain in the temple.

Once outside, return to the crystalline pool and cleanse and refresh
yourself in preparation for reentry to this world. Feel energy moving through
you.

Return to the riverbank or the shore and begin to reconnect with the
energies of this world. Feel the breeze as it blows through your hair. Hear the
birds. Listen to the sound of the waves as they roll in. Feel their power. Feel
the sunlight as it reflects off the water into your eyes. Know the warmth of
the sun on your face. Smell the smells. Feel the earth or the sand under your
feet.

When you have reconnected with the energies of this world, then return
to your starting place. Take your time in coming back. You are making a
significant transition. When you open your eyes, the room may be very bright,
so be prepared.

(A note: I do not mean this to be a commercial, but in doing workshops some people report that the journey process was much easier for them when guided. So, I have recorded the journey process on CD. You can order it from my web site: www.rossbishop.com)

This is the first real contact many people have had with their real inner feelings and the pain the child carries. Your relationship with her may move slowly. Be patient. This is a connection you will want to develop deeply. It is also the most important relationship you will ever have.

The child needs to know that you will be there to love her before she gives up her sanctuary of isolation. She does not know if you will follow through on the commitment you have made to be there for her. She may also be skeptical of adults in general. If she was seriously hurt or abused, she may be very wary. The secret is to open your heart and spend time with her.

Your childhood issues became hardened over a long period of time and through a good deal of emotional duress, so don't expect them to simply evaporate overnight. But you now have tools to help you address The Misunderstanding and all that goes with it.

If you stay with it, things will change. Go back as many times as you need until she is clear about what happened and that it was not her fault. Be sensitive to the fact that these may be substantial emotional issues for her. A lot of stuff may come up. Remain also sensitive that you may be resisting the process because you do not wish to address the pain that she holds. Unfortunately you are going to have to go there, and today is a great deal easier than sometime in the future. But there is a big difference between living in pain and working with it. No matter how difficult things are and no matter what comes up, you are now in the process of truly putting these things behind you. Every journey, each conversation with her, will help the process.

Some people are afraid they are making it all up. This is largely an ego defense against doing the work. If you persevere, the truth will become apparent.

For the rest of the chapter we will discuss dealing with specific issues using the journey process you have just learned.

ISSUES RAISED BY THE GRATITUDE JOURNAL

As you do your daily Gratitude Journal exercise, reactions to your attempts to feel gratitude will surface. These are not issues themselves but rather the ways some of these issues manifest. Your older inner child will be feeling and expressing her resentment for you giving love to others while ignoring her. Her reactions are not issues themselves, but they will point you to them. Use what she brings up to take you to the underlying issues. Go into the journey space and connect with her reaction, then ask her to tell you what she is really upset about, because this goes much deeper. There may be some overlap, as your initial work with the inner child may have already taken you to these issues, but most people need to return to these important issues several times anyway. Besides, it is always wise to be certain.

DEALING WITH REGRETS

You have undoubtedly done things you regret. After all, you are human and therefore fallible. Otherwise you would not be here. Some people carry a substantial burden regarding things they have done. Addressing this is a multi-part process.

The first thing to do is resolve the ego-driven motives that caused you to behave as you did in the first place. It is likely you were hurting, scared or needy (maybe all three) and your neediness and confusion drove you to act as you did. So the first thing to focus on is what was driving her behavior back then.

Set your intention to deal with this issue and proceed into the journey space. When you are in your temple or sacred place, ask the inner child who was involved in this incident to come and be with you. Speak with her about what happened, about her needs, fears and desires at the time. Those feelings did not originate with the situation you are concerned about. Tell her to take you further back and show you what happened to make her feel about herself as she did. At the core, you will find The Misunderstanding.

Talk with her about the Misunderstanding until she comes to see that what happened was not of her creation. She was a child. She did not create the environment or the events, nor could she control the adults in her world. If you are viewing a situation where she was being willful, you have not gone back far enough.

When you feel as though she has come to a new understanding, then return to the situation you have regrets about. Show her how this situation was being driven by the conditioning from The Misunderstanding and not by who she really was. It reflected what she believed, but that is not who she is. Talk with her about how she has been driven by her Misunderstanding. Help her to see that even though her behavior may have been regrettable, it was also understandable. When you have brought her to accept this truth, then forgive her for her behavior. I find it is helpful to do this last part aloud, by the way.

Make it clear that there will be changes. This is your act of sacrifice. Do everything you can through your sacrifice to see that she does not have to face these issues again. Make certain she understands her days of facing life alone are over. She knows you are not perfect and that you may relapse, but if you have earnestly made a commitment to change, she will be forgiving.

If you are still angry with the person (or group), you need to address your residual feelings. Perhaps the other person contributed to the problem and you may have some feelings about what they did. Use the Dealing With Anger procedure found later in the chapter. Being around them at this time will probably not be a good idea, either.

Do not be in a hurry to make amends. If you rush to forgive her or others before you have addressed The Misunderstanding or your anger, your forgiveness will not hold. You will repeat the behavior you have tried to heal.

People sometimes rush into forgiveness as a way to avoid the anger and pain they carry. In order to make amends, you need to feel safe. As long as she feels intimidated or frightened by the other person, forgiveness will be very difficult. Do the Dealing With Anger process until you feel your anger is resolved. It is important to deal with your anger, because it empowers your inner child. If you do not do this, your attempt to make amends will be premature and will likely fail.

When you have forgiven her and you are ready to proceed to make amends, then create a neutral place away from the temple where you can meet with the other person. Then ask the spirit of the other person to join you. (You can do this with groups, too.) When they come, speak your piece. Explain your behavior. Tell them what is in your heart and what was going on for you at that time. If you want to hear from them, that is fine. If not, that's okay too. Do not be invested in getting a particular response from them. You may not get what you desire, and this is just your ego setting you up, anyway. If you find yourself yelling at them, you have some more anger work to do. When you are finished, thank them for coming and send them out.

Repeat this process for everything you carry that you feel responsible for or guilty about. Do it until you feel finished with each piece. Call in your siblings, your children, former lovers, previous friends, old co-workers, etc. Get the rejection and self condemnation out of your system. If, after you have done this process, you want to make amends to the actual person, do so. Just don't set yourself up for further abuse or recrimination. You do not have to do it in person, you can write them, and even then, you do not have to send the letter.

DEALING WITH OTHER ISSUES

If life is pushing on you, The Universe is asking you to look at something important. There are several doorways you can use to access what is going on. You can use your current feelings, your behavior or your memory as portals to take you back to The Misunderstanding. It is helpful to remember that the charge you place on what is happening has little to do with the present situation. You may be upset with your partner, for example, and although your feelings may be legitimate and well founded, the emotional charge you put on the situation has little to do with them. It is your history, your Misunderstanding, that is being triggered by your partner's behavior. That is the source of your reaction.

The most reliable way to connect with what is really going on is to use your current feelings, and the best way to do this is through an event. Assume, for example, that something happened that brought up your feelings of unworthiness. Do a journey, and when you are in the temple, get in touch with the pain you experienced (you do not have to use an event, you can just use your feelings, but events are usually easier). Use your feelings like an anchor. Then ask your inner child to take you back to when she first felt this way. You will find The Misunderstanding.

Using your behavior is effective when you are not sure about the origin of your feelings or the reason you sometimes act as you do. It gives you an alternative way to connect with the issue. For example, you might shrink from having real relationships with people, but you may not know why. Perhaps you are easily frightened, or maybe you move quickly to anger and are unsure as to why you do that. You can use any response or behavior to connect with the originating Misunderstanding. (By the way, recognize that behaviors are reactions and not causes.)

Talk with your inner child about why she acts as she does. Have her take you back to show you what caused her to respond as she did "back then." You will go back to what was happening when the feelings and beliefs were created that drive your current behavior.

The third way to get to the source of a problem is through your memory. Perhaps you know what the issue is. Maybe you know for example, that your mother was not there for you emotionally. You can use what you remember from your childhood to get your inner child to take you back so you can address what happened, but this is not totally reliable. Use what you remember to generate feelings, then use those to go back. Memory is a mental function and as much as it would like to, we don't want your mind controlling things here. However, she knows everything that has ever happened to you. Simply ask her to take you back.

Don't be surprised if what you find is somewhat different from what you expect or remember. She undoubtedly had to pigeonhole and rationalize away what was going on, but her feelings will be reliable. We already know that your understanding of reality was not complete, so be willing to allow the whole truth to come forward. I mention this because she may have an investment in protecting someone who hurt her but who also gave her love. We see this often in situations involving sexual abuse. As I mentioned earlier, she may also possess a strong motivation to not upset the family apple cart. When she knows your love and support will be there for her, she will be freer to live in the truth.

DEALING WITH ANGER
(TAKING BACK YOUR POWER)

This process can be a bit tricky because 95% of what we call anger isn't actually anger at all. Real anger comes from compassion and connects us. Anger will be expressed as: "I care about you enough to tell you I am angry about what happened." As I said, we don't see this often.

Most of what we call anger is really rage. It is a fear-based response which says, "I am hurt and afraid. I don't know if I can take care of myself, so I am going to turn the dogs on you in order to back you off so I can create emotional distance for myself. That will allow me to feel safer." Where anger connects, rage separates. Rage condemns, it punishes, it pushes away. It is important for you to recognize which you are dealing with, and both can be present at the same time.

If what you carry is rage, get in touch with your fear of being hurt, and journey to deal with the issue. Look for feelings of helplessness, powerlessness, abandonment and maybe even the desire for revenge. As you work through your childhood issues, you will eventually get to the real anger. It will be wrapped in sadness.

As you continue to work with your inner child, she will reach a point where she feels sufficiently resolved about what happened and safe in your love and support that she will allow herself to feel real anger toward those who hurt her. This is a very healthy and important place. She had to give away her power back then, and she is approaching the time where she can begin to take it back. Note that for this exercise, we are going to focus on her feelings. The other people and their feelings are not particularly important. This is about her and her process. We are going to give her the opportunity, under your protection, to express the pain she has withheld all these years.

Dealing with rage and anger invariably takes us to family of origin issues. And dealing with parents and family presents special problems. These relationships are loaded with emotionality and long established patterns of behavior. The tendrils of our unfulfilled needs still reach out to parents for love and approval, even though it has never really been there. Plus, it is simply difficult to avoid family. You can ignore a boorish friend, but this is more difficult to do with a family member you see at holidays and family gatherings.

Even if the family environment was not nurturing, it was still the only source of love you had. Many people are reluctant to jeopardize those relationships. Your parents did the best they could, but that kind of thinking is a trap. It gives an excuse to poor performance. Protecting parents is mostly a cop-out. Not allowing your inner child to have her honest pain and anger about what happened cripples her. Besides, you are going to have to eventually deal with these issues, anyway.

Some adults just do not do well as parents. And when parents cannot express their love, their children get hurt. That hurt is really a gold mine for everyone involved. In addition to the pain that the child carries from these encounters, the child's pain offers a marvelous opportunity for the parent to look at his or her own behavior and say, "Hmmm, something is wrong here, maybe I should look at what I am doing." Unfortunately, this opportunity is rarely taken, but it does illustrate the perfection of the process. This is the real gift our children bring to us, by the way.

Your parents needed to hear your message thirty years ago, but they weren't ready to hear it then. Instead, they used their parental power and the threat of the loss of love to pressure you into submission. Addressing the pain their children carried would have required them to address the feelings they had avoided their entire lives.

In many families there are also strong prohibitions against speaking the truth. The message to the child was, "If you share your feelings, you will blow things up." You had to respond to that implicit loss of love. The dilemma, of course, is that repressing the inner child's pain cripples her emotionally.

Learning to speak your truth isn't about your parents, anyway. It is about you taking back the power you gave up to them so long ago. This is where your relationship with your inner child becomes especially important. If she knows your love and support will be there, even if the world goes totally to pieces, it is much easier for her to stand in her truth. This is true not only with regard to parents, but for any issue.

The way to deal with this is to go into the journey space and to find a safe place outside the temple where you can do this exercise. The first thing to do is to make her feel secure. To help with that, make her about seven feet tall. This insures that "big people" will not intimidate her. Then tuck her in safely next to you so she also feels the sanctuary of your love and protection.

Then call in the offenders, one at a time. Tell them to come to you. Feel free to contribute to this process, but ideally, we want most of what follows to come from her. Have her tell the other how much their behavior and choices hurt her and how difficult it has made life. Encourage her to let fly. Read them the riot act! Yell and scream (you do not have to do this out loud). The important thing is to hold nothing back. You may have to do this process several times.

The next step is problematic for some people, but if she wants to get physical with them, let her. Allow me to explain: In this space you cannot harm anything so there is no risk. Her feelings and emotions have been repressed your entire life. It is vital we break down her prohibition against expressing her truth. In addition, we need to move the energy of her frustration. I would never advocate violence toward another being. But, this is an important step in her taking back the power she gave up because of The Misunderstanding. There may be years of accumulated frustration in there. If she wants to kick them down the block, or beat them to a pulp, let her.

I would suggest that you not listen to the explanations or rationalizations of the other people unless you are certain they are sincere. Whatever they did, for whatever reason, they chose to sell you down the river rather than deal with their own pain and fear. Their decisions were motivated by their needs and fear, and they exhibited little real regard for you, no matter how they rationalized the situation. Don't let them off the hook, but if they have something sincere to say, it might help her to hear it.

PHYSICAL PROBLEMS

Did you know you could speak with your heart or your stomach? How about your hurting shoulder? Crazy as it may sound, it is true. It may not be the kind of conversation you would have with a friend, but you can learn to communicate with the parts of your body. As practice, right now, close your eyes and ask your nervous system what it needs.

The question now is, what are you willing to do about it? This gets us down to how really serious you are about your healing.

If there is some part of your physical self that is experiencing a problem, focus your attention there and ask to communicate with it. You may get words, or perhaps just feelings that you will have to interpret. The tissues of the body are where you store your unresolved fear, pain, anxiety, anger, etc. Use what you have learned about the journey process to go back and deal with the emotional issues your physical self is pleading with you to address.

Once you open communication with this part of yourself, then tell it (or you can use the inner child) to return to where the contraction or energy disturbance began. Heal the wound you uncover there. You will be back to The Misunderstanding. You will find it was not your fault, and she can now let go of the contraction.

Ask this part of your body what it needs. Then ask it what changes it needs you to make. This is where you get to take responsibility for the emotions you have been unable, or perhaps unwilling, to resolve. How much are you willing to change? Are you willing to change your diet or get more exercise? Will you reduce your level of stress?

THE WOMB

This surprises some people because of the way we are taught to view infants, but your awareness was well developed in the womb. To further shatter what science teaches us, we can go even further. You had conscious awareness even before your conception. Science sees you as this body, this mind. You are SO much more than that.

As a fetus you had a good sense of what was going on outside your mother's womb, and you were, of course, directly connected to her emotions. Ask the child to take you back to the womb and show you what she was feeling. Ask her to tell you what coming into the world under these circumstances made her feel, and especially what it made her feel about herself.

She may not have wanted to come out at all! It is almost certain she took on unjustified negative feelings about herself. Show her the truth. She has done nothing wrong. If it would help her, create a perfect womb for her in a sacred place. Take her there and let her develop under your love and care.

OTHER INNER CHILDREN

Most people have several inner children. They tend typically to constellate around infancy, 3 to 4 years old, 6 to 9, and then the early teen years. These seem to represent the major emotional developmental phases in people's lives.

If your inner children are different than these do not be concerned. Recognize that each age will have its own needs and issues that will need to be addressed.

It is frequently useful to create working relationships among the various inner children. They can share perspectives, address conflicting needs and support each other with, of course, your help.

PAST LIVES AND NEGATIVE ENTITIES

Each of these topics is a discussion in itself and will be addressed in the next chapter. As you work with your inner child, if she seems somehow "off" to you, if her behavior is erratic or if you see dark clouds or tar-like blobs around her, you have an entity to deal with.

Here is a summary guide to use for your journeys:

THE JOURNEY PROCESS

• Find a comfortable place where you will not be disturbed. Close your eyes and imagine yourself alone at a special place where the land meets the water.

• Dawn is just breaking. Feel a gentle, warm breeze blowing through your hair. Feel the incredible energy in the water. Feel the sun on your face. Listen to the sounds. Smell the smells. Feel the earth or the sand under your feet. Feel the sunlight as it reflects off the water into your eyes.

• Walk along the shore or the riverbank until you come to a crystalline pool. There should be no other creature or being there. Enter the pool and cleanse yourself of the energies of this world. As you leave the pool there may be a ceremonial robe for you to wear.

• After cleansing in the pool, look up and you will see a temple or other sacred place.

• Go to the door of the temple or the perimeter of the sacred space and ask permission to enter.

• Once you are inside, you may find an altar. Spend a moment there and declare your intention.

• Ask your inner child to come and be with you.

FINISHING YOUR JOURNEY

• When you have finished your journey, gather the inner child or children you have worked with, and either leave them in a safe place or bring them back with you.

• Spend a moment at the altar and give thanks for your journey.

• Go to the temple door, or to the perimeter of the sacred space, and ask permission to leave.

• Once outside, return to the crystalline pool and cleanse and refresh yourself in preparation for reentry to this world.

• Return to the riverbank or the shore, and begin to reconnect to the energies of this world. Feel the breeze as it blows through your hair. Listen to the sounds.

• Feel the power in the water. Know the warmth of the sun on your face. Smell the smells. Feel the earth or the sand under your feet. Feel the sunlight as it reflects off the water into your eyes.

• When you have reconnected with the energies of this world, then return to the room and open your eyes.

SHAMANIC DRUMMING

I like a CD called "Journey Of The Soul" by Donna Callaghan and Patricia Fares O'Malley. Track four is great. You can order it from: www.peaceplace.net. ($15 plus s&h).

"The Ultimate Shamanic Journey," by Melinda Rodriguez and Dirk Barkemeijer de Witt (www.drumdiva.org) is also very good, and adds the sound of the didgeridoo. $20 (incl. s&h).

AROMATHERAPY TEST

This test may seem like something of a parlor trick, but it works. I like this test because it is simple and you can do it by yourself.

Stand still with your legs about shoulder-width apart. If you have a friend with you, have her observe you from the side.

Clear your mind of thoughts, and focus on the issue you wish to address in your journey. Hold the bottle of oil against your abdomen, just below your navel.

Close your eyes and hold the bottle in place for 15 - 20 seconds. Feel if your body wants to move forward or backward. The movement will come in waves. The first wave will be smaller, and the second wave will be stronger. If your body moves forward, you are getting a yes, and if it moves backward, it is saying no.

Test various oils to see which one or ones you react to strongly. This will tell you which one(s) will help you with the issues you have identified. Test frequently, because what you need will change as you progress.

There are a number of aromatherapy oils on the market, and I am not pleased with the quality of most of them. They sacrifice too much in quality. One blender I have worked with extensively, and can highly recommend, is Mikael Zagat from Quebec. Mikael is a seventh-generation blender, and his intuitive gift is unparalleled. His distributor is www.4Dshift.com. You can order from their website or email info@4Dshift.com for a catalogue.

Life was one damned problem after another.

Elbert Hubbard

CHAPTER 9

Entities and Past Lives

This being human is a guest house.

Every morning a new arrival.

A joy, a depression, a meanness,
some momentary awareness comes
as an unexpected visitor.

Welcome and attend them all!
Even if they're a crowd of sorrows
who violently sweep your house
empty of its furniture,
still, treat each guest honorably.
He may be clearing you out
for some new delight.

The dark thought, the shame, the malice,
meet them at the door laughing,
and invite them in.
Be grateful for whoever comes,
because each has been sent
as a guide from beyond...

Rumi

ENTITIES

Throughout history, few subjects have aroused the fear, fascination and terror that entities have. Our folk history is filled with tales of ghouls, goblins, evil spirits, bewitchings, demonic possession, devils, spells, ghosts, angels, curses, the occult, demons, miracles and magic. Our lore about entities is also replete with ignorance, fear-mongering, hyperbole of unimaginable proportions, enough lies to fill the Vatican, and manipulation for political and religious ends that has no equal. What we can say for certain is that some people have learned to work successfully with these beings. We can also say that no one fully understands the subject.

There was once a time when our ancestors worked the land, were close to each other and had a strong reverence for nature. These people lived with and depended upon the nature spirits. Their spirituality was personal and experiential. They did not learn it from books. All things, good or bad, came from either the individual's or the clan's relationship to spirit.

These people experienced spirituality and it, in turn, bestowed meaning to life. There was not an outer world of form and inner world of mythology. They saw the world and their experience with it as an interrelated complex of gods, spirits and humans. Their struggles and accomplishments were integrated into the culture and brought to us through their stories and sagas.

Although people depended on and respected nature, they also feared her. Their lives were run by something intellectuals pejoratively call superstition, which ignores the positive (non-intellectual) values of having a spiritual life. Our ancestors may have been scientifically ignorant, but they possessed a respect for nature and the world of spirit that has been lost to us. That faith gave them an anchor through which to address and manage the challenges presented by life. It is possible that they respected nature because they feared her, but I suspect that their respect came more from their intimacy with her. Modern man's desire to "conquer" nature has distanced him from her and allowed him to massively, perhaps irreparably, damage her.

Most ancient cultures believed in gods and saw spirits as otherworldly beings possessing an assortment of mystical qualities. Our word demon comes from the Greek word daimon, which referred to beings with special powers who could place themselves between people and the gods, often to our detriment. Homer wrote frequently of daimons. He said, "A sick man pining away is one upon whom an evil spirit has gazed." Socrates and Aeschylus both thought that insane people were under the influence of daimons, and Plato believed that daimons sometimes obsessed mortals.

In Greece, the Arcadian nymph Nicostrate or Themis represented the balance of the natural order. She epitomized not only earthly unity, but also the balance of the great universe itself. The Greeks believed that when the natural order was violated through human hubris, i.e., "defiance of the gods," that the forces of righteous anger (Nemesis) and shame (Aidos) would rise to right wrongs and then reweave the web that had been disturbed.

The Greeks saw the interplay of these forces inherent in human behavior and believed that they also moved everything toward balance. Themis was often shown with the wheel of life, representing the wholeness of the universe, the ceaseless process of change and the interconnectedness of all things. She gave out "What was due." In time, she became associated with the principles of morality and justice that brings people into harmony with The Universe. She is the blindfolded statue of Justice that holds the scales of balance (the natural order of things) seen over many courthouses.

To the Greeks, Aidos the butterfly was the quality of reverence for life that encourages us to do no wrong. Aidos is one of the balancing spirits that manifested the natural shame we feel when we witness injustice or do something unloving. In her book on illness and healing, Kat Duff wrote:

> *Originally, shame carried a sense of the sacredness, of the great Mystery that infuses all life, instilling a healthy respect, reverence, and humility. It served to remind humans so prone to hubris, that we are not God, and that we have made and will make mistakes. It allowed us to acknowledge our mistakes and prompted us to remedy them to the best of our abilities. To the Greek understanding, shame was the antidote for human hubris, the remedy for wrongdoing, our means of mending the web.*[43]

In the eighth century B.C., the Greek poet Hesiod predicted that there would come a time during what he called the Age of Iron when people would become so depraved that Aidos and Nemesis would depart out of frustration and leave us to reap what we had sown. Hesiod described that time:

> *A father will not be in harmony with his children nor his children with him, nor guest with host, nor friend with friend, and a brother will not be loved as formerly. One will destroy the city of another. No esteem will exist for the one who is true to an oath or just or good; rather men will praise the arrogance and evil of the wicked. Justice will be might and shame will not exist . . . Then Aidos and Nemesis both will forsake mankind and go, their beautiful forms shrouded in white, from the wide earth to Olympus among the company of the gods . . . and there will be no defense against evil.*

The natural connection between people develops out of compassion, respect and understanding. Hesiod observed that when the natural web of connections is broken, violence prevails. He said that when the web is violated, our capacity to feel righteous anger and shame is lost, and then our natural protection from evil and wrongdoing dissipates. He also pointed out that when the social law of people replaces the natural law or balance of The Universe, then people's ability to perceive the natural order and respond accordingly, greatly diminishes.

In Greek mythology, the Muses were nine goddesses or spiritual guides who embodied the arts and inspired the creative process. Creative people were thought to be possessed by a genius (the word comes from the same root as djinn or genie), which gave them inspiration. It is but a short jump from muse to entity, and the Muses often depicted and discussed in literature may be more literal than people realized. The Great Library of Alexandria and its circle of scholars was formed around a mousaion, a "museum" or shrine of the Muses. The museum was close to the tomb of Alexander the Great, a king with legendary communication with beings from other realms.

Unwilling, or perhaps unable to disturb the pantheon of the gods, the Greeks were content to appease them. Instead, they focused their efforts on attempting to break the daimons' spells or create protection from them.

Assyrian tablets offer the first written accounts we have regarding the treatment of illnesses by doctors. People would visit doctors seeking cures for illness, emotional issues or bad luck. A malady was a malady it seems, and it did not matter where or how it manifested. Bad luck and cancer were both afflictions that came from the gods.

Physicians in ancient cultures were shaman. They healed primarily through exorcism. This included incantations and prayers to the gods, as well as direct challenges to the daimons, which the people felt caused disease and disharmony. Ancient Babylonian priests would ritually destroy a clay or wax image of a daimon, freeing the afflicted person from its influence.

In our dismissal of these practices as superstitious, we forget that these were also very practical people. They may have been primitive and crude by modern standards, but they were not stupid. They would not have tolerated these practices for so many years if they did not produce results. These ancient healers were using methods we know to be effective, because many of their practices are used successfully today all over the planet. An interesting question, by the way is, "Where did the Babylonians get the images of the daimons they destroyed?" They could have invented them, but as you will learn later, that was not necessary.

Mystical teachers through the millennia have told us that energy could be made to move in and out of physical form. It sounds complicated, but in principle it is not. You do it all the time. Heat water for your morning coffee, and you put energy into the cool water. Apply heat to ice, and it will change form and melt. Eat lunch, and the food is transformed into energy for your body.

The trick is to make nature respond to your intention. In the hands of a skilled practitioner, energy can be introduced into objects and substances, given form and otherwise manipulated. We read in the Bible how Christ turned water into wine and created loaves and fishes. The shamanic literature we have has many examples of energy/mater manipulation. After all, what is healing?

If priests and physicians could break spells and manipulate energy, then others with skills and training could create spells and curses, too. So we find in the profane world the development of the black arts as dark witches and sorcerers sought to compete with the daimon for power over life. These practitioners used all manner of rites, spells, talismans, potions and curses to afflict their clients' enemies or satiate a client's desires.

Some of these manifestations are so spectacular that they capture our attention. We know them as spells and curses. When an Aboriginal in Australia commits an offense that the elders feel requires capital punishment, the elders will empower a carved wooden stick, known as a "killing stick" to exact the sentence. Once empowered, the stick is covered. When it is to be used, it is uncovered and pointed at the offending person. This person will die soon afterwards. Interestingly, not so much from the killing stick's power, but from what it does with the energy of guilt held by the offender.

Curses are uncommon, yet we see the effects of some curses today, although most of them were created thousands of years ago. This is craft. It is witchwork and sorcery, the stuff of legends and folk tales.

Confronted with the natural spirituality of native people, the church felt compelled to convert these pagans to Christianity and to destroy their competing religion. When the Church "saved these poor, ignorant savages" it replaced individual, experiential spirituality with a learned one of abstract faith and belief. The Christian God was inaccessible. He could not be felt; he had to be imagined. God could no longer be found in woods or streams. He was an ephemeral deity who could only be accessed through the Church.

God went from being known and expressed through the events of life to a remote and distant heaven where he communicated only with the Church hierarchy and rarely bothered with the common people. The Bible written in Latin, was for the theologians. In the Middle Ages, commoners were forbidden to read or interpret Christian teachings. The possession of even a single page of the Bible by a common person was an offense punishable by death. Priests told people what they should believe.

The result of this transition was that the divine was removed from the realm of experiential knowing and reinterpreted as a mental exercise, robbing it of its "mysterious relation to the inner man." And when people cease to experience God, they are forced to believe in him, and belief, as Paul Tillich pointed out, is a commodity subject to loss. William James also noted that belief is fragile because it is usually "faith in someone else's faith," and as the cliché goes, "Theologians know a great deal about God but very little of God."

The Christian religion in those days was not a positive faith that created an affirmation of life and taught the interrelatedness of all things. The entire focus of the Church was on salvation and the afterlife. Nothing else mattered. Having taken people's natural spirituality, the Church replaced it with fear. Church faith was a negative religion of intellectual concepts. The Christian God was a punishing being who condemned people for their sins and made them suffer for their misbehavior. So that along with salvation came a new kind of insecurity and uncertainty. Jules Michelet wrote of the medieval church:

> On Sundays after Mass the sick came in scores, crying for help -- and words were all they got: "You have sinned, and God is afflicting you. Thank Him; you will suffer so much the less torment in the life to come."[44]

The Catholic Church of the 12th through the 17th centuries was also corrupt beyond imagination, and it held itself above criticism or reform. In the words of Dietrich Von Nieheim, Bishop of Verden, written in 1411:

> When the existence of the Church is threatened, she is released from the commandments of morality. With unity as the end, the use of every means is sanctified, even cunning, treachery, violence, simony, prison, death. For all order is for the sake of the community, and the individual must be sacrificed to the common good.

As institutional rigidity grew and moral corruption spread, people began to question the Church's trusteeship of their faith. Its traditional base of power began to erode. People searched for other forms of spirituality that spoke more directly to their needs and allowed a direct connection to Spirit. They began to participate in non-Christian practices such as the Wiccan Sabbath, which had become a popular alternative to strict and severe church services. Since the Church was only interested in salvation, people turned to witches, conjurers and sorcerers to manifest spells and curses that would help them with the events and concerns of daily life.

The Church's response was to tighten control. The Inquisition had been in use for some time on a limited basis. Now the Church squeezed the populace to the full extent of its power. Using the Inquisition in Spain and witch-hunts in central Europe, the Church sought to eliminate practices it considered contrary to Christian dogma. Seizing upon people's natural fear of the supernatural, the Church also found a way to, once again, thrash the competition.

Although the witch population in Europe had never numbered more than several thousands, millions of innocent women who practiced everything from herbalism to midwifery were tortured and burned alive along with gypsies, gays, the mentally ill, Jews, Muslims and anyone else who disagreed with the Church.

In addition to its unadulterated brutality and total desecration of Christian tenets, the really unfortunate thing about the Inquisition was that the Church had it completely wrong, and history suggests this was purposeful. Although the Church had the knowledge and experience to deal with possession and help these troubled people, it chose instead to torture and burn alive everyone it deemed a threat. It did nothing to address the very real problem of possession that had plagued mankind for centuries, even though Christ had taught it, and Christians had practiced exorcism since the founding of the Church.

Exorcism was a common practice in the ancient religions, and in tribal societies, shaman had been dealing with these problems for millennia. Yet the Church rejected what it knew, either because it did not believe in its own processes or. what is more likely, felt that it was more expeditious to terrorize the populace into submission in order to ensure its position in society.

Later, split by the Protestant Reformation and weakened by ongoing corruption and opposition to the Inquisition, the Church was in no position to resist when physicians suggested that possessed people might actually be ill. Physicians urged that people be confined to asylums rather than being tortured and burned at the stake (note the word "asylum" rather than "hospital"). This was a sincere humanitarian gesture by the medical profession, and it added another bone of contention between the Church and the emerging scientific community.

Doctors split the treatment of spirit possession, which they referred to as "mental illness," from its traditional spiritual roots. The men of science had little choice, they had to protect themselves from the subjective judgments of a desperate Church, but they were also not about to support "superstitious beliefs," anyway.

Doctors viewed possession as a condition more akin to cholera or measles than demons, and they began a long quest to look for physical causes to mental disturbance. This has always been the approach of the medical community in regard to mental issues, and although it has produced some results, it has never provided real answers. But in their quest for certifiable truth, the early physicians and scientists threw spirituality out the window with the ecclesiastical bath water, and the damage to the fabric of Western society has never been healed. We are paying a terrible price for the lack of spirituality in our culture today.

Early physicians observed that possession occurred more frequently in women than in men and placed a gender designation on the condition. They called it "hysteria," a loss of self-control, which they concluded came from the fact that one possessed a womb (hystere), a situation best cured by the removal of that dangerous organ, thus demonstrating for all time, the inherent fallibility of rational logic.

There was another source of conflict between the early physicians and the Church. Christ was a psychic healer and the premier exorcist of all time. At least twenty-six references to Jesus' exorcisms are found in the Bible, and in addition to bringing Lazarus back from the dead, he performed many other healings. Since science cannot reproduce these miracles, it puts them in a special category marked, "We don't necessarily dispute them. We just don't understand them."

Science has always had a difficult time with psychic phenomenon because, as I pointed out earlier, these phenomena exist outside the realm of rational thought. These things are impossible to measure and repeat using scientific criteria. It isn't that they do not exist; it is that they do not fit into a rational context. You cannot adequately assess phenomena in one realm from one below it. It is like our fla- world two-dimensional character trying to measure height. It cannot be done! In one of the examples we have of Jesus performing a physical treatment, he took dirt in his hand, spat on it and then applied the mud to the eyes of a blind man. The man's blindness was cured.[45] They do not teach that technique in medical school today.

The Bible speaks eloquently of Jesus' healing abilities. Christ was trying to show us that through faith (not religion, but faith) we are all capable of compassionate healing. People view His healing work as an extension of His special connection to The Creator, but there have been numerous shaman and other spiritual healers over the years whose ability to heal has also been well documented. Yet even though the field has always been filled with charlatans and phony faith healers, there are a few legitimate healers practicing in the world today.

I spent some time with John of God, the renowned miracle healer from Brazil. John doesn't do healing himself. He allows the spirits of other great healers to come through him to do the healing work. John the man is actually something of an emotional train wreck, but the work the entities do through him is nothing short of miraculous.

People come by the busloads to John's Casa seeking help from the entities. Some people are cured, and this has been well documented, while others come away with nothing. I stood in John's line and watched as people came to him. I could see in people's energies the ones who were sincerely willing and ready to receive healing, and those who still had things to learn from the experience of their affliction. These people sincerely wanted to heal, but they were not ready to surrender their egos or beliefs so that healing could happen. It was as though when they came to John they held up shields to block the healing energies. Others had learned and grown from their experiences and were so sick and tired of hurting that they would have done anything to heal. They opened to the God Space and readily accepted it.

I remember one man who was in his fifties and had not walked since he was eight or nine. He was so ready to heal it just poured out of him, but he could not find his way through the tangle of his rational mind. I watched the entities crack this fellow's resistance open like an egg and reawaken the faith that had been suppressed in him for years. The man stood without his crutches and walked on his own, badly mind you, for the first time in forty-some years. He spent that afternoon "walking" around the Casa grounds, exercising leg muscles that hadn't pulled weight in a very long time.

The people who received healing most easily were the "simple" people who didn't clog the process up with a lot of analytical analysis and anxiety. This intrigued me, so I spoke with some of them. They were Brazilians, mostly farmers or simple working people. They were not spiritually educated, although Brazilians in general are very spiritual people. They have developed a charismatic Catholicism that goes well beyond the faith of Rome. Most were religious but some were not. But what they shared was faith in something greater than themselves. Most of them had faith in God, and that faith gave them the confidence to surrender to the healing process.

I kept thinking of what Western doctors call the "placebo effect" or "spontaneous healing," and how they misunderstand what is happening to their patients who heal through belief, which is ultimately what all healing is about anyway.

For millennia, Oriental physicians have achieved remarkable healings through working with the energy meridians of the body. Because it represents an alien philosophy, Western doctors have resisted these approaches. But some Western physicians are beginning to accept these time-tested and proven concepts. Dr. Oz, of "Oprah" fame, says,

> We're beginning now to understand things that we know in our hearts are true but we could never measure. As we get better at understanding how little we know about the body, we begin to realize that the next big frontier ... in medicine is energy medicine. It's not the mechanistic part of the joints moving. It's not the chemistry of our body. It's understanding for the first time how energy influences how we feel.

In Chapter One, I mentioned the book The Biology of Belief by Dr. Bruce Lipton. Dr. Lipton's premise is that the fundamental assumptions about life made by biologists since before Darwin have been in error. He is proving that the function and development of living organisms has much more to do with their reaction to their "beliefs" than with cell genetics or Darwinian evolution.

Shaman, white witches and the healing entities that work through John of God stand at the intersection between mind, matter and energy. That discussion has occupied some of humankind's brightest minds and has garnered no small amount of myth and misunderstanding. One of these original investigations, that of alchemy, gave birth to much of what is modern science.

If you saw the movie *"What the #$*! Do We (K)now!?,"* you saw the ice crystal photographs of Masaru Emoto.[46] Emoto has demonstrated that water retains the energy of the thoughts to which it has been exposed. Good thoughts make elegantly beautiful ice crystals, and unpleasant thoughts make ugly ones.

Emoto's beautiful images of joy and peace contrast vividly with the unpleasant images left in the water by messages like, "I hate you" or, "you are ugly."

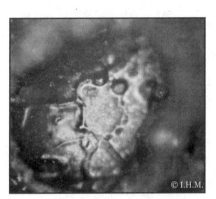 

Ice crystals made from water taken from the Fujiwara dam in Japan before (left) and after (right) prayers were said over it.

This idea reinforces further the ancient concept of saying grace to give thanks for a meal, the notion of holy water or the Eucharist where Christ blessed the bread and wine at the Last Supper.

Keeping Emoto's work in mind, remember that not only are you 70% water, but also that the other liquids and tissues of your body are susceptible to this kind of imprinting! How many negative messages do you give the cells of your body every day? If you recall the story of the Aboriginal killing stick, even though we may not be able to manipulate them like a sorcerer or shaman, our beliefs do manifest in the physical realm. Pooh-poohed by the sciences for years, there is a growing body of evidence in support of the idea that our beliefs do have a powerful impact on our physical and emotional well-being.

As physicists delve deeper into the nature of matter, they begin to discover the impact that our thoughts and intentions have. A textbook of quantum mechanics or a paper about string theory today reads more like a mystical text with numbers than a treatise of Newtonian mechanics. Although they may take a long time to admit it, scientists are at the very edge of understanding that our thoughts do manifest in reality.

Universal Law does not operate like the laws of physics you were taught in high school. Scientists are just beginning to figure out that fixed laws aren't so fixed. If a Universal Law is broken - actually I should say bent - for the sake of compassion, for example, there will be no penalty. Christ brought Lazarus back from the dead because of his love for him. He healed in this same way. If, however, Universal Laws are broken, let's say because of malice or greed, the price will be substantial. A curse, for example, comes with a very high price. The traditional image we have of witches looking like old hags was not just an artistic invention. It is real. These women have aged tremendously as a price for their transgressions. That is why you do not see true psychics or clairvoyants going to the horse track or playing the lottery.

When a person asks a witch or a sorcerer to conjure something or cast a spell, she is asking for power over life. "Love Potion Number 9" is simply an attempt to obtain through magical means what one does not feel confident enough to get on one's own. Similarly, placing a curse on an individual or a family is revenge, and it exacts a very great price. We tend to think in terms of external punishment, but what happens "inside" an individual when she commits an evil or unkind act is actually more important. What has been historically called "hell" is when that disturbed energy begins to mix with the harmonizing energies of The Universe.

The same principles hold true for thoughts. If you are in a natural state of consciousness, your thoughts flow naturally and freely. If, however, you lock your thoughts up with fear, you create disharmony – a disturbance in The Universe. You will then live in, and must compensate for, the disturbance. The manifestations can range all the way from anxiety and mental rigidity to personality disorder, dementia, schizophrenia or paranoia.

We do not do these things alone. Actively involved in the process of contracting our energy will be a negative entity. The relationship with entities ranges from simply having an entity reside in our shadow, a fairly common occurrence, to full-blown entity possession. Thus far, we have discussed the more serious side of entity possession because these situations create a great deal more disruption, and history tends to focus its attention there. So, they get more publicity. And, although entities residing in people's energy fields are actually fairly common, phenomena like possession and curses are not. For the rest of the chapter, we will speak of our more ordinary relationship with entities.

The first thing to consider is the idea that conscious beings can exist without having a physical body - in other words, outside the physical realm. When we see a human spirit that has been disconnected from its physical form, we typically call it a ghost. These beings are actually fairly common, but most people are not consciously aware of them.

Our folk literature is filled with ghost tales, and even after accounting for a good deal of story-telling embroidery, most of the tales are remarkably similar. These are souls who either have become stuck between realms or have remained here because of a special connection to an event or a place or trauma.

Similarly, the literature of near-death experiences is filled with stories of people who have observed events that took place while their bodies were "dead." One of my favorite stories is of a young man who drowned and was brought to a hospital. He was technically dead. The emergency room crew tried to revive him with a defibrillator that didn't work, and after a valiant effort, the physicians accepted defeat and gave up. Lying on the table, the boy recovered spontaneously, and later told the doctors he had watched their efforts, especially one physician who had accidentally knocked the defibrillator plug out of its socket.

In addition to human spirits without form, there are also non-human beings without physical form that inhabit our space. Although angels and light beings are dismissed by science, the thousands upon thousands of similar encounters people have had with these beings over human history are simply too prolific and too consistent to be merely the hallucinations or delusions they are dismissed to be.

If you consider that when people have visions, as just an example, their experiences vary widely. Their experiences are influenced by their beliefs, culture, their emotional state and a host of other considerations. Yet when people encounter angels or light beings, their experiences are remarkably similar. People's encounters with beings of light are a part of our cultural history, and the telling of these old stories does influence how people interpret their own experiences. But when you take these stories apart and examine them in detail, they are so incredibly similar that the influence of folklore simply does not account for their consistency, especially when you consider that these experiences have been separated by oceans, cultures and thousands of years in time.

There is another group of beings that we have even more experience with, and they are the most common of all. These are the entities. We generally are not aware of their presence, but their influence can be most powerful. There are discussions about whether entities are actually separate beings or extensions of our consciousness, and there are good arguments for each point of view. But the disagreement is largely an academic one. Is this the perfection of the system or simply the soul's own vast conscious awareness? Each of us is much greater than our waking consciousness, so it is possible that entities are "just us" in some expanded form. What is important is that entities act in limited and predictable ways, and that we know how to deal with them, whatever their status or origin. Entities present themselves as separate beings with a limited consciousness and can be effectively dealt with as such, so I treat them as separate. After all, there are teachers like Ramana Maharshi who maintained that life itself was a "waking dream," developed out of our vast consciousness.[47]

In the shamanic journey environment, entities mostly appear as dark, tar-like blobs or shadow clouds around the inner child. You can also sometimes see them around the people you call into the journey space. When you tell an entity to manifest in its true form, most of the time you see a tar-like mass with awareness and eyes. Sometimes entities will take the form of spiders, snakes, scorpions, bats and even an occasional dragon, underlying our general dislike of bugs and reptiles. Sometimes entities will even appear two dimensional and "cartoon-like."

Entities have different eye colors. The most common eye color is red, but yellow, green, white and black are not unknown. These are subtle differences and not of concern to us here.

Entities are single-minded in purpose. They seek to protect the inner child by creating psychological distance between the child and a perceived threat. Like all otherworldly beings, entities have no overt power in this realm. What the entity does is to amplify the child's existing feelings of fear and then through a number of ploys, encourage the child to avoid potentially difficult situations. The entity will encourage the child to withdraw, repress her feelings, rationalize pain or deny or not remember what happened. The entity will numb the child to her feelings, dull her memory, urge her to deny what is happening, get her to blame herself, devalue her worthiness or through a hundred other schemes, encourage the child to pull back from life. The child has already been conditioned to act in this manner, and the presence of the entity simply intensifies her reaction. The behavior the entity seeks to elicit is similar to what the ego does, however having an entity is like having an ego on steroids.

Sometimes, in the opposite, the entity will encourage the child to project her pain out onto the world through rage or other dysfunctional behavior, but the end goal is still the same: to create a feeling of separation from a threat. These are not behaviors that resolve situations. They exist for the sole purpose of creating a sense of separation.

Entities do not have the power or malevolence attributed to them throughout history. Entities operate through influencing and amplifying the thoughts and emotions of their host. I do not believe that they are evil, per se; in fact, they seem to have no moral convictions at all. What entities bring into every situation is perfectly matched to the needs of the child. The entity provides a sense of sanctuary at a painful and uncertain time.

The vast majority of convicts imprisoned for violent offenses, both men and women, report being physically and emotionally abused as children. The percentages for women by the way, are usually much higher. Violent criminals report that their abuse was severe. Do you think that there just might be a connection here? Psychiatrists have tried for many years to help these people change their behaviors with the disappointing outcome that prison recidivism rates are astronomical. From the Shaman's perspective, prison psychiatrists have not been addressing the real problem.

Although they are not the scary beings depicted by Hollywood or in folk tales, entities can have terrible effect on a fearful or hate-filled human mind. That is something we all should be far more concerned about, because such influences have caused more mayhem and pain in human history than can possibly be imagined.

We do not appreciate the cost to society of our dysfunctional families, and although sexual abuse, drug use and physical abuse are more common in low-income environments, it is not isolated there by any means. Mass school shootings have all been done by middle class boys. The Amish school shootings at Nickel Mines, Pennsylvania and the killings Virginia Tech were both done by a middle class, male adult.

Perhaps the most damaging aspect of the entity relationship is that the entity will cultivate and expand the feelings of unlovability and unworthiness the child already carries. It does this so that the child will not take risks and subject herself to additional emotional abuse. If the child can be convinced that she is not as good as other people, for example, then she will not be inclined to expose herself to potential rejection. This is a shortsighted strategy, but it is unfortunately very effective, and the long-term implications can be devastating. Yet, in the moment, with few other resources available, it works.

How the entity becomes attached is rather simple. When a child is overwhelmed with pain, fear or anxiety, and has no real recourse for resolution through her caretakers (most of the time the caretakers are the ones creating the problem), the traumatized and vulnerable child will make an agreement to accept an entity's "protection." The entity offers separation from pain in much the same way that alcohol or heroin does. Drugs don't make our problems go away - we just don't feel the problem in the moment. That is what an entity does, without the drugs. When you collapse feelings into yourself, you tighten your entire system. You go numb. You do not feel. When you explode out at someone else, the smoke and thunder obscures the great pain in your core.

Unfortunately, once the pattern of behaviors is established, the child, later adult, will continue to react to life in this way because these defenses do work (to a certain extent) in the moment and have provided a feeling of protection to a vulnerable psyche. They will also have led to the creation of a set of personal beliefs that can be virtually impervious to outside influence. Life may be miserable, and the external circumstances may no longer warrant this level of protective response, but the pattern has been established, and it is safe and familiar. It also reflects the way the person has come to see herself and the world based on The Misunderstanding.

Earlier, I spoke of possession. In a normal entity relationship, the entity has access and can influence the thinking of the wounded child. However, if the trauma suffered by the child is severe enough, the child will sometimes simply surrender control of her emotional self over to the entity. This is a condition traditionally known as "possession." With possession, the person is still there, but speaking with her is like addressing a hollow shell with a bomb attached to it. The behavior of the inner child will be erratic, sometimes rageful and mean. If you look into the eyes of a possessed inner child, they will flash or in the alternative, appear like the blackness of infinity. This tells us that the trauma to the child was serious (to her) and that it will require a more dedicated effort to straighten things out.

If a person's healing process requires it, an entity can also masquerade as a light being or wise spirit, purporting to share wisdom, exposing the person's naiveté and gullibility and leading to no end of confusion, frustration and consternation. Looking at it energetically, the entity's masquerade is a mediocre imitation of the real thing, but to a person unfamiliar with these matters, the charade can be convincing. This is why dialoguing with an entity is never helpful. Entities sometimes work in pairs, by the way, one protecting the other. One will create a distraction when the other's connection to the inner child is threatened.

Your relationship with your entities is thousands of years old, reaching back through many lifetimes. The pain you experienced in childhood is familiar. The events will be different, but the feelings and dynamics will be old. Remember, you have been working with these issues for a long time. And, no, you haven't failed. Look around you. The rest of us are all here too. But just to reinforce the point, some part of you is familiar with these beings.

A few entities are more effective than others. They possess an ability to influence that is significantly greater than the rest. They generally work with groups, and have an excellent access to psychic information. This kind of entity is not common, and they appear in response to special circumstances, bringing exactly what each person in the group needs. These higher-level entities (of which there are few) exhibit a deep understanding, generally well beyond the conscious awareness of the people affected. The web they weave can be complex and is usually disturbing, disruptive and perfect. At the time, their influence can seem very manipulative, but there is always a greater goal to these encounters.

These entities can often be found influencing the religious process. Thousands of years ago, one rather skilled entity went around masquerading as God in the ancient Middle East, passing judgment and smiting things, giving rise to the image of the wrathful deity depicted in the Old Testament and Southern Baptist sermons.

These more sophisticated entities are involved in the creation of curses that are passed down from generation to generation, interestingly, most often from mother to daughter, though sometimes they skip a generation. As an aside, the majority of these curses began long ago in Eastern Europe and the Middle East.

Entities have a strong influence in the arts. Creativity, it seems, is often rooted in pain and the creative process can be palliative. Creativity flows from a combination of personal pain and psychic insight and, therefore, the arts and literature are ripe arenas for their influence. Art can awaken us to the artist's pain and sometimes to her joy. How poor our world would be without the emotion-driven expressions of artists, writers, actors, dancers, comedians, composers, musicians, poets, sculptors and painters. They reflect life back to us. They are the great mirror.

In your own life, as you work with your inner child, you may become aware of a dark energy around her, like a cloud or dark tar. This is an entity. Another clue is if your inner child acts abnormally. She may be very angry or sad, but if her behavior is excessive, and this is a judgment on your part, there may be an entity present. A less reliable way to tell is by your dreams. If the images are vivid and disturbing, the odds are that an entity is present.

To find out for certain, when you are with the inner child, tell the entity to manifest. Tell it that you want to see it in its true form. When it comes, if you have any doubt about what it is, then ask, "Are you a negative entity?" Use those exact words and watch for an energy shift. Pay no attention to what the entity says, especially if it says, "No." Listen with your heart. Watch its eyes and feel its energy. An entity's energy has a flat, lifeless quality. If you are not sure, asking a second (or third) time should convince you.

If you are dealing with a light being, there will be no question about its origin. The response to your question will be an unequivocal, crystal clear, "No." The energy will be stable, bright and clear. It will feel alive.

Once you have determined that you are dealing with an entity, do nothing with it. There is nothing to be gained by engaging it. You won't (usually) get the truth anyway, and by engaging it, you distract yourself from the task at hand, which is exactly what the entity would like. Just be aware of its presence and be careful of fantasy journeys. They just waste your time. Your inner child made the agreement with this being because she had no other alternative. Give her another way.

Knowing that an entity is present is one thing; bringing your inner child to believe that you will be there for her so she will be willing to let the entity go is another matter altogether. Remember, the entity is here because your inner child felt it was necessary. It has been her protector. She very likely still feels that way. She felt unsafe, and she will maintain that relationship as long as she feels vulnerable. Your task is to give her another alternative, and you must be mindful that you have come to the party only recently.

Her need for the entity will be based on The Misunderstanding, and as you help her see the fallacy of her earlier perceptions, her need for the entity's protection will dramatically diminish. Knowing you are there to love and support her also makes a significant difference.

At some point, and this may take several journeys, when you feel that a base of trust has been created between you and your inner child, and as she comes to understand she was not the cause of what happened, ask her if she would be willing to let the entity go. If she agrees, then see the dark energy, and everything associated with it, being lifted away and then send it back to the Creator. He only loaned it to you, anyway.

If your inner child is possessed, you may have problems communicating with her. The easiest way around this is to make a direct connection from your heart chakra to hers. Let her feel the truth and warmth of your love. This may take a while, but stay with it. She wants out of this situation even more than you do. When she finally agrees to release the entity, see it as being lifted out through her back and then send it up to the Creator as before.

If you have problems, your inner child is hanging onto the entity because she does not feel sufficiently safe to release it. As difficult as this may be to accept, this speaks to a shortcoming in your relationship with her, and this is something you need to address. Most often it is because you have been unwilling to give up your worldly concerns and make her more important than the needs of other people. This is about your unwillingness to disconnect from your dysfunctional external relationships and give up your beliefs. Unless she is possessed, her demands will not be unreasonable. You need to look at what is going on for you.

When she lets go of the entity, remember that she has just given up her protection, and she is going to need a great deal of love and support.

I am frequently asked about protection from entities. There is a problem with the concept. The "vulnerability" to an entity comes because of the pain carried by your inner child. So having an entity is really an "inside job." It's like trying to "protect" yourself from contacting a virus. You can't. But, what you can do is to keep your system healthy so that you are not vulnerable to these pervasive outside influences. Doing something external can help to focus your intention, but without her support, it will not last long. There are rituals and spells that can help by creating conditions in your energy field that make it difficult for entities to enter, but they are far from foolproof. If you want a real solution, go to the source of the problem and heal the pain carried by your inner child.

For a quick fix you can say, "I refuse this negative energy," and it will buy you a little time as your thoughts create an energy disruption, but don't count on anything external for a long-term fix. Mary's experience teaches us a lot about working with entities:

MARY'S JOURNEY

I had been working diligently for many months, doing journeys that addressed issues in this lifetime as well as previous lifetimes. Massive internal shifts were occurring. One day, I received guidance that I needed to address one of the biggest wounds of all—that moment when I separated from the Creator, the moment when I went from being in joyous union with Him to being separated from Him, the moment when the ego was created.

I didn't begin the journey the minute I got that guidance. See, even THINKING about addressing this brought up a depth of fear in me. The MIND started trying to get out of it, give all sorts of reasons for not taking this journey. Finally, with gentle nudges from that guidance, I began the journey.

When I went in, I found the Child waiting for me, tapping her foot, ready to light into me. She was ANGRY, saying how she resented this process, how we always seemed to be dealing with pain. She didn't understand the necessity of all of it. In fact, she didn't understand the necessity for having pain there in the first place. And she was angry with God for the whole thing. And she was angry with me for trying to make her go back to a pain that we BOTH knew would be enormous.

I opened my heart to her. The fear, even before attempting to go back, was large enough to warrant this massive anger. She needed help. I cannot remember what I said—I wish I could. Whatever I said, it came effortlessly, easily and had the desired effect. She became willing to go.

Once she was ready, it was instant. We were there with and in the Creator, full, complete, whole, peaceful, surrounded by light and love, sort of like floating in a golden womb. Then suddenly, we were moving outwards, away from the light, away from all we had known, away from the love and the peace towards darkness. We floated in it and towards it. And the darkness seemed to go on forever. The emotional pain of this is indescribable. How does a ripping of soul energy feel?

When the pain hit, I was sobbing uncontrollably. I held her, sank with her into the pain. At this point, I lost all objectivity. I wasn't working with the Child anymore. I WAS the Child. And the pain was so intense that I WAS the pain.

I cannot recall exactly what happened in detail next. There were prompts from that same guidance, but in between those prompts were what I have come to call "infusions." A profound depth and amount of knowing, of understanding, is infused into me in a few moments. There are no words— just pure knowings. It's amazing, but seems completely natural while it's happening. The infusions came. I understood the vastness and the nature of the Separation, that it wasn't a rejection or abandonment of me for some internal flaw. It was intended to guide me to realize the essence of my true nature, that God is not separate from me even if I was separate from God. And I began to know, really know who I was, the Truth of that Presence inside. Love was coming from me, pouring out of me in waves. I was the golden light now, radiating, still separate, but not separate really.

The prompts from that guidance and these infusions were a perfect, glorious interplay, a sort of dance with God. Gradually, as this dance continued, I began to gain a more ordinary state of mind. Objectivity returned and I saw the Child again in front of me. She was glowing, radiant, and my love for her was enormous. I wanted to hold her, hug her deeply.

But as I continued to look at her, it became clear that something was attached. It didn't look like a negative entity. (I had seen negative energy before in other journeys, entities of negativity.) This attachment was like a shadow of her, a reflection, a dark reflection. Attached to this dark reflection were several negative entities—red, yellow, black and green. The entities seemed to sort of feed this shadow. And I knew somehow that this shadow was the ego, or at least a very large piece of it.

Once she saw it as separate from her, it was easier to point out how it had been damaging her for so long. I reminded her about all the lifetimes of ego interference as we tried to follow a path, all the repetitions, all the anger at the Creator and the interference in this process of becoming whole and coming home. The entities were making a brilliant show during this time, but it was more like posturing. They knew the effect was not impressive. The dark reflection waited for her decision when I asked if she'd be willing to let the reflection and all the entities go. She was ready, but she wanted to thank it for all the protection that it had provided her for so, so long. We watched it all swirl upward in silence.

When it was gone, she looked very fragile. I held her and stroked her hair. After a minute or so, she stood straighter and started to glow. She looked right at me and said, "There is no forever darkness, is there?"

"No, Little One, there isn't," I said. Tears of relief came for both of us.

I felt very disoriented and cried more, only this time the tears were from a deep gratitude. I began to try to put words on the "infusions" I had received. "There is no forever darkness. There is nothing to fear. Nothing can be harmed—or rather, there is no harm. The Original Separation was an Act of Love." I knew I was worthy. I understood who I really am and I had to laugh because I got that it was nothing and everything, a sort of wave in the ocean of God. I felt peace.

my mom aftersaw "were wake from the dream of life" and say "of course"!

PAST LIVES

As a shaman, I deal with some odd subjects – entities, spirit possession, the shadow, psychic energies, ghosts, evil, and whatnot. Although there is doubt about some of these topics, nothing generates the skepticism that the idea of past lives does for a few people. The nature of their reaction and its intensity pushes on deep-seated denial. The subject seems to threaten the control over life these people have gained through their rational minds. I have also found that these individuals are usually sitting on some very painful past histories and are understandably reluctant to return there. When I encounter these people I am often reminded of something Saint Thomas Aquinas wrote:

To one who has faith, no explanation is necessary.
To one without faith, no explanation is possible.

Is there such a thing as a past life? My answer is absolutely. I have a good memory and a vivid imagination, but I could not possibly conjure the vast amount of detail found in my past life journeys. I regularly challenge clients to do historical research to corroborate what they find in their past life excursions. I tell them to look for historical accuracy, authenticity of dress and tools or weapons, etc., especially for things and events they have no conscious knowledge of. We get few firm points of cross-reference, but when we do, the accuracy is extraordinary. Also, the perfection of past events in the way they line up with the issues each individual is working on, convinces me that there is something far more significant going on than mere imagination.

One of the rather snide comments about past life work I have heard is that everyone was an Egyptian princess or someone famous. In my 25 years of healing work I have done thousands of past life journeys and in that time we have encountered few famous people. The vast majority of past life journeys have been about people you've never heard of, but there is another consideration here.

The past lives that will be the most prominent will be those of intense trauma or conflict. Through much of history, most people were farmers or herders who died peacefully of natural causes. They lived in poverty and their traumas were familial. This was not as often the case with the nobility. Theirs was often a violent existence. It seems that intrigue, murder, poisonings, etc. were a staple in the lives of some of our noble ancestors as they clambered over each other for positions of power. Someone, it seems, was always scheming against someone else.

That level of violence is going to generate a great deal more emotionality, and that is going to make those lives more prominent in past life work, because at this stage in our evolution, it is the unresolved pain from our previous lives that we carry forward. Your old pain influences how you experience this life and the amount of pain you have. Until your past life traumas are resolved, the old pain will continue to affect your life.

In your previous lives, as in this lifetime, The Universe exerted pressure on your beliefs. Your attachment to your beliefs caused you to become crosswise with life as it does today. That is because it all originates from the place in you that is afraid to surrender to the God Space.

In the past lives that will be prominent in your initial journeys, the conflict between your ego and other people caused things to go badly. You died, usually at the hands of these people, feeling abandoned and betrayed. As things went badly you probably looked to God for rescue and when it was not forthcoming, you felt abandoned. Life definitely felt unfair.

Of course, you have had many other experiences in your past, but as I said, the ones that will stand out are those that were marked by significant pain and trauma. These are the experiences that at this stage in your development give you the greatest opportunity for growth and change.

In our work with your inner child, we have operated from the premise that the child had done nothing to create the problems that affected her. Children are innocent, powerless and incapable of creating the dysfunctional behaviors of the adults in their world. This gives you the opportunity to see yourself in a reasonably pure and unblemished state, free from the affectations of ego. This is a most useful perspective for healing.

However, in the painful interactions in your past lives, you were probably not so innocent. As an adult, your ego pushed you to create the situations you got yourself into.

If it were important to heal your former childhood self, we would go back to that childhood as we have done with your present lifetime, and then progress forward in time. But it is not necessary for us to do that. We can accomplish the healing we need by working with the adult former you. Our interest is to work with the ego drives that got you into trouble because it is the unresolved pain from those situations that bleeds through into your life today. Although there will be some consistency to the patterns of each childhood, once you have dealt with The Misunderstanding from your present life, it is generally not necessary to heal the childhood issues of your previous lives.

The events we will work with from your past will typically (although not always) have developed when you were an adult. Resolving those struggles will begin to drain the dysfunctional drive underlying your present life conflicts and struggles. If we look for the most prominent painful events from past lives, we typically find: persecution by the authorities, violent death in war, the abuse of spiritual privilege and then some sort of palace intrigue.

In order to limit confusion, you will want to focus your efforts by using your intention. Choose a particular issue that is significant today. Choosing something current helps insure a more direct connection to the past life that is influencing the present.

When you have set your intention, then move into the journey space and connect with your inner child. She will be your guide to the past. Tell her to take you back to the lifetime most directly connected to the issue or feeling you have identified.

Most of the time you will be shown a scene near the end of a particular life. Remember, that life probably ended badly and so you are being shown a time just before the high point of the crisis. In other instances you may only see an object or a scene. If that is the case, continue to ask to be shown more until you have a good grasp of what was going on. Do not be shy about asking. You need to know what happened. In one client's journey, all we saw at first was a white blouse. We worked with that image by asking to be shown more. Eventually we were able to learn the rest of the story. It turned out that she had been brutally raped and murdered while wearing that blouse, but the event was so traumatic that the inner child just couldn't blurt it out all at once. Showing us the blouse was her way of easing the client into a very painful occurrence.

Once you have an understanding of the critical moment, then go back a little earlier in time to see what led up to the difficulty. Since you would typically have been an adult, we want to look specifically for the role you played in creating the situation. We are looking for ego issues. Consider your motivation back then. When we journey back we will often find someone who has been apprehended for speaking her "truth" in the face of injustice. And, although the cause may have been noble, when we look at your motivation, we will see the fear-based rage that is driven by woundedness rather than the legitimate anger at injustice, (which is likely to be present also, but in a subsidiary way).

When you have a good understanding of the past life person's motives, then travel to that time and introduce yourself to the former you. Tell her who you are. Talk with her about her pain and show her how her fear and ego pushed her to set the situation up so things would turn out badly. Help her to see that it was not necessary for events to go as they did. Once she sees the truth, then encourage her to let go of the beliefs she holds about herself. In most cases she will be ready to change.

Once she has made the shift, then replay the situation you found her in, but this time, have her operate from her new beliefs. The situation will probably have a different outcome. Then be with her as you fast-forward to the end of her days. I will address several other concerns next, and then we will finish this exercise.

In some cases you will not be able to change what happened. This is because in that lifetime, you were making a sacrifice for the learning of others. If this is the case, then explain this to your previous self, and help her to see that she was playing a part, i.e., making a sacrifice, in God's greater plan.

What we want to achieve, whether you are able to change the karma of what happened or not, is for the previous you to die peacefully. If you were unable to alter events so that it was necessary for you to die violently, then work with the past life you so she is able to pass from a place of peace, even in the midst of chaos and pain. If you were able to change events, then be with her as she passes from this life peacefully. What we have done in either case, is to remove the shock and trauma that you have carried from these lives for centuries.

The last thing we will do in this process can be quite profound. For some people it brings a moment that changes their lives. When the former you passes from this world, then bring her spirit back with you to the present. When you have returned, have a pen and paper handy. Ask the spirit of this person what it has to say to you. You are going to hear less than six words, and these may be the most important words you will ever hear. This truth will be perfect and will speak to the core of what you have come here to resolve.

You can ask this spirit if it will remain to help you through your daily struggles. Notice please, that if the spirit does decide to stay, that something about you must be worth saving. You must not be as unworthy as your ego maintains!

Sometimes when we journey to past life events, we find an innocent person. We may find a waif who has been abused by life or a young man on a battlefield who is about to be killed. In these cases, the issue the person is up against will be her relation to The Creator. Her assumption will be that she was unworthy and caught up in difficult circumstances because she was unlovable and undeserving. As with any other life circumstance, your challenge will be to help the former you to see the truth. The situation has been created to give her the opportunity to move to a new understanding.

After you have talked with the previous you, then ask to be taken to meet with The Creator. If there are entities active in your system, they will muddle the process, so I would recommend that you not do this until you have done the essential work on your present lifetime issues.

When you are in The Creator's presence, (and it will be an energy not a being), ask to be shown or told the truth about who you are. You may hear words or receive an image. Whichever it is, make certain that you take in this truth. I would urge you to use what you receive as an anchor for the rest of your life.

Here are the thirteen Principles we have developed through the book:

LOVE EVERYTHING

ANYTHING YOU DO NOT LOVE WILL BECOME A LESSON

WHAT GETS YOU INTO TROUBLE ISN'T YOURS

YOUR LIFE IS PERFECT

THE EGO CANNOT LOVE

DO IT NOW

TRUTH MUST BE FELT

IF YOU DIDN'T BELIEVE IT, IT WOULDN'T MATTER

YOU DETERMINE YOUR EXPERIENCE

NOTHING CAN BE WRONG WITH YOU

MAKE HER THE MOST IMPORTANT THING IN YOUR LIFE

CHOOSE COMPASSION

HEALING MEANS LETTING GO

SOME FINAL THOUGHTS

For many lifetimes The Universe has urged you to deepen your spiritual connection in preparation for your reconnection with the God Space. It has nudged and sometimes pushed, you to change. This comparatively relaxed pace has allowed you the freedom to move at your own speed. That is changing.

If you look around, you will find that the process of change is accelerating. Life, which has never been peaceful or tranquil in the first place, is going to become a good deal more tumultuous. Everyone will be placed under stresses they have never experienced. For those who have taken this time to address their spiritual disharmonies, the changes will be far less disruptive.

On an increasing number of fronts, life as we have known it will be seriously threatened. For the first time in human history, we will face the prospect of the extinction of our species and quite possibly the end of life on earth. Individually and as a species, we are going to be asked, ever more forcefully, to move from our present beliefs and behaviors to live in the God Space. As with any disease, humanity is being given the choice, "Change or die."

You may not be able to do much about the larger picture, but you do have control over how you will react to what is happening. Start making changes now, start today. It is a great deal easier if you do it on your terms rather than waiting until you are pushed into a corner where you will be forced to make the same changes.

Make your spiritual growth the most important thing in your life. If you don't do it today, circumstances are going to demand it of you tomorrow.

Footnotes

[1]There are estimated to be 100 stars in the universe for every grain of sand on the earth!

[2]Ramana Maharshi, *The Essential Teachings of Ramana Maharshi.*

[3]Dr. Bruce Lipton, *The Biology of Belief,* (Mountain of Love/Elite Books, Santa Rosa CA, 2005) P. 146.

[4]Gay Hendricks has been teaching this idea for years and I am grateful to him for the concept.

[5]I am indebted to Salemla (Sukie) Colegrave for this perspective. Sukie's insightful book, *By Way Of Pain,* (Park Street Press, 1989), is unfortunately out of print, but if you can find a copy, I encourage you to read it.

[6]Juan Ramon Jimenez, (Ortiz-Carboneres, ed.), *Selected Poems of Juan Ramon Jimenez,* (Aris & Phillips, 2005).

[7]Matthew 7:39. Also see Leo Tolstoy, *The Kingdom of God Is Within You* (1894).

[8]Matthew 7:44. There is a difference between the person and their actions. You do not have to like what they do, but love them for who they are.

[9]Matthew 26:52.

[10]As with Christ's teachings of non-violence, many church leaders find The Beatitudes from The Sermon on The Mount to be too "utopian and unrealistic" to put into practice. So for centuries, Christians have been taught "Christianity Lite" because church leaders were reluctant to offend their source of income. They therefore (conveniently) ignore Christ's admonition to not hoard earthly things.

[11]Matthew 6:19.

[12]The Christian Bible has a number of significant mis-translations. Dr. Rocco A. Errico of The Noorah Foundation, (amongst others), offers interesting insights into these "errors." One of his books is: *Let There Be Light, The Seven Keys, The Noorah Foundation,* www.noohra.com

[13]"Ancestral Versus Original Sin: An Overview with Implications for Psychotherapy", by V. Rev. Antony Hughes, M.Div St.Mary Antiochian Orthodox Church, Cambridge, Massachusetts, www.stmaryorthodoxchurch.org/orthodoxy/articles/2004-hughes-sin.php.

[14] Arnold Patent, *You Can Have It All,* www.arnoldpatent.com/books.html.

[15]Rivkah Scharf-Kluger, *Satan in The Old Testament,* (Northwestern University Press, 1967).

[16]Hakuin Ekaku (1685-1768)

[17]John Ruskan, *Emotional Clearing,* (R. Wyler & Co, NY, 1993). www.emclear.com/Articles_orig.html,

[18]Ellen Goodstein, Bankrate.com, "8 lottery winners who lost their millions," http://moneycentral.msn.com/content/Savinganddebt/Savemoney/P99649.asp

[19]Eckhart Tolle, *A New Earth, Awakening to Your Life's Purpose*, (Dutton, 2005) p. 12.

[20]David Hume, *An Enquiry Concerning Human Understanding*, (1740).

[21]Gregory Bateson, *Mind And Nature, A Necessary Unity*, (1979).

[22]Lao Tsu, *The Tao Te Ching*, trans. by Gua Fung and Jane English, (Vintage Books, 1972).

[23]Antoine de Sainte-Exupéry, *The Little Prince*, (Harcourt Brace, 1943), P. 70.

[24]Jalal ad-Din Rumi, *The Masnavi*, 1250 CE.

[25]From a speech made by Krishnamurti in 1929 when he dissolved the Order of the Star. The organization was built around him by Theosophists who selected him at the age of thirteen to be the vehicle for the return of the Christ, or Maitreya. He was raised accordingly, but after his enlightenment, he refused the role that had been prepared for him, disbanded the organization, and continued to teach on his own.

[26]Mohandas Gandhi, *An Autobiography, The Story of My Experiments With Truth*, (Beacon Press, 1957).

[27]This is a commencement address deliverd by Steve Jobs, CEO of Apple Computer and of Pixar Animation Studios to Stanford University graduates, June 12, 2005. www.mayanmajix.com/art2986.html, and www.cotwest.com/1/cotw/spiritual_browsing.asp?artID=2748

[28]Sura 9:5.

[29]Sahih Bukhari Vol.9 Number.57.

[30]A. Guillaume, *The Life of Muhammad*, Oxford Univ. Press, P. 369.

Also: Muhammad said: "If you gain a victory over the men of Jews, kill them." - Abu Dawud (hadith) Book 19, Number 2996.

[31]Dr. Robert Emmons, *Thanks: How The New Science of Gratitude Can Make You Happier*, (Houghton Mifflin, 2007) p. 11.

[32]Emmons, P. 113.

[33]Emmons, p. 41.

[34]Viktor Frankl, *Man's Search for Meaning*, (1946).

[35]www.todoinstitute.org/naikanretreat.html

[36]John 8:1-11

[37]Bernie Siegel, *Prescriptions for Living: Inspirational Lessons for a Joyful, Loving Life*, (Harper, 1999)

[38]Emmons p. 171, 182

[39]Fred Luskin, *Forgive For Good: A Proven Prescription for Health and Happiness*, (NY, Harper Collins, 2002), P. 116.

[40]Carl Jung, *Alchemical Studies, vol. 13, The Collected Works of C. J. Jung, The Bollingen Series XX* (Princeton: Princeton University Press, 1968), Par. 54.

[41]Being healthy and holy both come from the same Proto Germanic word "khailaz," which meant "to make whole." To be more whole was to be more holy. Both speak to the return to the God Space. There was also hal or haeli, which meant to be "entire, unhurt, healthy." Old English had the derivative "haelan," which meant "to make whole or make well," which ultimately gave us heal.

[42]Crisis Magazine, July/August 2005.

[43]Kat Duff, *The Alchemy of Illness*, (Harmony/Bell Tower, 2000)

[44]Jules Michelet, *Satanism and Witchcraft* (1862).

[45]Mark 8:22-26.

[46]Masaro Emoto, *The Message from Water, Vols. I, II & III* (HADO, Kyoikusa Co. Ltd). Also: www.hado.net

[47]Ramana Maharshi, *Talks With Ramana Maharshi* (Inner Directions, 2000).

Index